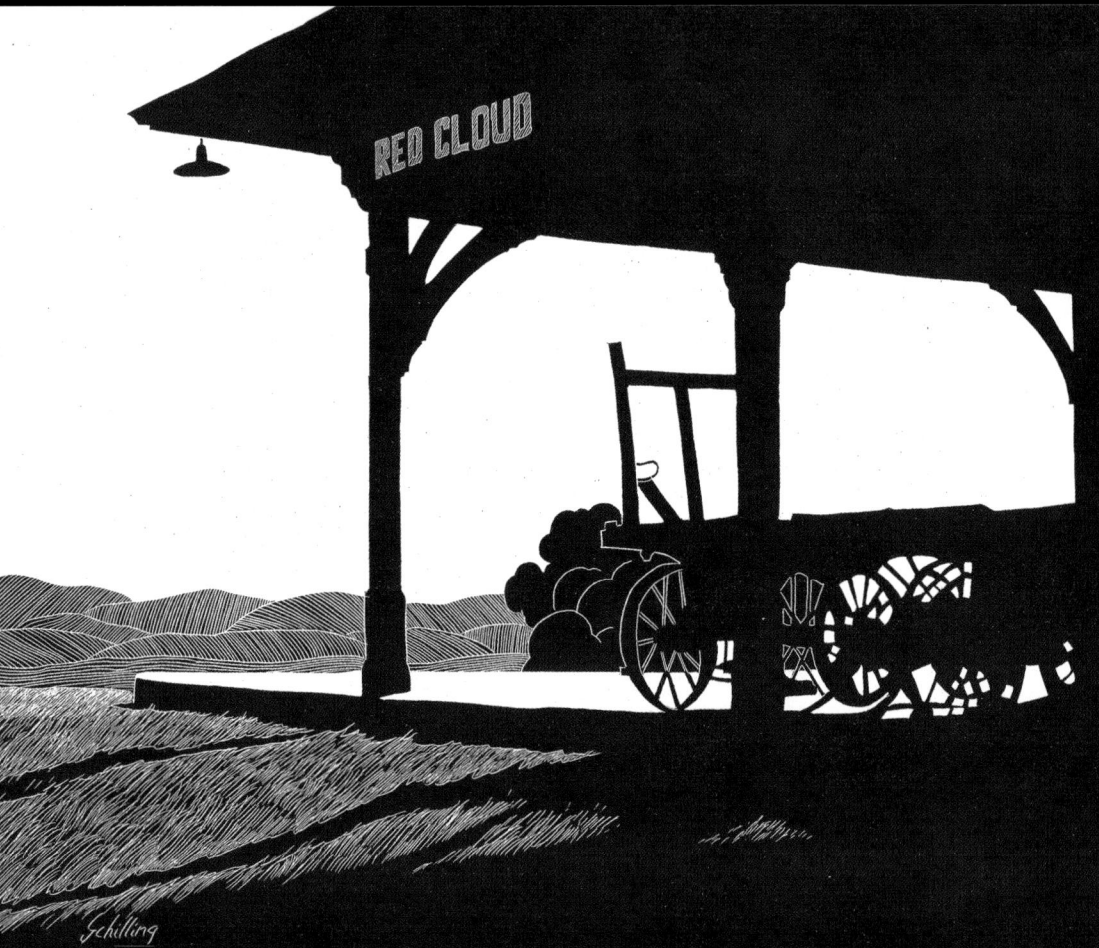

We stumbled down from the train to a wooden siding, where men were running about with lanterns. I couldn't see any town, or even distant lights; we were surrounded by utter darkness. The engine was panting heavily after its long run. In the red glow from the fire-box, a group of people stood huddled together on the platform, encumbered by bundles and boxes.

MY ÁNTONIA

Red Cloud Station

Prairie grasses invade an abandoned roadbed.
Baggage carts stand guard over
Obsolesence.
No clicking of a wireless key to excite my senses.
Only memories, fading memories.

RICHARD SCHILLING

PORTRAITS OF THE PRAIRIE

PORTRAITS OF

THE PRAIRIE

The Land that Inspired Willa Cather

Richard Schilling

Foreword by Ted Kooser

UNIVERSITY OF NEBRASKA PRESS | LINCOLN AND LONDON

Publication of this book was made possible through a generous grant from William D. and Betty Ruth Hewit, founding benefactors of the Hewit Place building, home of the University of Nebraska's Center for Great Plains Studies and Great Plains Art Museum.

Set in Electra and designed by Nathan Putens.

Library of Congress Cataloging-in-Publication Data
Schilling, Richard, 1933–
Portraits of the prairie : the land that inspired Willa Cather / Richard Schilling ; foreword by Ted Kooser.
p. cm.   Includes bibliographical references.
ISBN 978-0-8032-2260-1 (cloth : alk. paper)
1. Schilling, Richard, 1933–
2. Prairies in art. 3. Nebraska—In art. I. Title.
ND1839.S335A4 2011
759.13—dc22
2010026337

In memory of

Gladys Renfro Schilling,

who, like Willa,

lived her formative years

in Red Cloud.

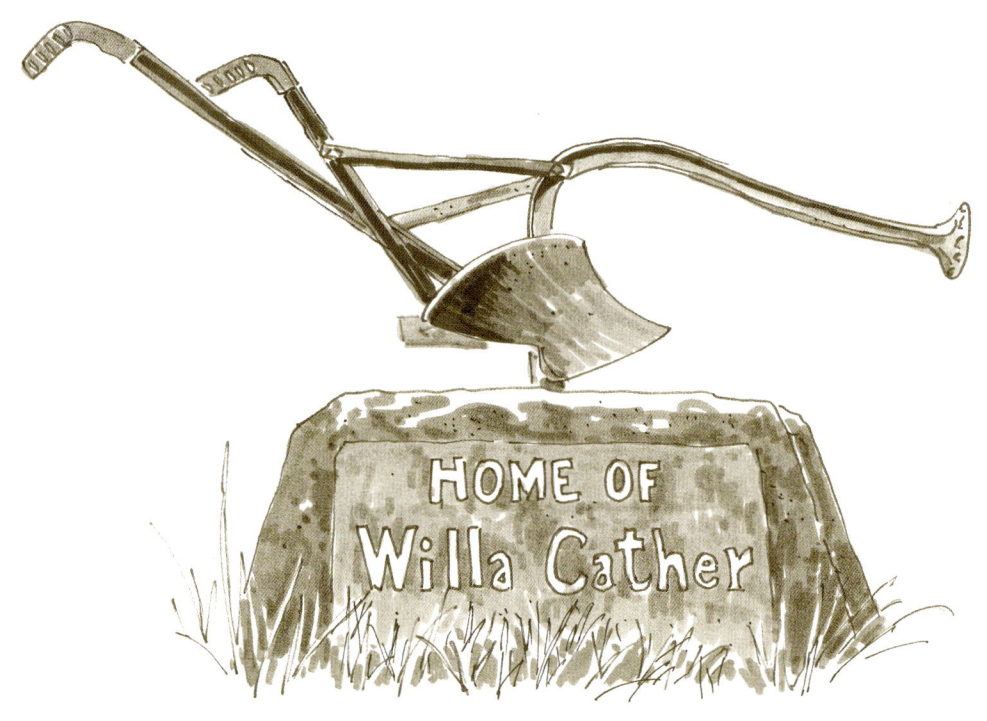

Contents

On some upland farm, a plough had been left
standing in the field. The sun was sinking just behind
it. Magnified across the distance by the horizontal
light, it stood out against the sun, was exactly
contained within the circle of the disk; the handles,
the tongue, the share—black against the molten red.

MY ÁNTONIA

Foreword by Ted Kooser *ix*

Preface *xi*

Acknowledgments *xiii*

Introduction *xv*

The Land *1*

Country Roads *29*

Waters of the Prairie *45*

Seasons of the Prairie *55*

Trees *93*

Art in Unexpected Places *103*

Homes and Prairie Towns *109*

Churches and Cemeteries *139*

Bibliography *155*

Foreword

Ted Kooser

It's been a delight to observe the progress of this handsome book toward publication. I met Dick Schilling in 2008, over coffee, and he told me about his plans to honor Willa Cather by making paintings and sketches of the prairie landscapes her stories and novels had evoked so memorably. I liked him at once, and admired his humility in the face of a project that proposed to lean itself up against the towering accomplishment of one of our greatest American authors.

And it seemed to me that the result might be a book that Cather herself would have received with enthusiasm, for to her the arts were all one grand enterprise, the creation of an abiding testimony that mankind could rise above its animal baseness. Her works are full of reverence toward the arts and their redemptive power, and the surname of her character Lucy Gayheart suggests the human soul in that state of ecstasy and celebration that is our natural response to great art. This book has made me feel that way, and I am immensely grateful to Dick for creating it.

Though artists gather with other artists from time to time—enjoying each other's company, relishing the shop talk, the gossip—the real work of the painter, the sculptor, the composer, and the writer is always accomplished in solitude, that state in which the truth begins to show through the surfaces. All through Cather's fiction there are passages like this one from *O Pioneers!*: "She had never known before how much the country meant to her. The chirping of the insects in the long grass had been like the sweetest music. She had felt as if her heart were hiding down there, somewhere, with the quail and the plover and all the little wild things that crooned or buzzed in the sun. Under the long shaggy ridges, she felt the future stirring."

Perhaps I needn't point out that these words describe the understanding revealed to a person in solitude. Dick Schilling, studying the works of Cather and walking in solitude over the landscapes she described, has had a great deal revealed to him, and the pages you are about to immerse yourself in are testimony to that. One singular and notable isolation, that of Willa Cather, has inspired another purposeful isolation, that of Dick Schilling, and the two artists, together in spirit, walking the divide of time, can be seen in this book to be looking upon and celebrating their common subject, a singular place, the great open prairies of Nebraska.

Preface

The Nebraska prairie has inspired me in a painterly way, as it inspired Willa Cather in an authorial way nearly a century ago. There certainly have been many changes since the days of her youth, yet much of the land remains the same. I felt that it was time, "before the color fades," to paint my impressions of the prairie that was a creative force in the life and art of Willa Cather. These paintings are not illustrations of Cather's stories and books, but are images of the land as it appears today.

I attempted to search out scenes that might have been the locations, or possibly, the inspirations for her works. This was difficult at times since Cather's settings were often a collage of several locations from her childhood. Occasionally, I have used similar artistic license to improve a composition by removing obtrusive objects or to adjust the colors of ambient light. Also, because my paintings are not exact illustrations of her stories, the weather, colors, and seasons of the year may vary from her excerpted text.

In essence, my paintings are as fictional as Cather's. This is not to say that the land did not have tremendous influence on both of us. The prairie provided the overarching spirit that made her a much-loved American author and inspired me to interpret it in my own way.

I relied most heavily on Cather's descriptive writings in *My Ántonia* and *O Pioneers!* as I consider them to be among the finest and the most sensitive portrayals of the prairie landscape. With her quotations, I have used Cather's own voice to bring the illustrations to life, while my comments and field notes describe my painting techniques and impressions of the landscape.

A SENTIMENTAL JOURNEY

Not only did my research provide a deeper connection to the land that inspired Willa Cather, but it was a sentimental journey of discovery as it revealed much about my own mother, who had hidden her childhood memories in a corner of her heart, rarely sharing them with her own children. Like Cather twenty years before her, my mother, eight years old at the time, was uprooted from her birthplace and moved with her family to Red Cloud. She graduated from high school, received her certificate, and while still a teenager, began teaching school in the nearby town of Inavale to earn money for college. Reading "The Best Years" helped me visualize my mother as a young lady, teaching students not much younger than herself, in a rural one-room school.

Where there is great love, there are always miracles.
DEATH COMES FOR THE ARCHBISHOP

Acknowledgments

This project began as a dream fifteen years ago when I felt a yearning to rediscover the land of my birth. I was born in Lincoln and graduated from the University of Nebraska but moved to Colorado after returning from the service.

Willa Cather said that during her first year in Nebraska she "had to have it out with the land," which was so different from the scenic hills of Virginia. Eventually she succumbed to the mystery of the prairie. My own absence fostered a growing sentiment for my home state, and like her, I finally could appreciate its unique beauty. As I grew older, I continued to develop a longing for the prairie and reread the works of Willa Cather. I wanted to paint scenes of the Nebraska prairie, especially the land that had inspired her stories.

But sometimes a dream is only a dream until people with imagination catch the vision. The first was Susan Norby of the University of Nebraska Foundation, who saw some of my Webster County paintings and encouraged me to enlarge the collection and publish the work. She brought the prospectus for this book to the attention of Ladette Randolph, interim director of the University of Nebraska Press, who endorsed the project. Susan's enthusiasm, organizational skills, and experience in the New York art market have been the driving force behind the project. If it were not for her, this book would have remained only a dream.

I am indebted to the team of creative people at the University of Nebraska Press, especially Thomas Swanson, editor of Bison Books and Alicia Christensen, who skillfully led me through the mysterious maze of printing and publishing. Thank you to Joeth Zucco, senior project editor; Annie Shahan, senior designer; Nathan Putens, designer; and Cara Pesek, publicity manager. They were a team of champions who brought this book to print.

I am sincerely grateful to Ted Kooser, the U.S. Poet Laureate (2004–6) and Pulitzer Prize–winning author, for his introductory remarks. His books have delighted me, restored my appreciation of poetry, and proved to me that poetry need not be haughty or esoteric. Ted is a master painter of word pictures. His discerning eye, manifested in poetry, leads us into beauty that lies beneath the obvious. This is an artist's mandate, and Ted does it so well. Though I have seen firsthand the hills of eastern Nebraska's Bohemian Alps, which he made so magical in his descriptive prose, I have also seen new things, places, and people through his writing.

I also wish to thank William D. and Betty Ruth Hewit for their generous support of this book project. As dedicated alumni of the University of Nebraska, the Hewits continue to provide leadership in philanthropy motivated by their thankfulness and appreciation for their alma mater. I am grateful for their shared appreciation of Nebraska's beautiful landscape and their understanding that this book strives to artfully represent that landscape as it is today while simultaneously honoring the creative genius of Willa Cather.

For the first time, perhaps, since that land emerged from the waters of geologic ages, a human face was set toward it with love and yearning. It seemed beautiful to her, rich and strong and glorious. Her eyes drank in the breadth of it, until her tears blinded her. Then the Genius of the Divide, the great, free spirit which breathes across it, must have bent lower than it ever bent to a human will before. The history of every country begins in the heart of a man or a woman.   *O PIONEERS!*

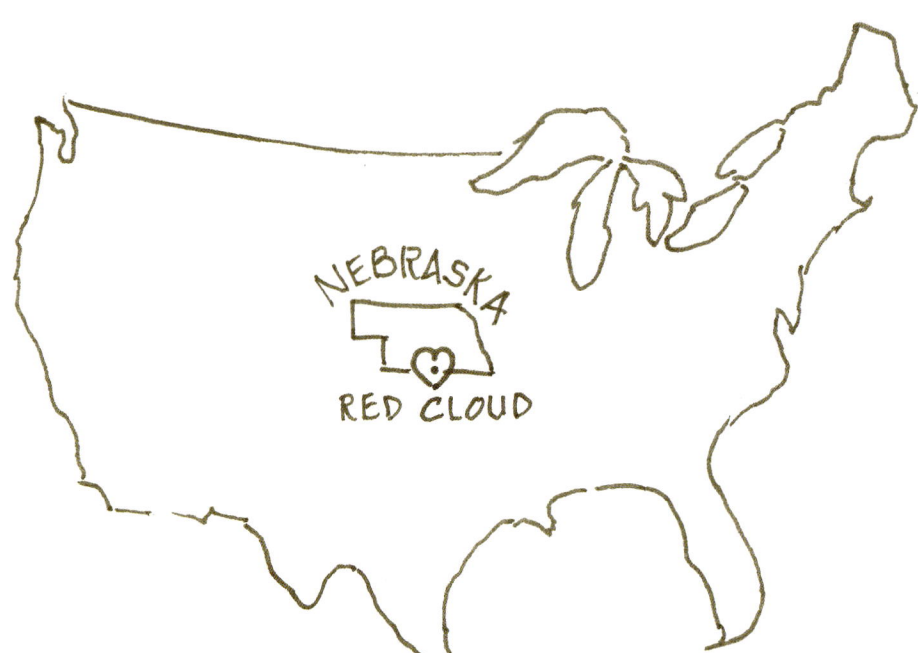

Introduction

There is a land—a land within a country—as far from one ocean as it is from the other. Beneath knitted roots of native grass was fertile soil that might sustain immigrant farmers. Patience, optimism, faith, courage, and strength would be needed to endure the tests that were to come. So early settlers labored, broke the sod, and produced crops. More often than not the crops were poor, but when all conditions were right—rain, sun, and temperature— they were bountiful and life was good. There were some settlers whose backs and dreams were broken, those who picked up what remained of their lives and deserted the land. But for those who endured, the rewards were satisfying and the souls of those people became bonded to the land like Alexandra's did in *O Pioneers!*

If you were to travel across the great American prairie, this flat land and its seemingly endless fields of corn and wheat would not immediately inspire rhapsodies of praise for its beauty and character. To discover the soul of this land, one must linger longer. This is Webster County, a small 575-square-mile county that sits on the Nebraska-Kansas border. "Catherland" lies between the Little Blue River in the north and the Republican River near the Kansas border. Cather called the upland between these two watersheds "the Divide." Today, cornfields, many with center pivot irrigation, reach to the horizon. The land is flat, but close to the Republican River it tumbles off into gentle, undulating hills separated by thicket-filled ravines. Nearer to Red Cloud, an eon of wind and water erosion has exposed clay cliffs beneath the sod. Settlers made their first homes in these cliffs and, as they prospered, built additional rooms with walls of stacked bricks of sod that were shared by mice, gophers, and snakes.

Some of the settlers had never farmed, so with enthusiasm that sometimes exceeded their knowledge or experience, pioneers set out to break the sod and plant their crops. The primary crop was corn. Initially, wheat did not do as well; however, in 1874 a new variety of wheat was introduced from the Russian Crimea that produced greater yields. In the years that followed, agricultural practices and technology improved. Settlers learned how to cultivate their farms so as to protect their soil from erosion by wind and rain while new planting and cultivating implements were introduced.

Success required more than just good sense. Nature is always capricious, and a good crop could be wiped out quickly by hordes of locusts that sometimes plagued the land. There were reports in 1870 of large, migratory grasshoppers six inches deep devouring the crops of hapless farmers. Moisture never seemed to come at the right time. Spring floods of the Republican valley were common. Even worse were the droughts that descended upon the land for long periods. Some cursed their misfortune, but Cather's Anton Rosicky made the best of what he had:

> "I asked your father if that hot wind all day hadn't been terrible hard on the gardens an' the corn.
> "'Corn,' he says, 'there ain't no corn.'
> "'What you talkin' about?' I said. 'Ain't we got forty acres?'
> "'We ain't got an ear,' he says, 'nor nobody else ain't got none. All the corn in this country was cooked by three o'clock today, like you'd roasted it in an oven.'
> "'You mean you won't get no crop at all?' I asked him. I couldn't believe it, after he'd worked so hard.
> "'No crop this year,' he says. 'That's why we're havin' a picnic. We might as well enjoy what we got.'
>
> "NEIGHBOUR ROSICKY"

If the drought was not enough for worry, there was the ever-present danger of grass fires that could race unimpeded across thousands of acres of dry grass threatening life and livelihood. Winter storms were hard on livestock and the loss of even one cow was a tragedy for a pioneer family who depended upon her for milk and cream. Worse, a blizzard could turn deadly within minutes, causing settlers and animals to lose their sense of direction. For instance, the blizzard of 1888, called the "school children's blizzard," began as an unseasonably warm winter morning, but ended with a blinding storm rolling across the prairie, claiming many lives.

Hard times lasted for decades. During the Great Depression and the dust bowl days of the 1930s some settlers, like the parents of Madeline Fitz, pulled up and left the land discouraged and broke. Fitz's photograph and letter are displayed in the Webster County Museum in Red Cloud. She wrote:

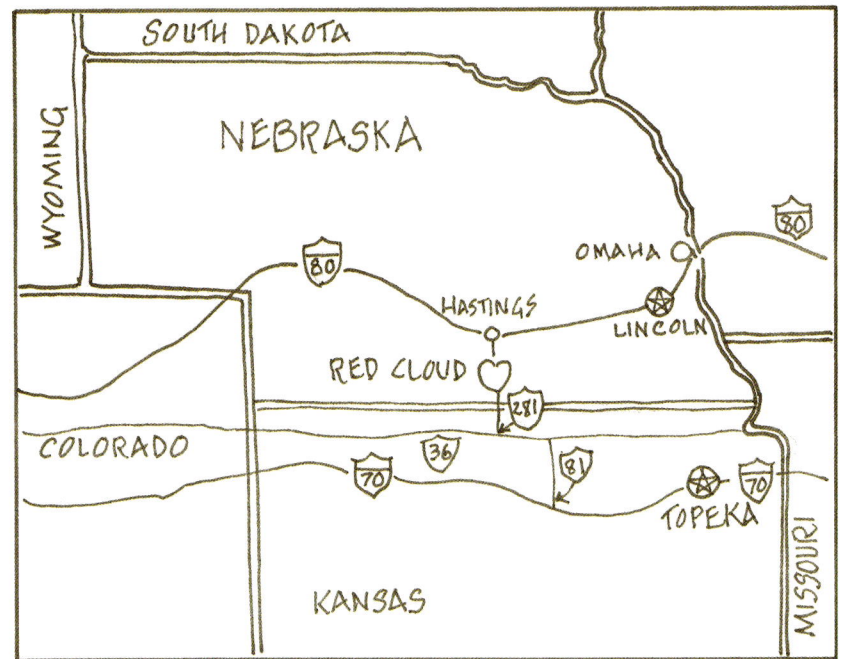

My dad's crop had burned up for so many years that the move in 1935 to land on the river bottom was the last stab to stay on the land. And wouldn't you know, that year the Republican River came up and flooded everything we had. We made it through Christmas and then sold everything at an auction, and we moved to Kansas City.

Those early settlers who stuck with the land, overcoming almost unbearable discouragement and losses, became the seeds of future generations of Americans who inherited the land.

> We come and go, but the land is always here. And the people who love it and understand it are the people who own it—for a little while.   O PIONEERS!

When the Cather family arrived in Nebraska in the spring of 1883, they moved into young Willa's grandparents' home on the Divide—the land that separates the watersheds of the Blue and Republican rivers. She was a nine-year-old girl who disliked the vast flat land, where she had been planted after being uprooted from the beautiful hills of Virginia. But following a winter of despair, she said that she had finally "had it out with the land," becoming infected with the allure of rolling waves of windblown prairie grass.

After one year on the Divide, Charles Cather, Willa's father, decided to move the family to the town of Red Cloud. The year spent on the prairie had molded the young lady's character and had a profound influence on her future writing.

After graduating from high school at the age of seventeen, Cather immediately entered the University of Nebraska. She wanted to be a doctor, but it seemed that events of the time were leading her to a writing career. She cut her journalistic teeth as a columnist and critic for the *Nebraska State Journal*, which was owned by Charles Gere, the father of her friend Mariel Gere. Cather's friendship with the Gere family and occasional contributions to the newspaper continued long after she left Nebraska for the East.

In 1895 she moved to Pittsburgh for a job as the editor of the *Home Monthly* and also joined the state's largest newspaper, the *Pittsburgh Leader*, as drama critic. Cather was eclectic in her themes and prolific in her production. Her reputation as a writer was growing as she was writing for three different publications. She produced nine short stories for the *Home Monthly* and columns for the *Nebraska State Journal* describing life in the big city of Pittsburgh to the folks back home. Soon after publishing her first book, *April Twilights*, she was lured to New York by S. S. McClure, owner and publisher of *McClure's Magazine*.

Cather may have lived out her life as a journalist if it were not for Sarah Orne Jewett. Cather was writing productively, but Jewett felt that she had lost some of her passion. Jewett thought the prairie and the wisdom Cather gained from older immigrant women would energize her work. Jewett said, "You must find your own quiet center of life and write from that to the world that holds offices, and all society, all Bohemia; the city, the country—in short you must write to the human heart."

Good advice! It proved to be a turning point in Cather's work. The prairie and the strong personalities of people who cleaved to the land became the inspiration for the books and stories for which she received many literary awards—including the Pulitzer Prize for literature in 1923.

PORTRAITS OF THE PRAIRIE

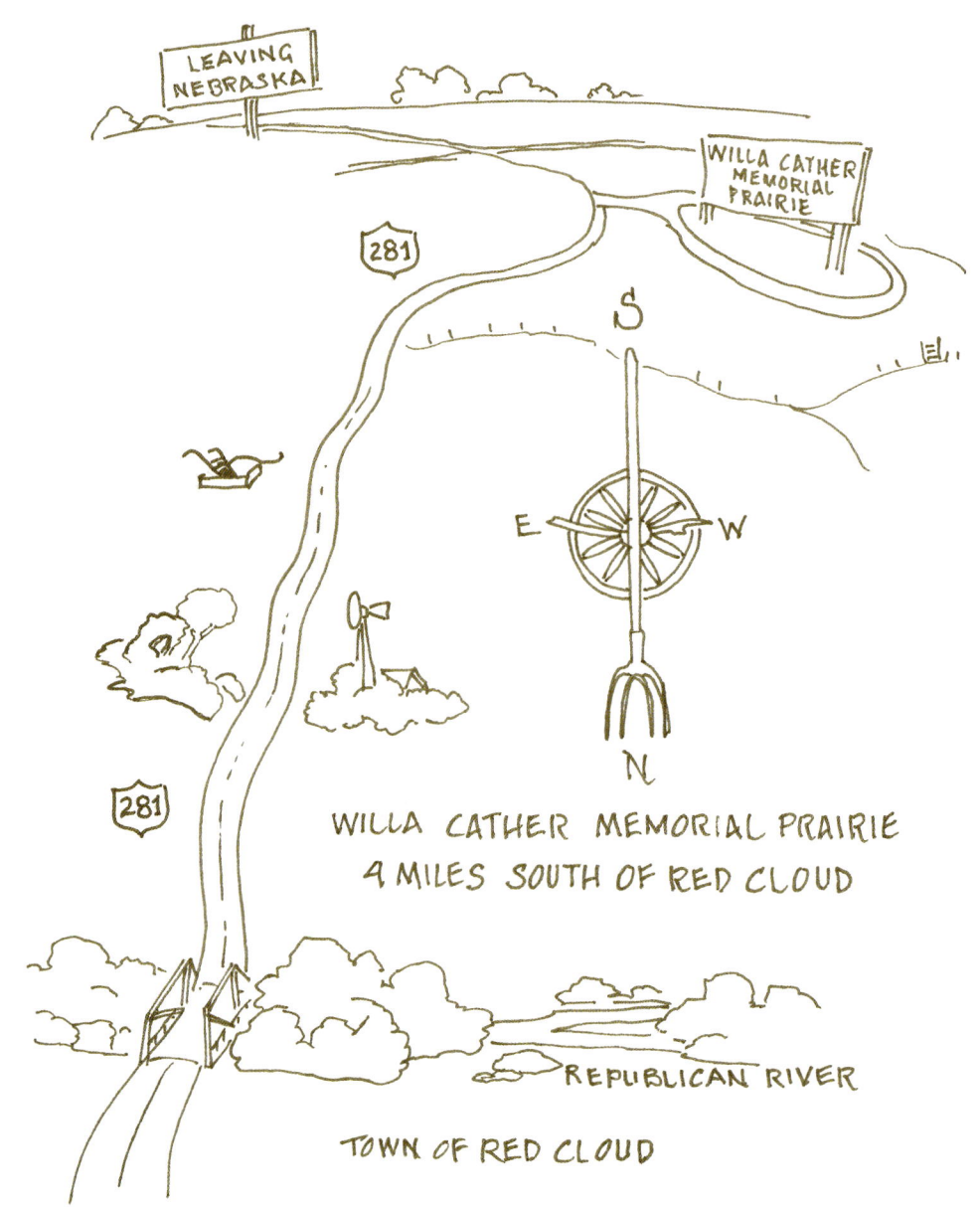

LEAVING NEBRASKA

WILLA CATHER MEMORIAL PRAIRIE

281

S

E W

N

281

WILLA CATHER MEMORIAL PRAIRIE
4 MILES SOUTH OF RED CLOUD

REPUBLICAN RIVER

TOWN OF RED CLOUD

This country was mostly wild pasture and as naked as the back of your hand. . . . So the country and I had it out together and by the end of the first autumn, that shaggy grass country had gripped me with a passion I have never been able to shake. It has been the happiness and the curse of my life.

INTERVIEW WITH CATHER IN THE *OMAHA DAILY BEE*, OCTOBER 29, 1921, *WILLA CATHER IN PERSON: INTERVIEWS, SPEECHES, AND LETTERS*, EDITED BY L. BRENT BOHLKE

The Land

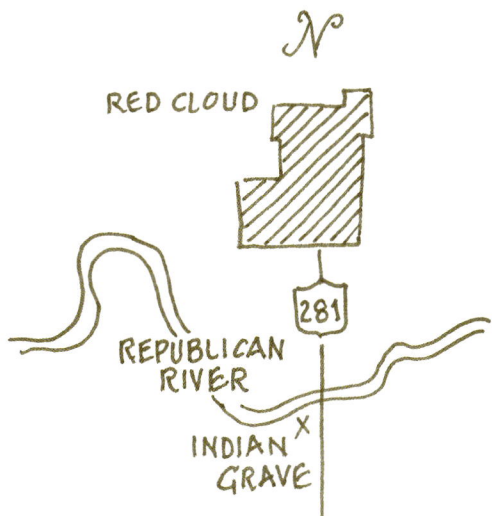

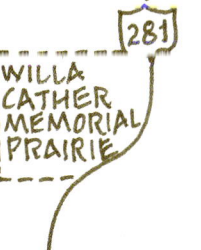

THE WILLA CATHER MEMORIAL PRAIRIE

This protected prairie is an example of the land that Cather loved. Here on the high land south of Red Cloud are 610 acres of virgin prairie grasses untouched by the tiller's plow.

On her left the Hereford cattle apparently wandered at will: the tall sunflowers hid the wire that kept them off the road. Far away, on the horizon line, a troop of colts were galloping, all in the same direction— purely for exercise, one would say. Between her and the horizon the white wheels of windmills told her where the farm house sat. "THE BEST YEARS"

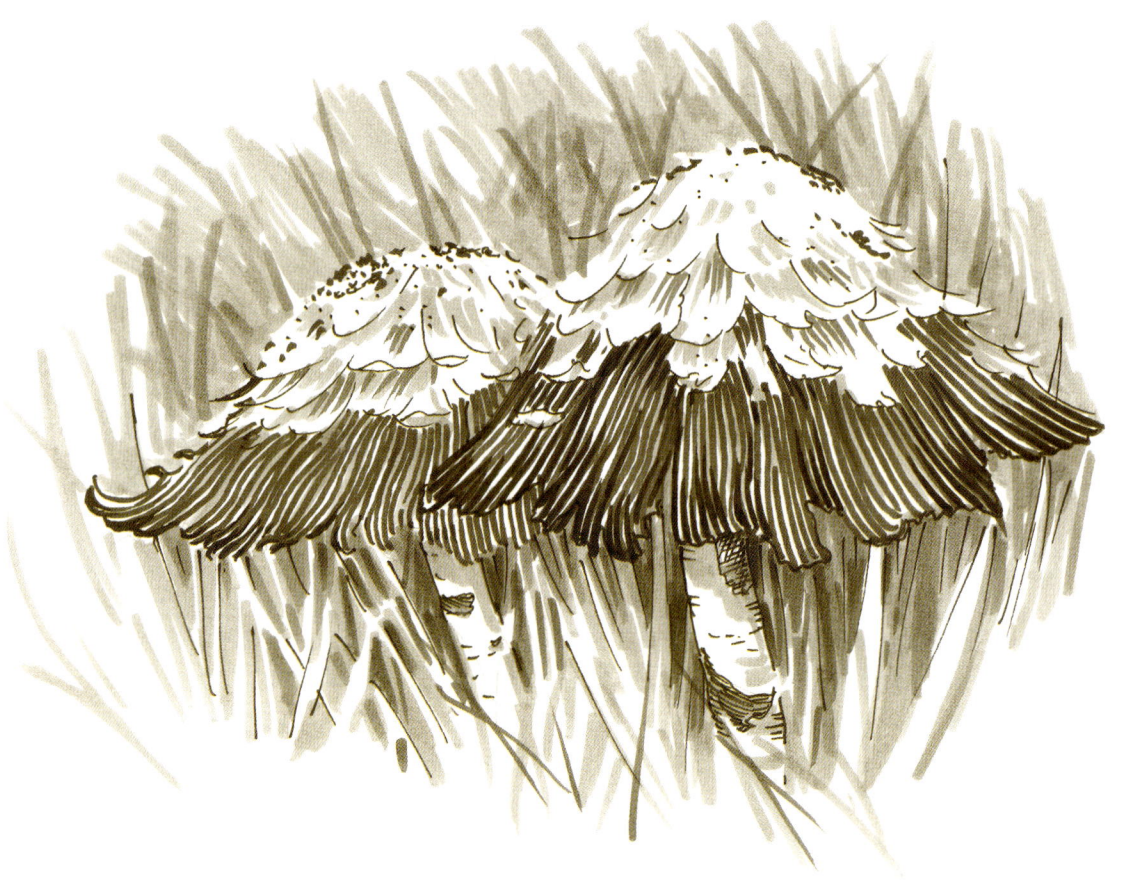

PRAIRIE MUSHROOMS

I separated the mantle of blowing prairie grass to expose other living forms. I found white, pancake-shaped fungi growing from short stocks. The edges of the mushrooms were circled with lace-like filaments that looked like dew drops. Little bumps on the upper surfaces captured sunlight and gave the organism a peculiar beauty. I learned later that they were meadow mushrooms, *Agaricus campestris*.

Here and there on the prairie path grew another fungal beauty—the shaggy mane fungus, *Coprinus comatus*. I had to lay prone on the path to study its morphology. Like a flowing ballroom gown, white feather-like down cascaded over a skirt of black dreadlocks.

Both of these mushrooms are edible and bring to mind an episode in Cather's *My Ántonia*. In the story, the Shimerdas gave the Burdens a bag of dried mushrooms. Not knowing what they were, Jim Burden's grandmother threw them into the fire, where they burned, but not before Jim rescued one and, on trying the tasty morsel, realized the great loss of this gift.

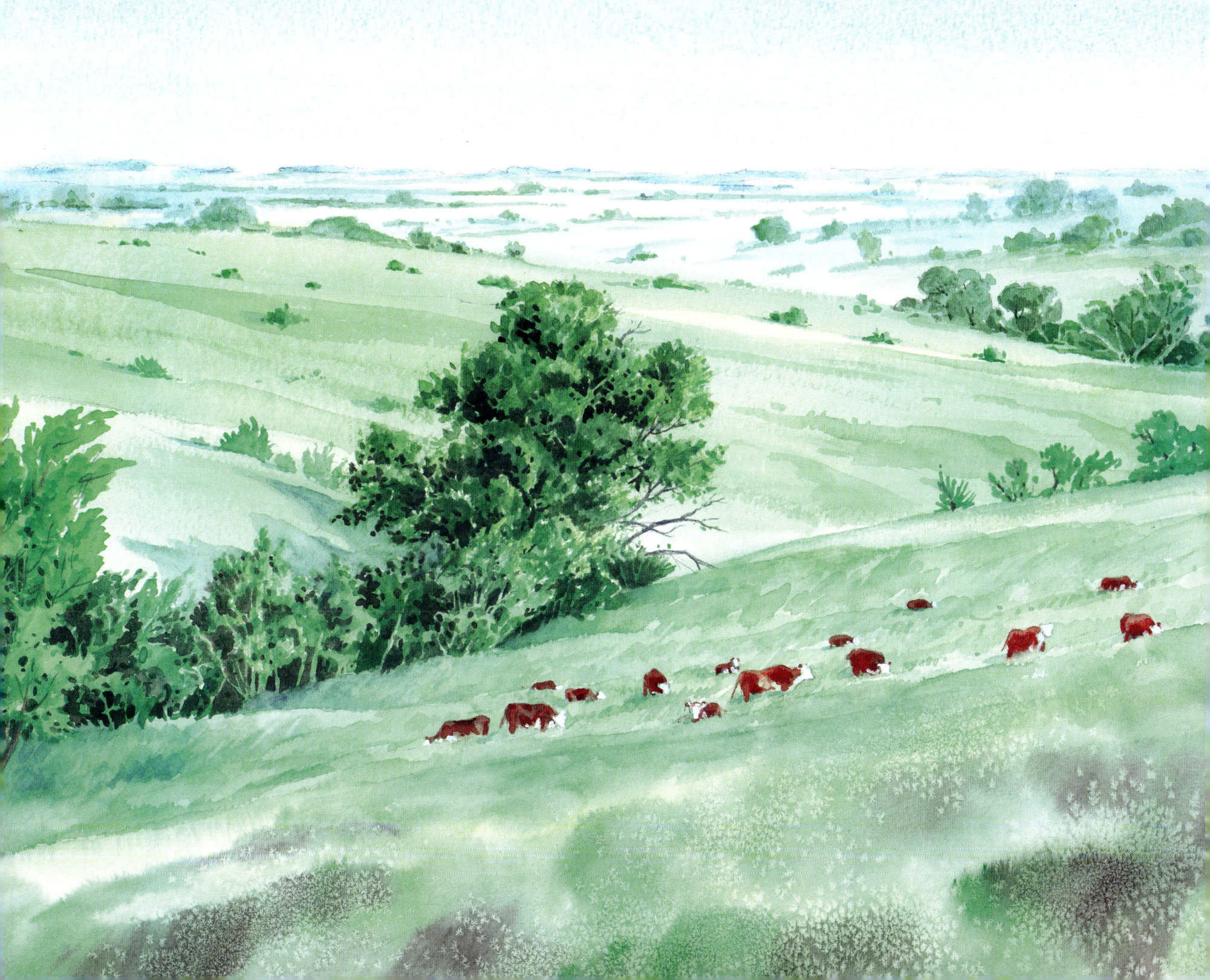

Once at the top and seated on the platform, they were silent. Margaret wondered if she would not hunger for that scene all her life, through all the routine of the days to come. Above them stretched the great Western sky, serenely blue, even in the night, with its big, burning stars, never so cold and dead and far away as in denser atmospheres. The moon would not be up for twenty minutes yet, and all about the horizon, that wide horizon, which seemed to reach around the world, lingered a pale white light, as of a universal dawn. The weary wind brought up to them the heavy odours of the cornfields.   "ERIC HERMANNSON'S SOUL"

In the summer Willa Cather and her brother Roscoe would sometimes climb their uncle George's fifty-foot windmill tower. In a letter to her friend, Mariel Gere, dated August 1, 1893, she describes one of these adventures: "Climbed the windmill in the evening and enjoyed the sight of moonlight glistening on ponds and corn tassels. Had to pull off skirts to climb down when a storm approached."

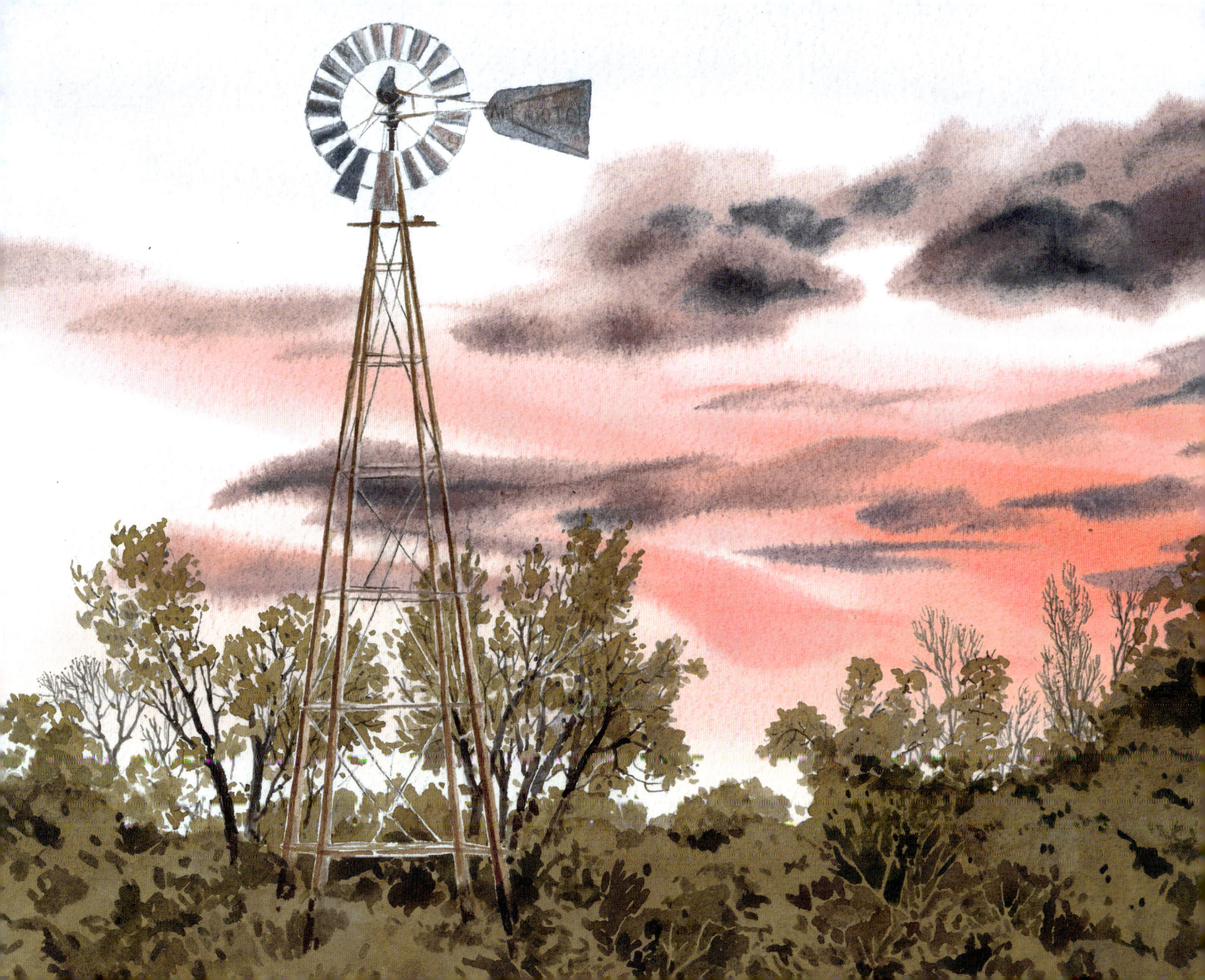

Isn't it queer: there are only two or three human stories, and they go on repeating themselves as fiercely as if they had never happened before; like the larks in this country, that have been singing the same five notes over for thousands of years.

O PIONEERS!

The Kansas-Nebraska Act in 1854 opened land formerly allotted to Indians for settlement. To encourage movement to the West, the U.S. Congress passed the Homestead Act in 1862, which gave 160 acres of public land to any head of household who lived on and improved the land for five years. The railroads were also given huge tracts of land to encourage development. Many people began to move to Nebraska Territory.

Charles B. Dempster was a visionary and saw a great opportunity. The immigrants moving to the territory needed water wells and pumps for livestock and domestic use. In 1878 he founded the Dempster Mill Manufacturing Company, which continues to manufacture windmills and pumps today in its Beatrice, Nebraska, plant.

THE CLAY CLIFFS

On one shore was an irregular line of bald clay bluffs where a few scruboaks with thick trunks and flat, twisted tops threw light shadows on the long grass.

"THE ENCHANTED BLUFF"

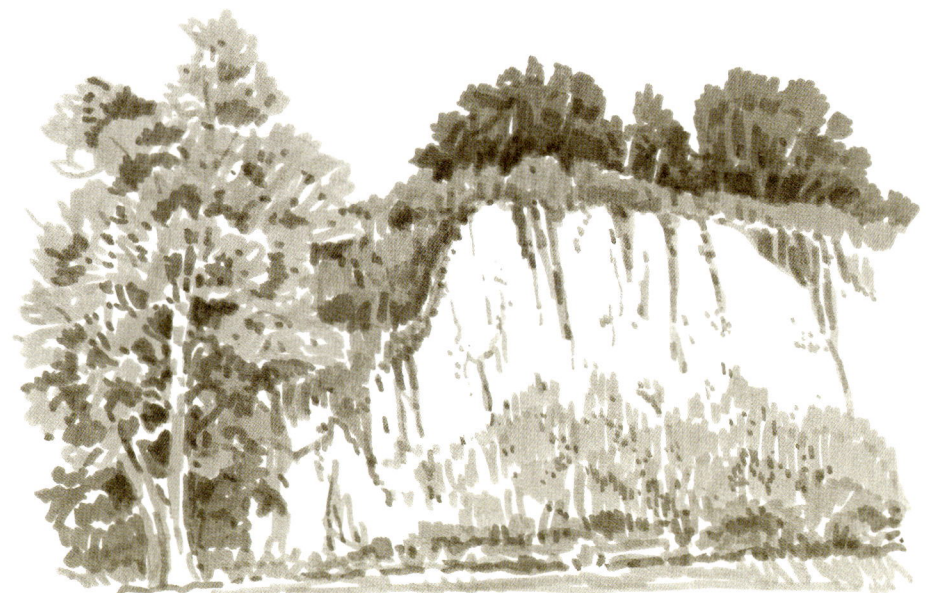

Before the land could be tamed and crops planted, the settlers had to construct shelters to protect themselves from the weather. The clay cliffs to the south provided the best temporary shelter. Dugouts were excavated and roughly lined with timbers. As time went on, additions were constructed outside the cliffs with more conventional building materials.

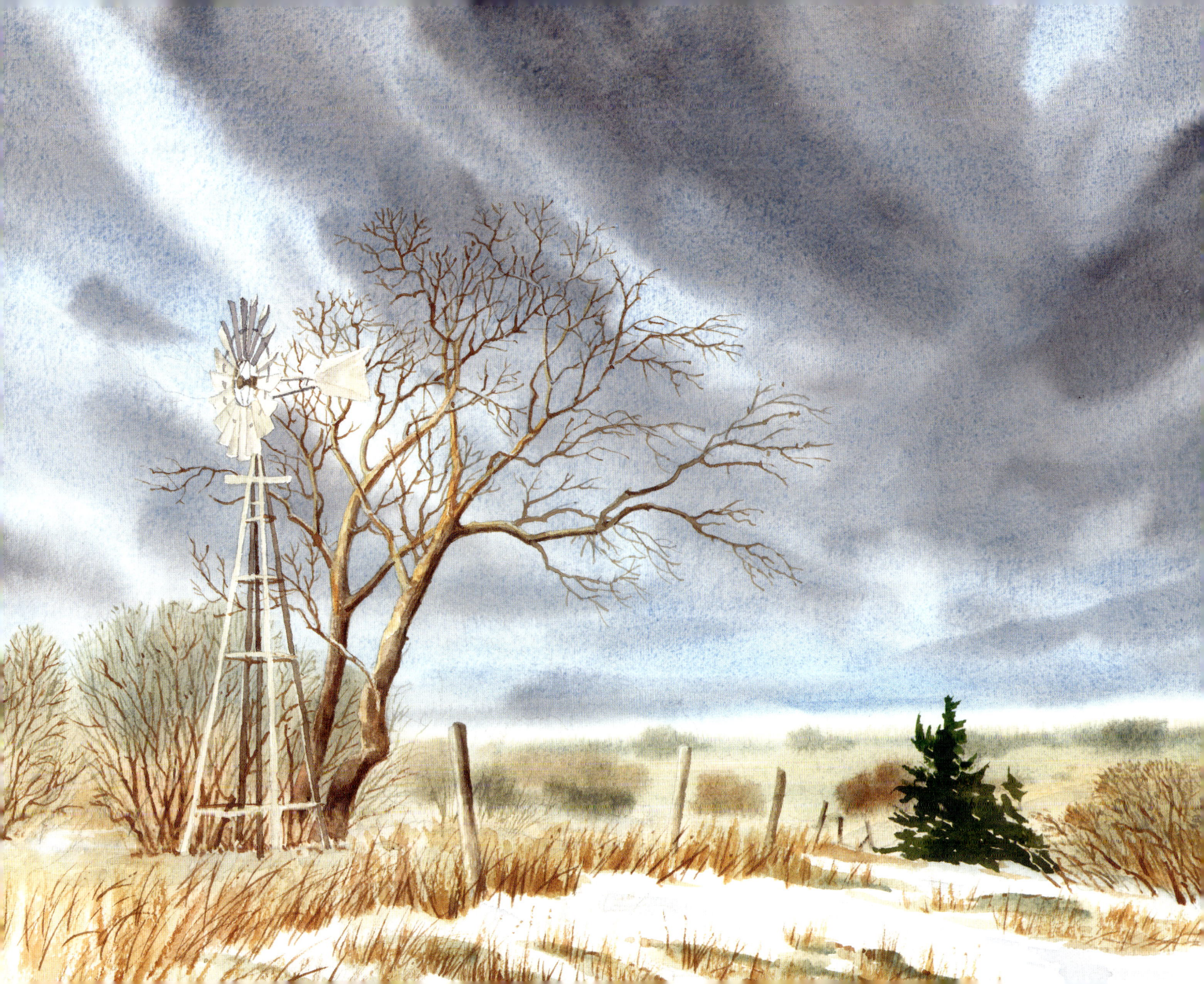

Presently they stopped before a little one-storey schoolhouse. All the windows were open. At the hitch-bar in the yard five horses were tethered—their saddles and bridles piled in an empty buckboard. There was a yard, but no fence—though on one side of the playground was a woven-wire fence covered with the vines of sturdy rambler roses—very pretty in the spring.   "THE BEST YEARS"

Cather's character Lesley Ferguesson taught in a little school called Wild Rose. The schoolhouse might have been like this one, which was moved in from the country and restored near Red Cloud.

I found the windmill next to this school of special interest. As this land was settled and farmed, a big market sprung up for windmills. On the vanes of these windmills were names like Everlasting, The Iron Screw, The Dandy, Favorite, and Aermotor.

In 1854 Daniel Halladay designed the first commercially successful windmill in the New World. Its unique design allowed the windmill to be self-governing and face changing wind directions. His machine had thin wooden blades that swiveled, adjusting their pitch and speed according to the velocity of the wind and reducing strain on the wind-wheel by keeping the pressure equalized.

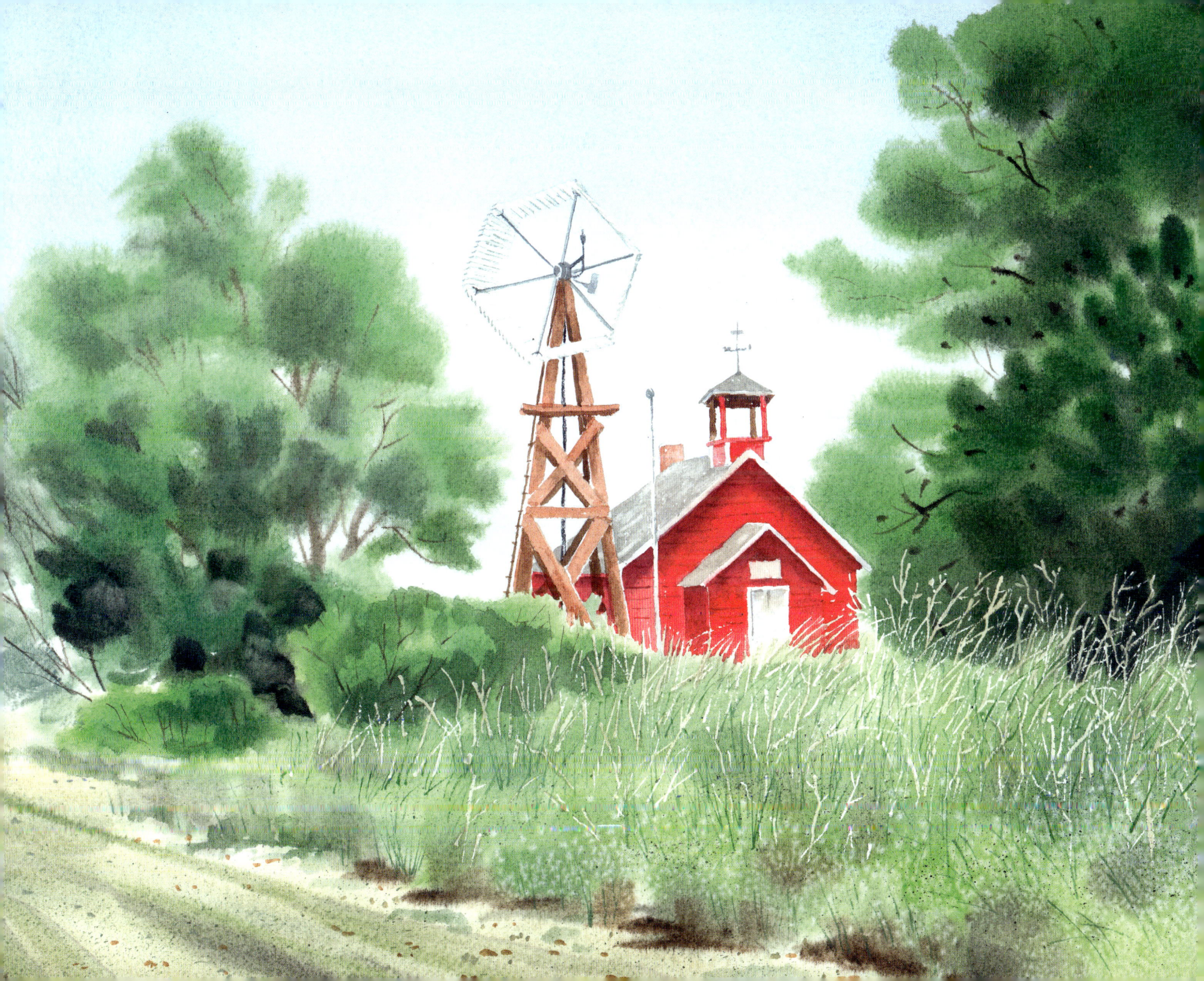

The sun dropped and lay like a great golden globe in the low west. While it hung there, the moon rose in the east, as big as a cart-wheel, pale silver and streaked with rose colour, thin as a bubble or a ghost-moon. For five, perhaps ten minutes, the two luminaries confronted each other across the level land, resting on opposite edges of the world. *MY ÁNTONIA*

Painting this scene presented a challenge because ambient light was coming from two sources—in front of me and behind me. The result was a surreal evening landscape where the warm pigments of the sky and field heightened the intensity of that magical evening time when both sun and moon encounter each other for only a moment.

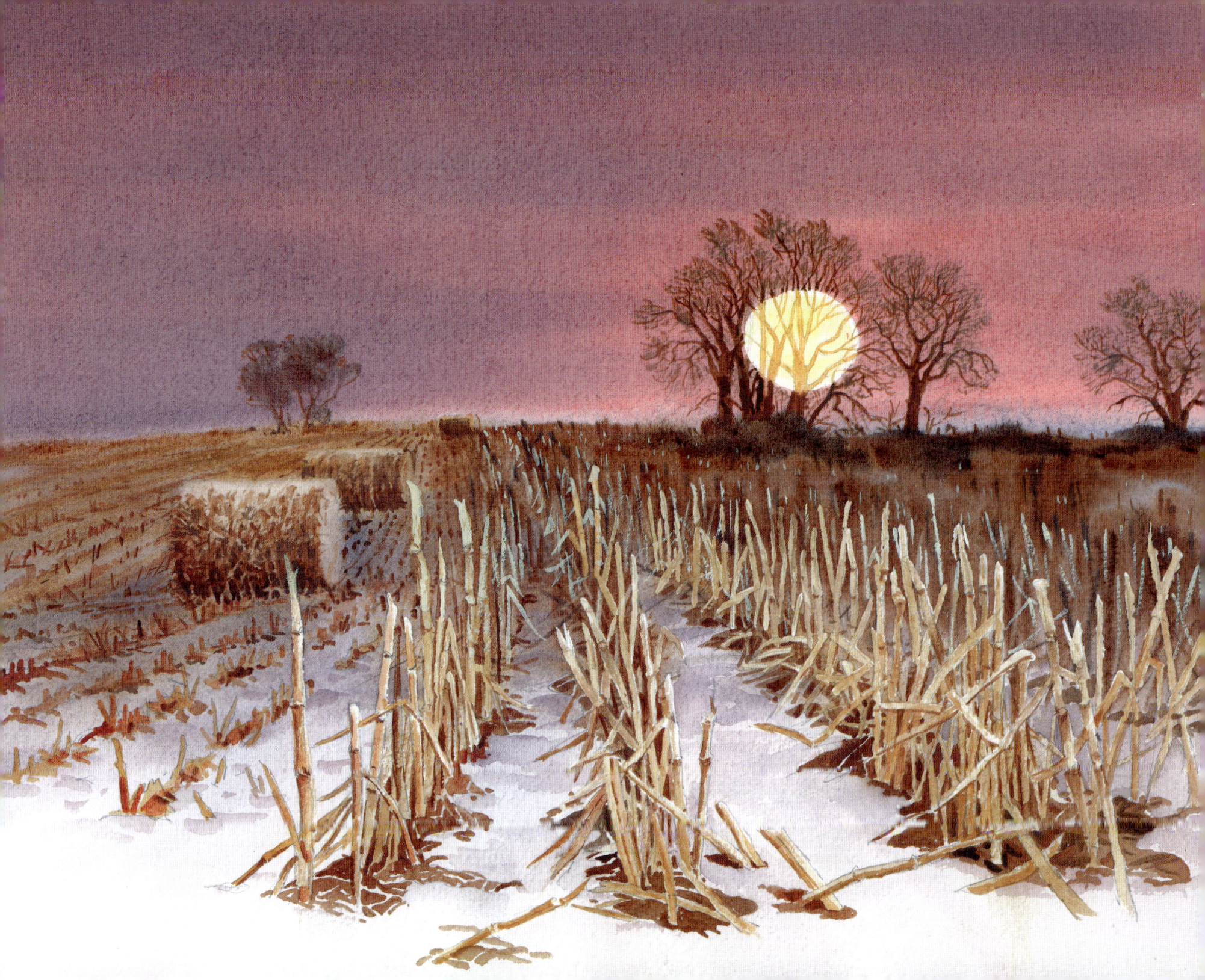

THE STARKE ROUND BARN

The Starke round barn, which is over a hundred years old, stands near Elm Creek, a few miles east of Red Cloud. I was curious to see the inside of this barn, possibly the largest circular barn in the country. I cautiously approached the three-level structure. It reminded me of a medieval castle with a drawbridge-like entrance to the second floor. On both sides of the planked ramp, the ground fell off to expose a lower level.

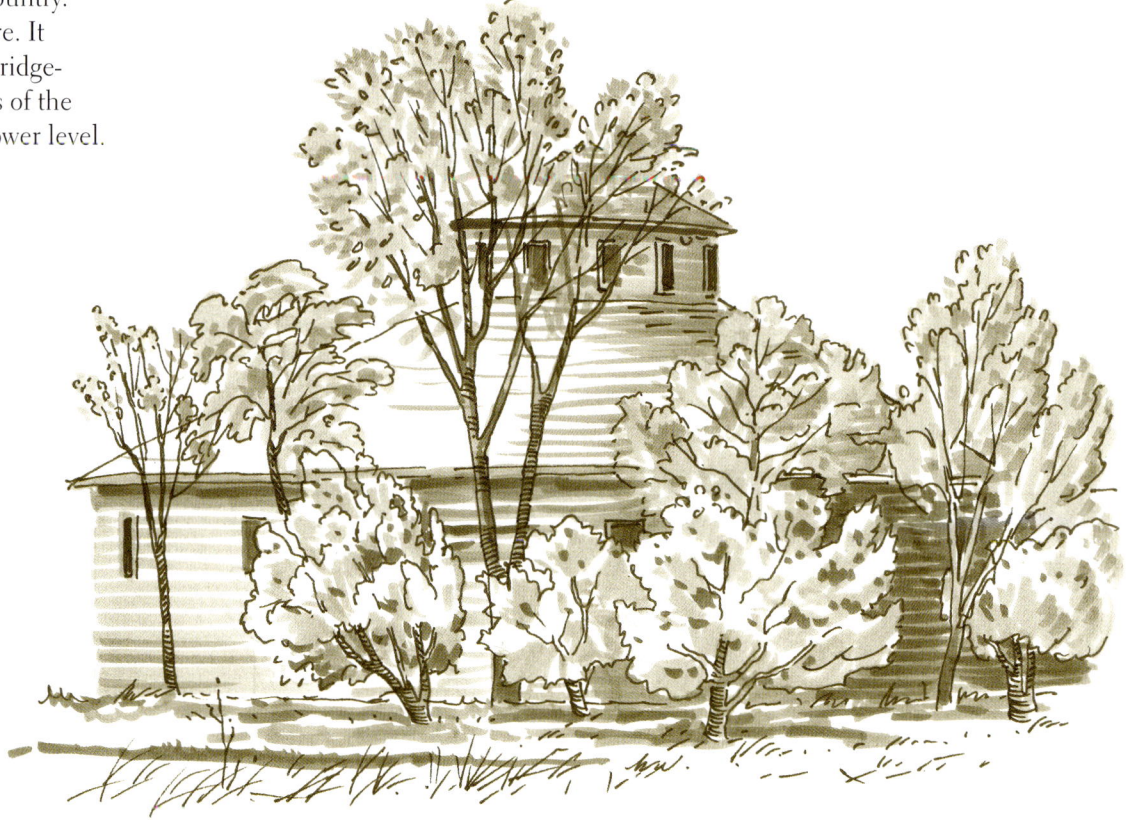

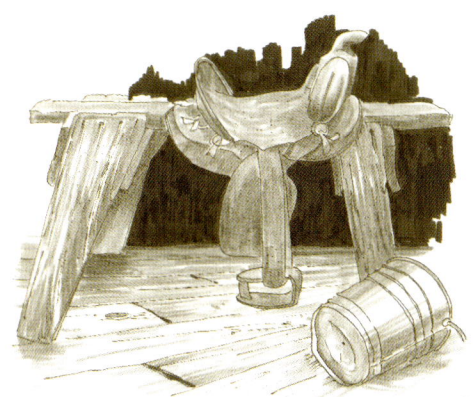

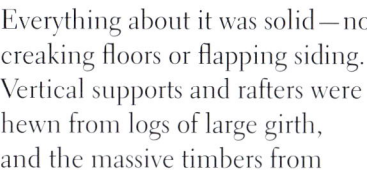

The sides of the round barn were clad with tin sheets painted white. The lower level had a row of closely placed windows that circled the barn like a ribbon. This level was reserved for livestock and milking the Holstein dairy cows that entered the barn from the lower side of the hill. The ground-level door that I entered opened to the second floor. It allowed entry of tractors and heavy farm equipment. There was another level above me that was used for hay storage and a track that was used to hoist hay into the loft from horse-drawn wagons below.

I stepped into the darkness of the cavernous structure hoping my eyes would adjust to the darkness before I fell into some exposed pit. My fear was not unfounded, for around the outside walls, dim light revealed a series of four-foot-square open holes in the flooring.

Suddenly, the slapping wings of a dozen pigeons taking flight from their roost in the rafters sent a chill up my back. My eyes were now starting to adjust to the low light, and I saw the skeletons of old farm machinery parked in the outer circle. In the center was a red brick silo surrounded by wooden cribs. Feed for the cows was dropped to the animals below.

The architect of this building masterfully created the best in form and function.

Everything about it was solid—no creaking floors or flapping siding. Vertical supports and rafters were hewn from logs of large girth, and the massive timbers from Wisconsin held the frame of the building together by balance and tension rather than nails. There were several windows in the upper level, and sunlight fell on a couple of old saddles that had been placed on sawhorses. There were other relics scattered over the floor.

Unfortunately, the Starke's farming operation was subject to periods of boom and bust. After losing millions of dollars, their farm, unique barn, and equipment were sold at auction on the courthouse steps at foreclosure.

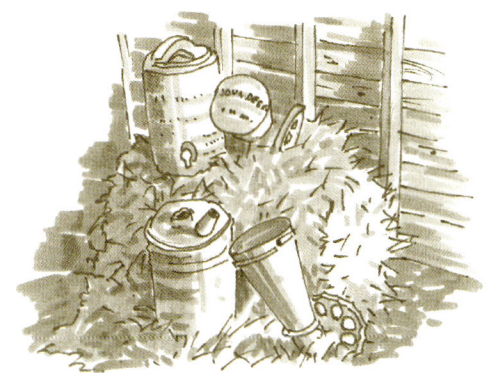

The moonlight flooded that great, silent land. The reaped fields lay yellow in it. The straw stacks and poplar windbreaks threw sharp black shadows. The roads were white rivers of dust. The sky was a deep, crystalline blue, and the stars were few and faint.

Everything seemed to have succumbed, to have sunk to sleep, under the great, golden, tender, midsummer moon. The splendour of it seemed to transcend human life and human fate. The senses were too feeble to take it in, and every time one looked up at the sky one felt unequal to it, as if one were sitting deaf under the waves of a great river of melody.

"THE BOHEMIAN GIRL"

A nighttime painting is one of the most difficult challenges facing an artist.

Colors are not discernable in moonlight because it is not intense enough to allow the retinal color cones in the eye to distinguish the pigments. A painting of varying degrees of blackness would not be successful. Therefore, the artist must work with certain representational pigments—Payne's grey (a beautiful blue-black color), neutral tint, sepia, and dark permanent green.

Frederic Remington was a master of nighttime western landscapes. He often used dark green mixed with black to achieve a realistic result. Here I have tried to create a nighttime image in which the moon hides among clouds in a partially star-lit sky.

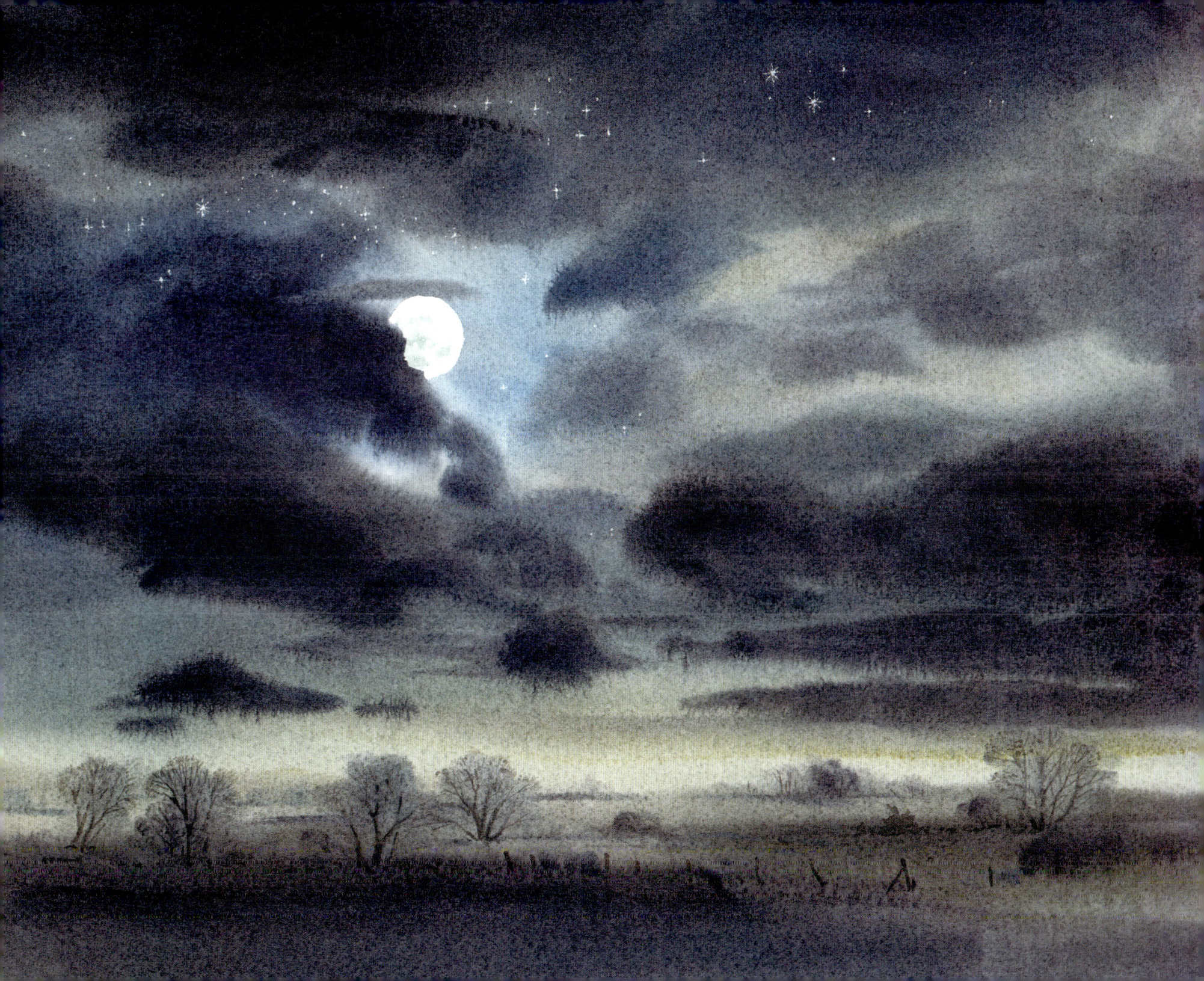

Elsewhere the sky is the roof of the world; but here the earth was the floor of the sky. The landscape one longed for when one was far away, the thing all about one, the world one actually lived in, was the sky, the sky!

DEATH COMES FOR THE ARCHBISHOP

During hot August afternoons, I have seen cumulus
clouds on the prairie that appeared to reach heights
of thirty or forty thousand feet. Virgas, which are
sheets of falling rain that vaporize before reaching
the ground, are often visible, as they were when this
picture was painted.

The wheat harvest was over, and here and there along the horizon I could see black puffs of smoke from the steam threshing-machines. The old pasture land was now being broken up into wheatfields and cornfields, the red grass was disappearing, and the whole face of the country was changing.

MY ÁNTONIA

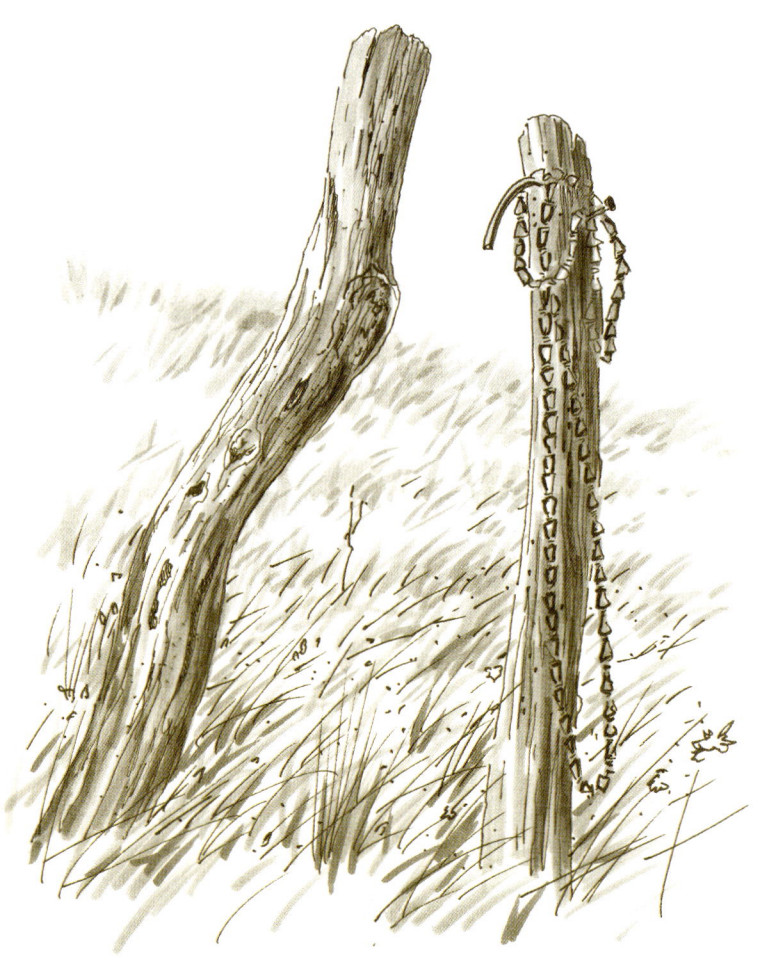

Beneath this prairie sky stretch miles of cultivated fields producing bountiful crops in most years. Center pivot irrigation has reduced some of the risk of sporadic and infrequent rains. In earlier days, farming an eighty-acre homestead was about as much as one man could handle, unless he had some able-bodied sons to help. Today, large, air-conditioned, music-filled tractors and combines roam the land guided by global positioning systems. Though technology has changed the way the land is managed, the prairie continues to mold the character of those who work it.

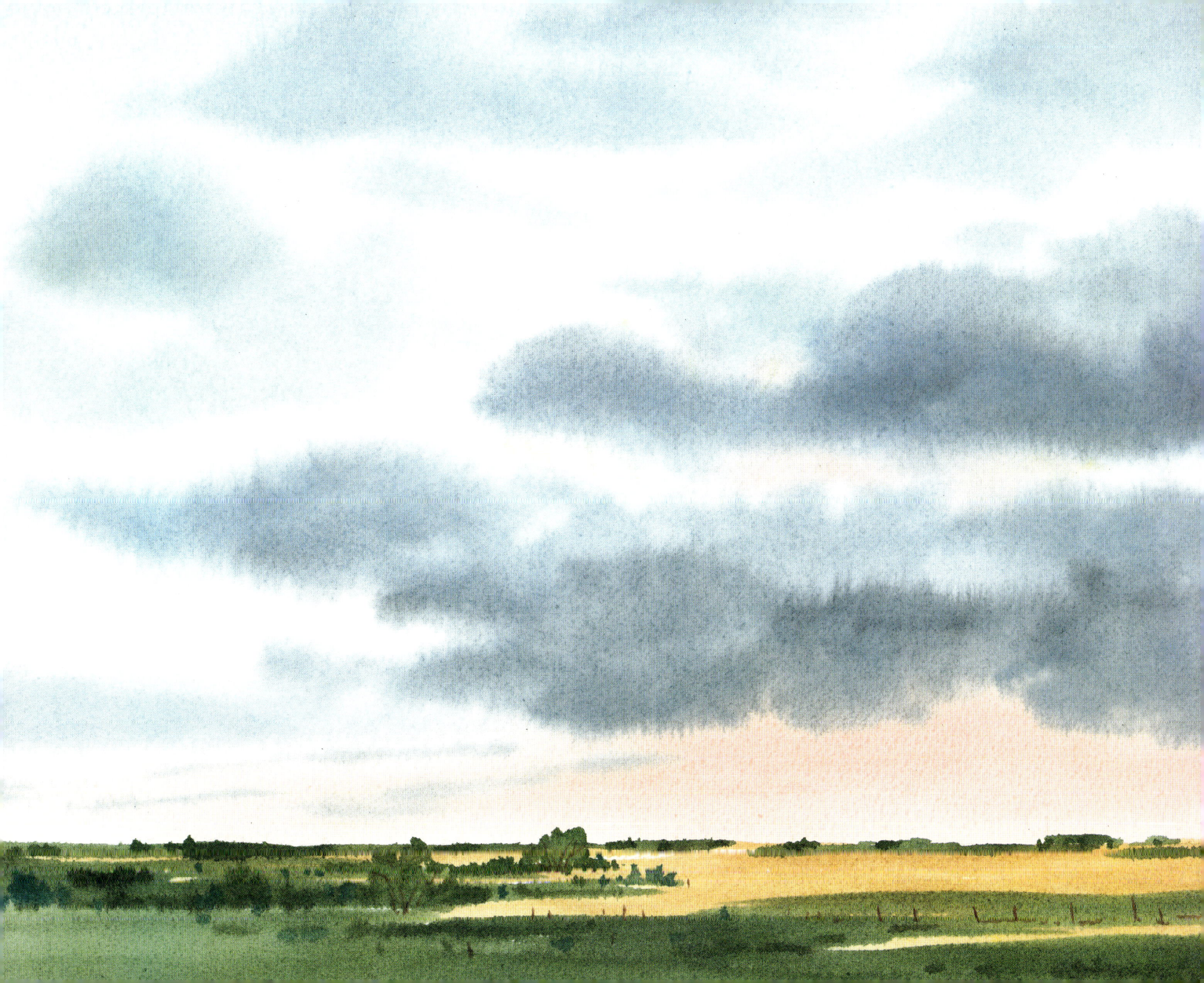

I understood. For her, just outside the door of the concert hall, lay the black pond with the cattle-tracked bluffs; the tall, unpainted house, with weather-curled boards; naked as a tower, the crook-backed ash seedling where the dishcloths hung to dry; the gaunt, molting turkeys picking up refuse about the kitchen door.

"A WAGNER MATINÉE"

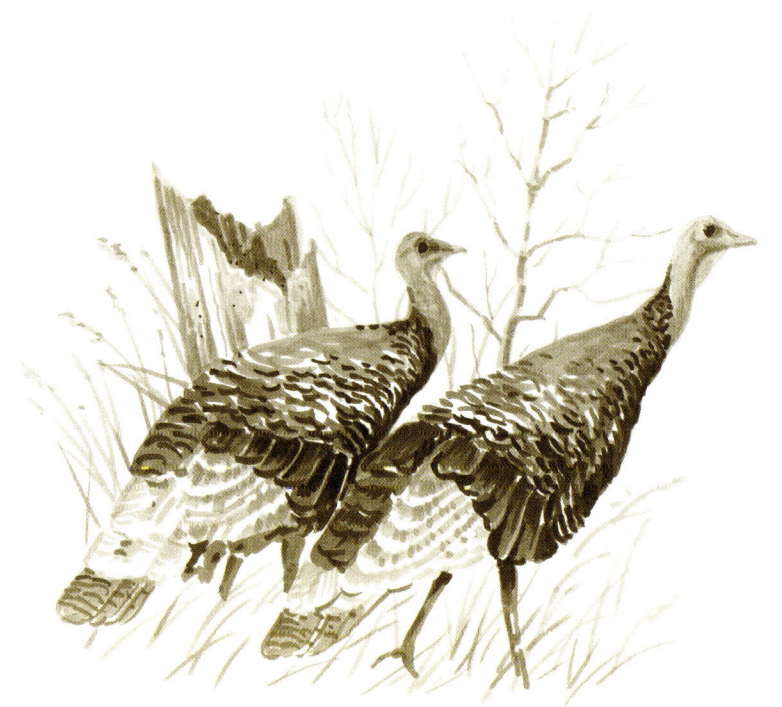

On a cold January morning I was startled with a vision on the hillside. A column of ancient centurions were plodding up the hill. Their heads were tiny and covered with equally tiny helmets. Their long necks and chests were thrust forward, their skinny legs exposed by wind that blew their great coats behind them—like cartoon characters of Roman knights. I squinted my eyes to see more clearly only to find turkeys trudging up the hill.

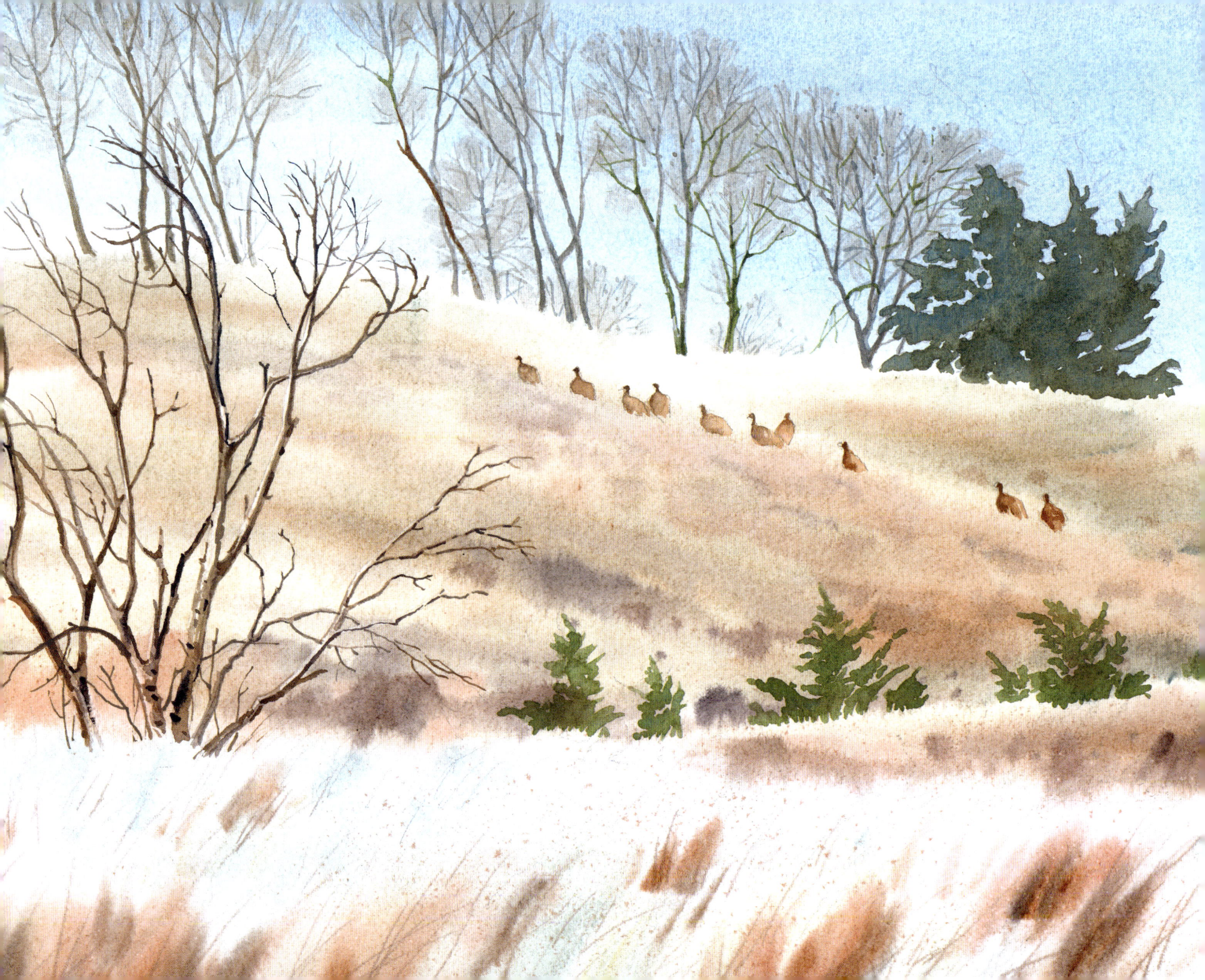

Prairie Dawn

A crimson fire that vanquishes the stars;
A pungent odor from the dusty sage;
A sudden stirring of the huddled herds;
A breaking of the distant table-lands
Through purple mists ascending, and the flare
Of water ditches silver in the light;
A swift, bright lance hurled low across the world;
A sudden sickness for the hills of home.

APRIL TWILIGHTS

Into the fields with the first flush of day, and
then the sun—oh hark! A burst of pure, heart-
lifting melody, the glorious song of the lark.

THE SONG OF THE LARK

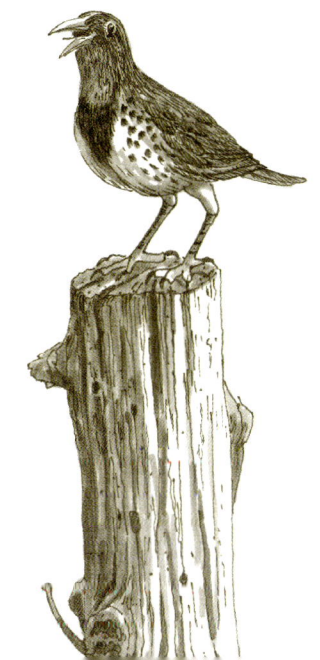

Sun rays pierced the morning vapor, casting painterly strokes in the rose-colored clouds. It was peaceful here, and barely a sound could be heard except for the larks. In the distance a cattle truck groaned as it down-shifted on the hill into town, puncturing the solitude of the moment until its grumbles were finally muffled by the trees of the valley. Then the silence of the prairie returned and the lark's song began again.

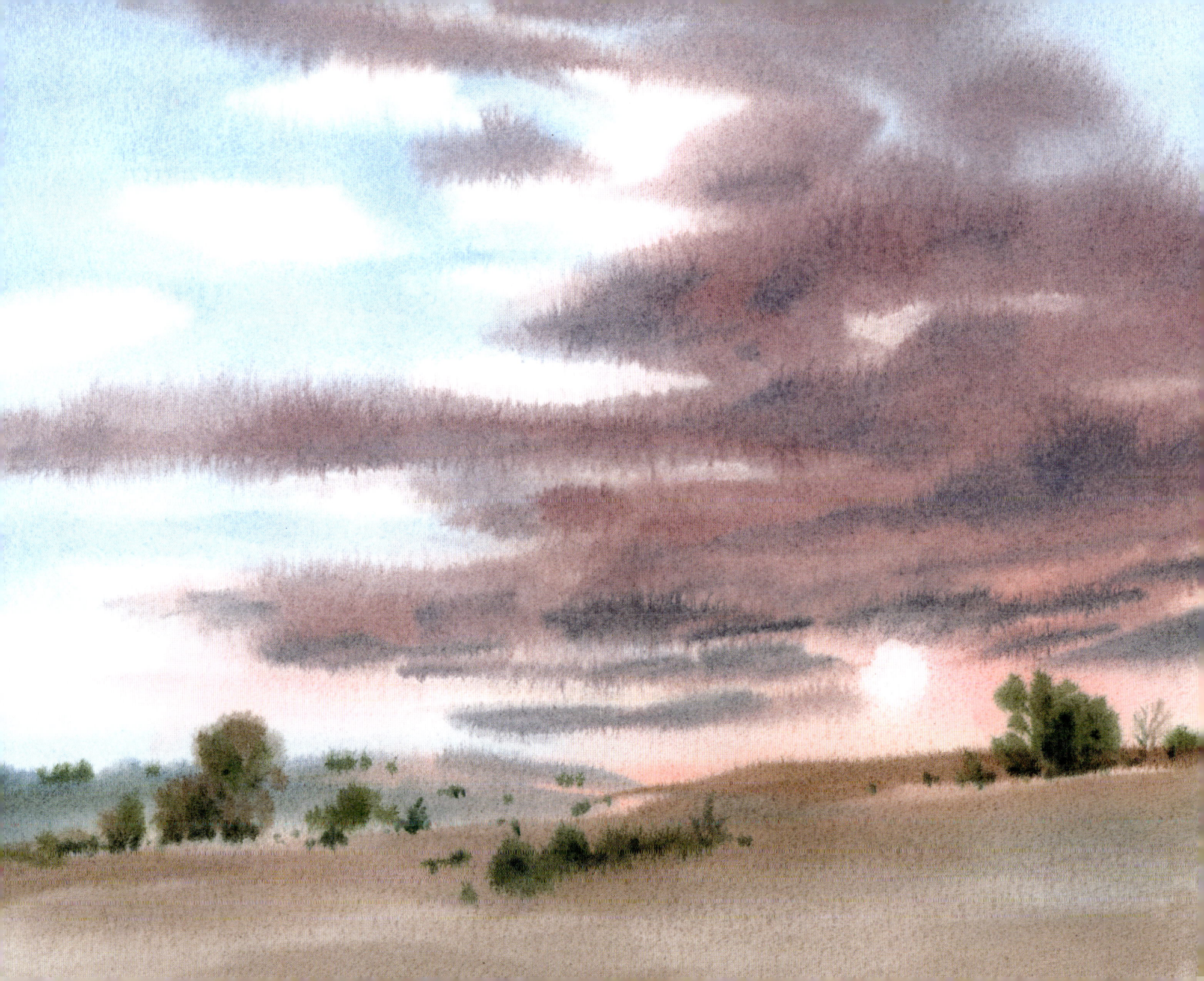

I still see some of these old threshing machines standing as iron-clad dinosaurs in corners of fields. Hiram A. and John A. Pitts of Winthrop, Maine, patented the threshing machine in 1837. Prior to that date, farm workers beat the stalks with a flail or used animals to trample them to release the grain. The invention of the thresher revolutionized the harvest by separating the grain from the husk, cleaning the grain, and then stacking it, eliminating some of the drudgery of fieldwork. Threshers were moved by horses into the fields, where they received wagonloads of wheat to be processed.

1904 RUMELY STEAM ENGINE

Soon the invention of the steam engine would further revolutionize farming. A portable steam engine that would drive the thresher was developed and simplified the process even more. Meinrad Rumely, a German immigrant, designed the hallmark of the industry with the Advance-Rumely Universal steam engine, which was equipped with a power take-off that provided up to forty horsepower on the belt that drove the thresher. I found this 1904 model in the Webster County Museum. Threshers like this were used for decades until the early twentieth century, when self-propelled monster machines called combines roamed the fields combining the operations of cutting and separating the grain from the chaff and straw.

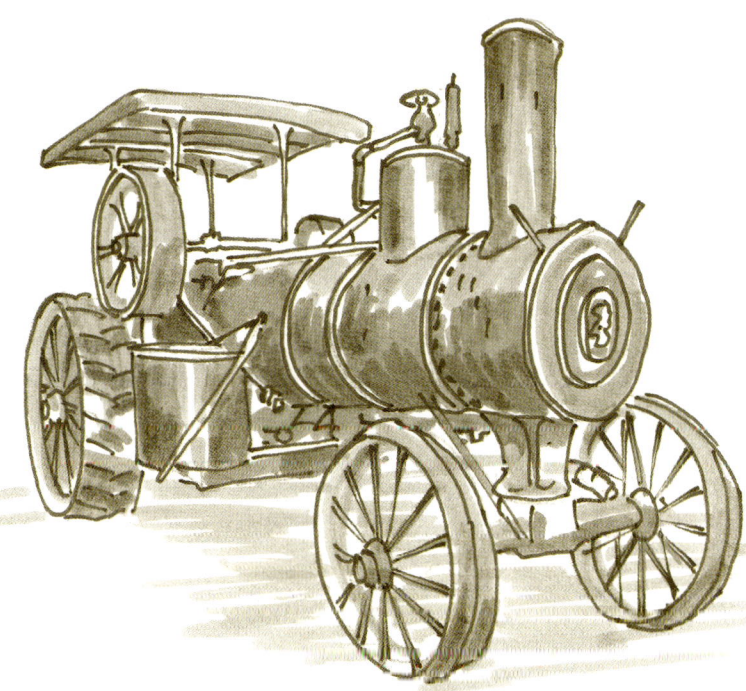

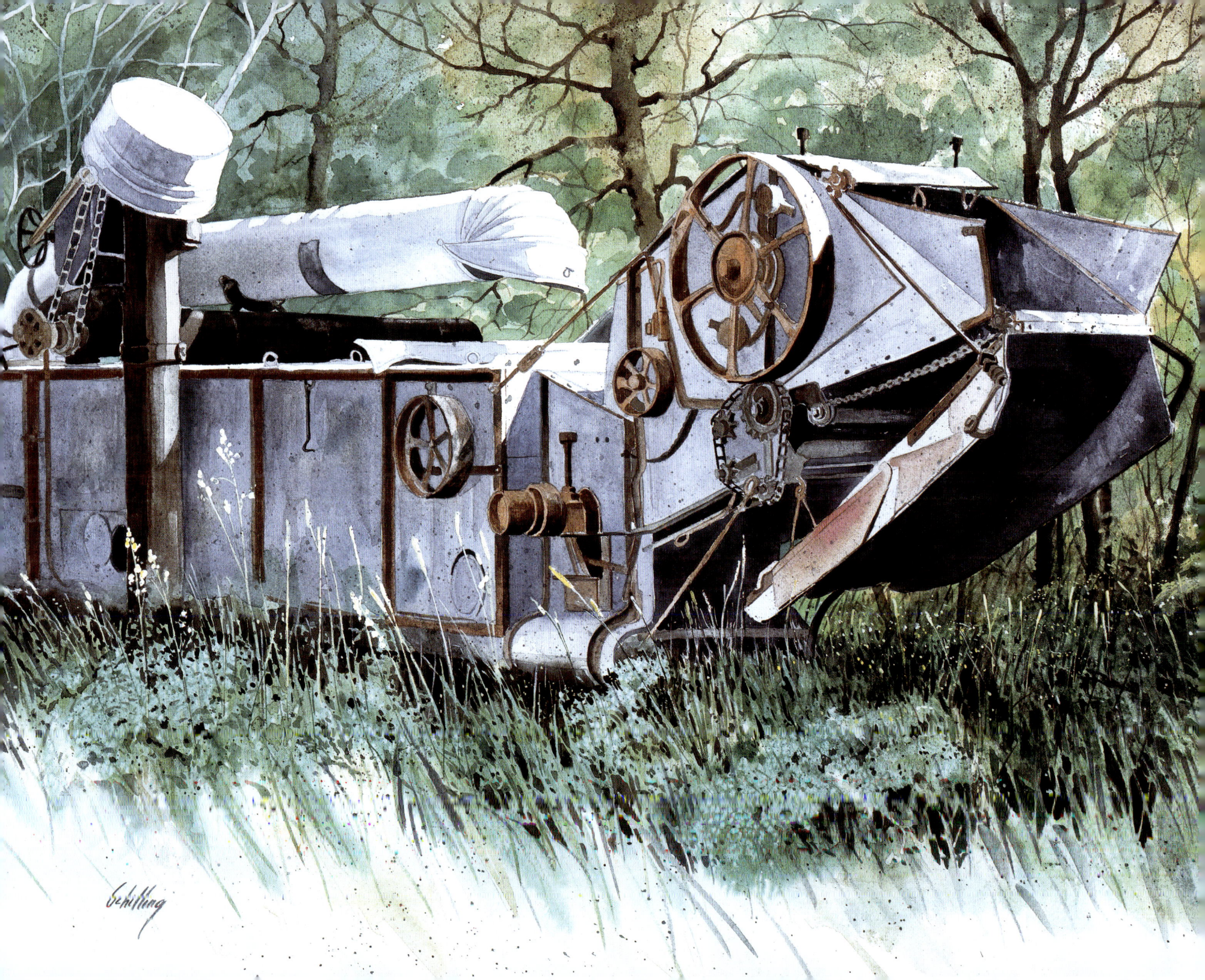

She had never known before how much the country meant to her. The chirping of the insects down in the long grass had been like the sweetest music. She had felt as if her heart were hiding down there, somewhere, with the quail and the plover and all the little wild things that crooned or buzzed in the sun. Under the long shaggy ridges, she felt the future stirring.

O PIONEERS!

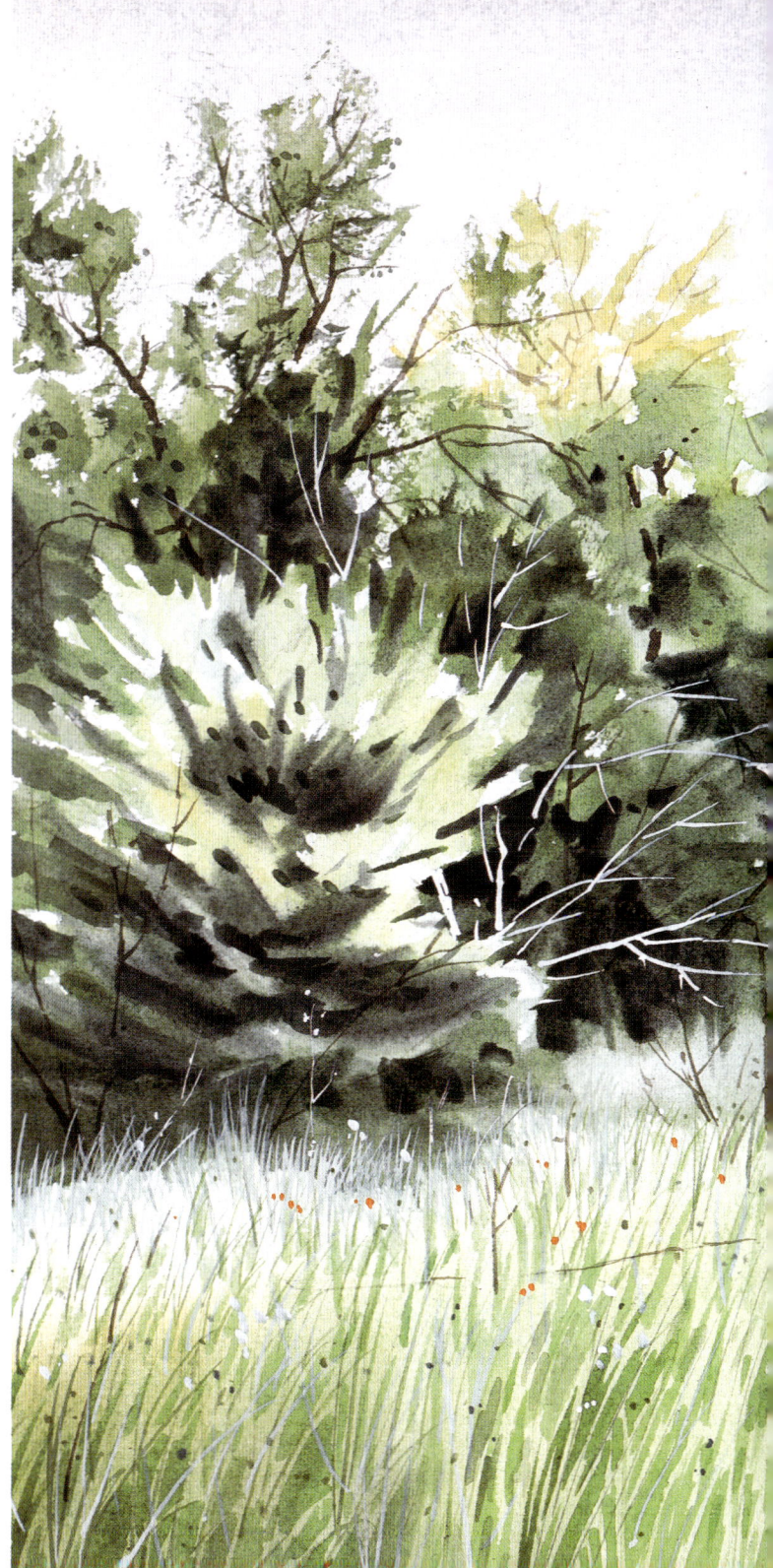

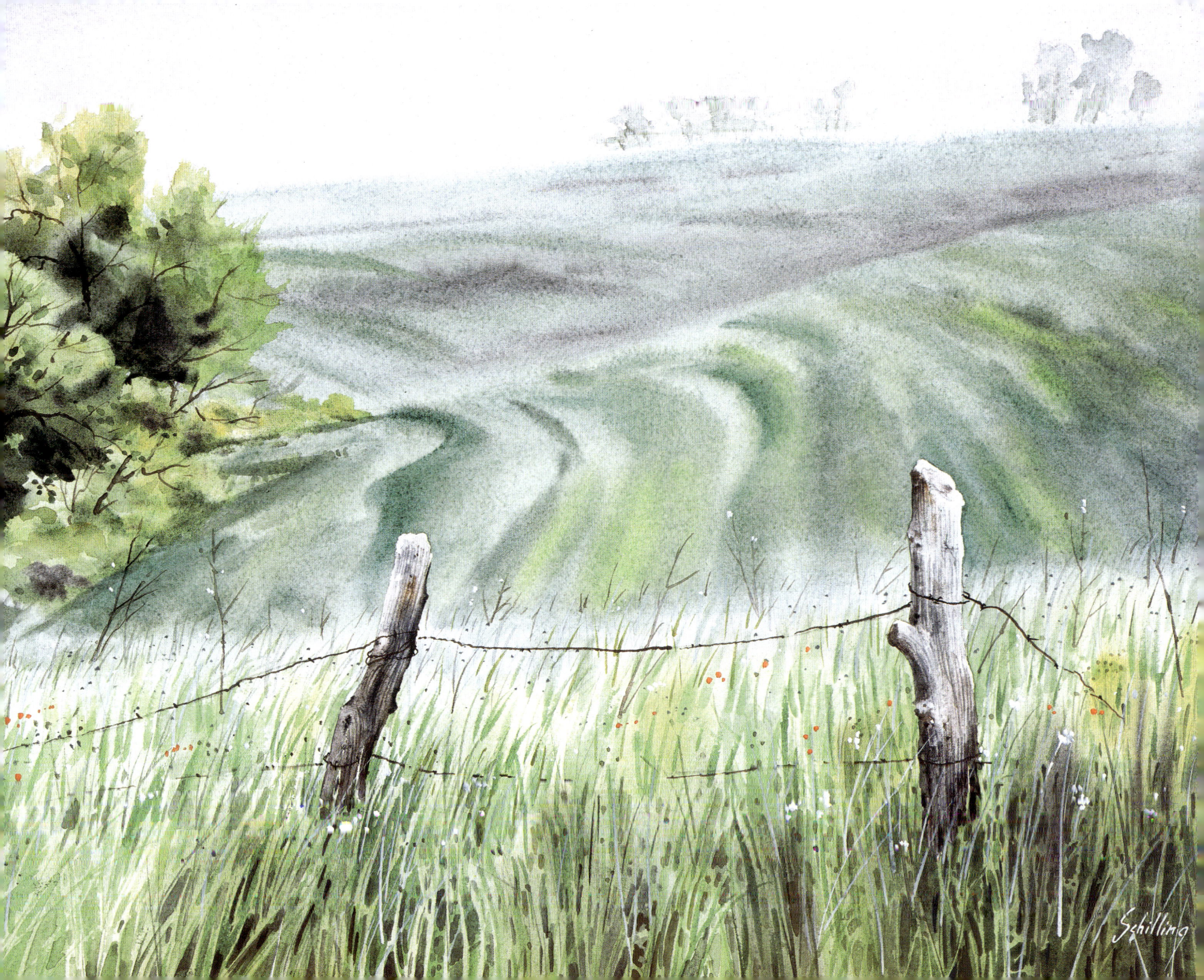

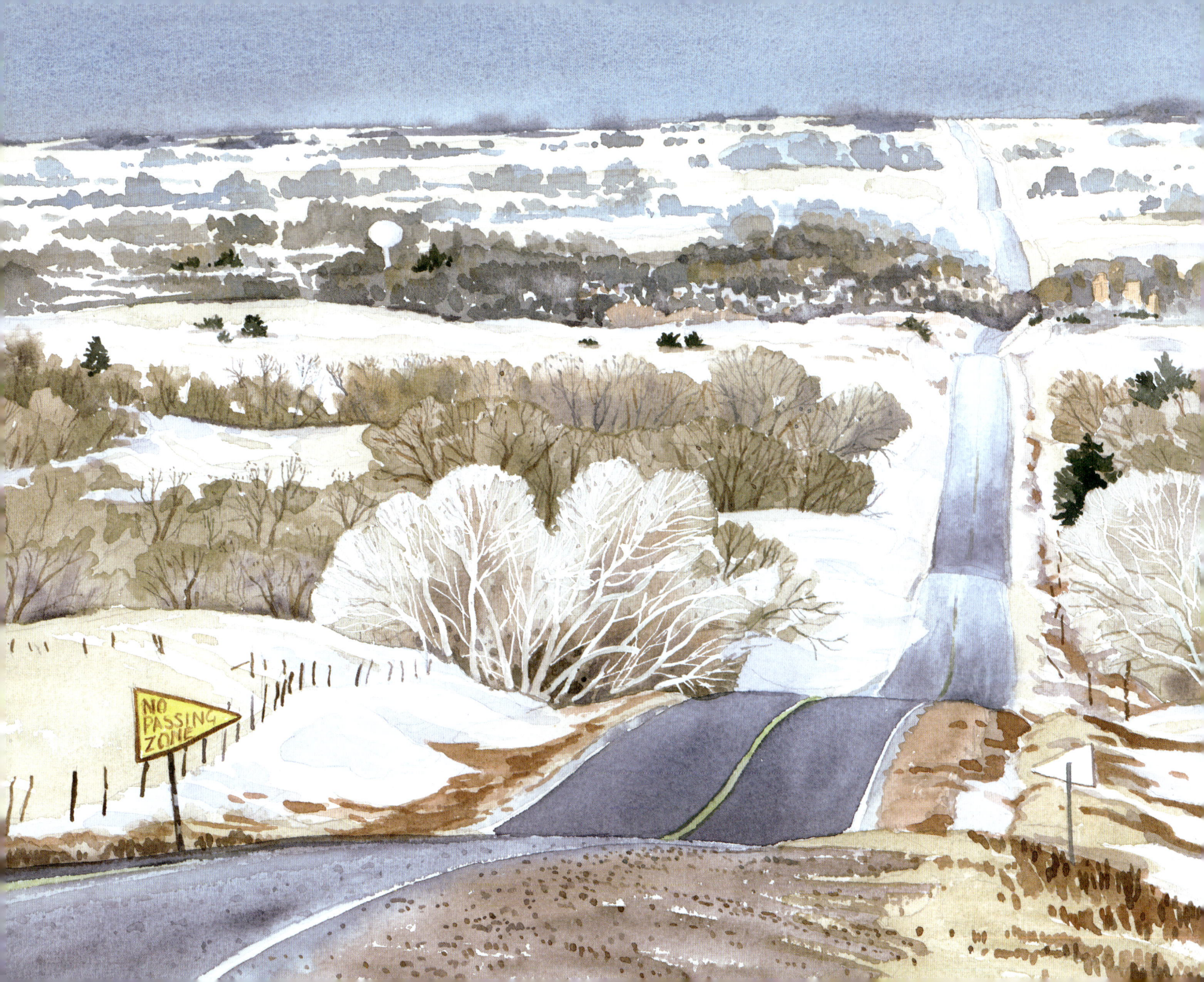

Country Roads

One January day, thirty years ago, the little town of Hanover, anchored on a windy Nebraska tableland, was trying not to be blown away. A mist of fine snowflakes was curling and eddying about the cluster of low drab buildings huddled on the gray prairie, under a gray sky. The dwelling-houses were set about haphazard on the tough prairie sod; some of them looked as if they had been moved in overnight, and others as if they were straying off by themselves, headed straight for the open plain. None of them had any appearance of permanence, and the howling wind blew under them as well as over them. *O PIONEERS!*

I headed north on State Highway 281 into Red Cloud on a winter morning. I was thinking of Cather's description of the trails that crisscrossed the prairie made by pioneers to reach their neighbors' places. These paths were usually the shortest distance between two points.

Today, roads intersect at almost every mile to form grids dividing the prairie into sections, townships, and counties. For me, the county roads have character. Their quirky personalities range from roads where rooster tails of dust chase farm trucks and wagons across the horizon, to hills swaddled with roads of brick-hard clay, called gumbo, which becomes a sticky, gummy mass when wet. Walking in this mud is nearly impossible. As one man commented, "you get taller with every step you take."

The windy springs and blazing summers, one after another, had enriched and mellowed that flat tableland; all the human effort that had gone into it was coming back in long, sweeping lines of fertility. The changes seemed beautiful and harmonious to me; it was like watching the growth of a great man or a great idea. I recognized every tree and sandbank and rugged draw. I found that I remembered the conformation of the land as one remembers the modeling of human faces.   *MY ÁNTONIA*

The sign said "Limited Maintenance Road." I thought this was an understatement. Even better-maintained roads of Webster County require a vehicle operator to be alert. I especially had to be watchful for approaching farm equipment on the crests of hills. The roads could be slippery even in summer when covered by a blanket of powdered clay, and I hoped I would not have to walk to a farmer's home and ask to be towed out of a barrow pit.

I used a yellow sky in this painting to indicate a hot, dry summer day. It would be unusual to see a sky of this color, but in this picture it denotes summer heat—an artist's trick to the senses.

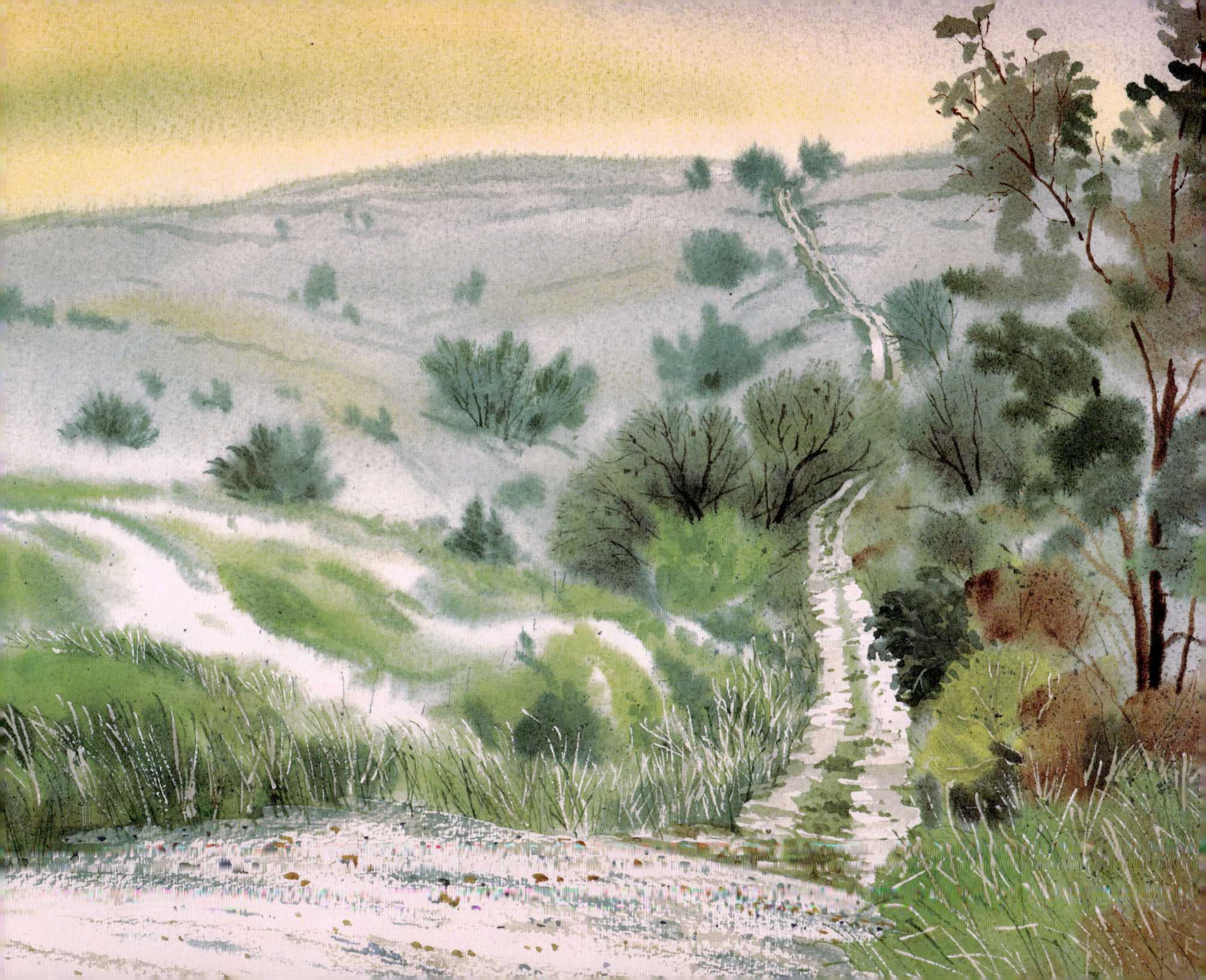

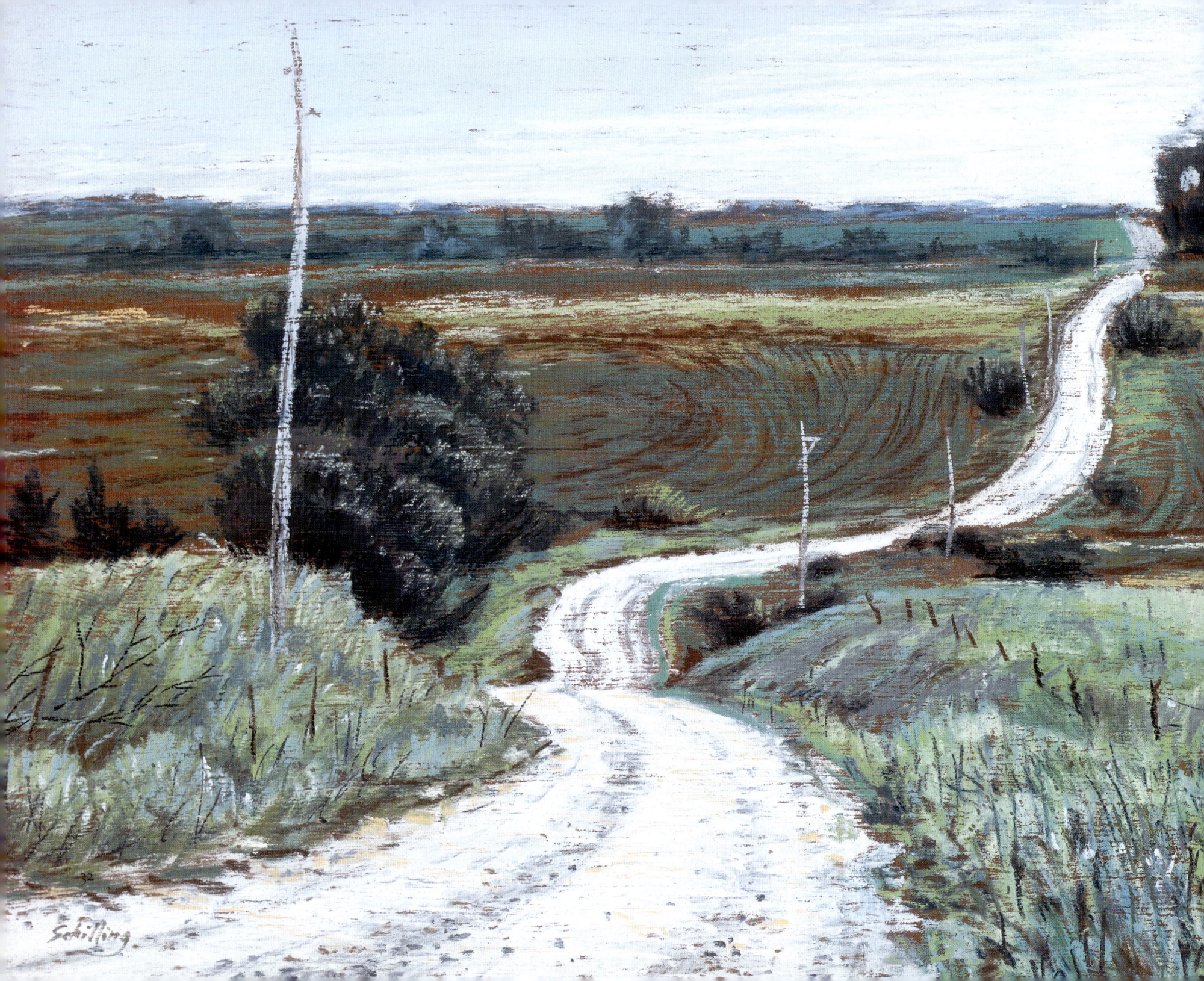

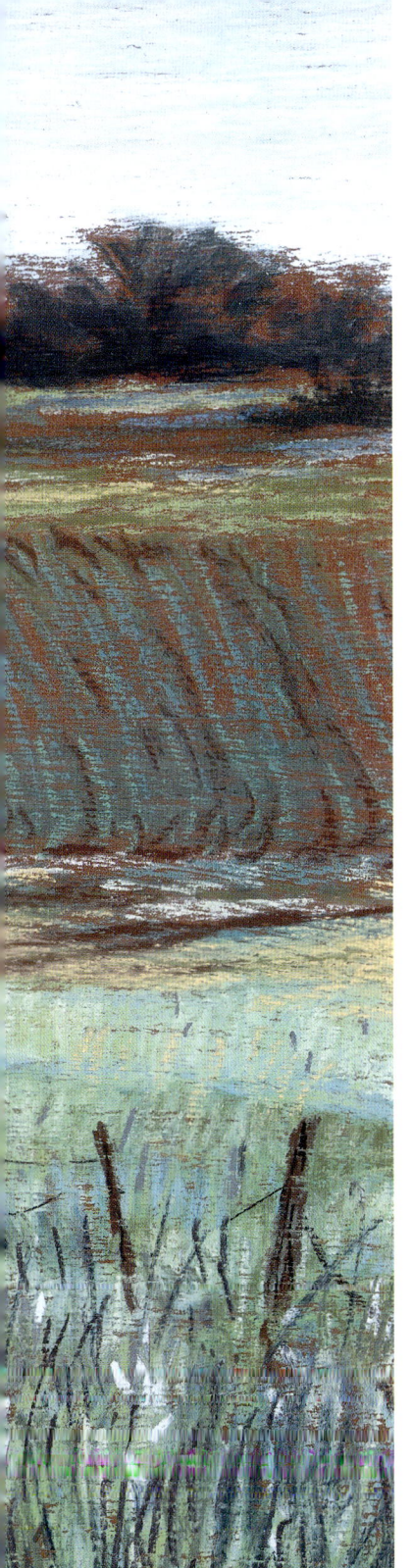

I could hardly wait to see what lay beyond that cornfield; but there was only red grass like ours, and nothing else, though from the high wagon-seat one could look off a long way. The road ran about like a wild thing, avoiding the deep draws, crossing them where they were wide and shallow. And all along it, wherever it looped or ran, the sunflowers grew; some of them were as big as little trees, with great rough leaves and many branches which bore dozens of blossoms. They made a gold ribbon across the prairie.

MY ÁNTONIA

Sunflower-bordered roads always seem to me the roads to freedom.   *MY ÁNTONIA*

The roads of the hill country north of Red Cloud exhibit character like human faces sculpted and wrinkled by time. County roads twist and deviate, occasionally yielding to a creek or an eroded hillside.

This pastel painting's point of interest is the twisting road and the sense of distance and expectancy it imparts. Roads like these are lonely and void of travelers, but for me, they are filled with promise as I eagerly anticipate the view from the next hill.

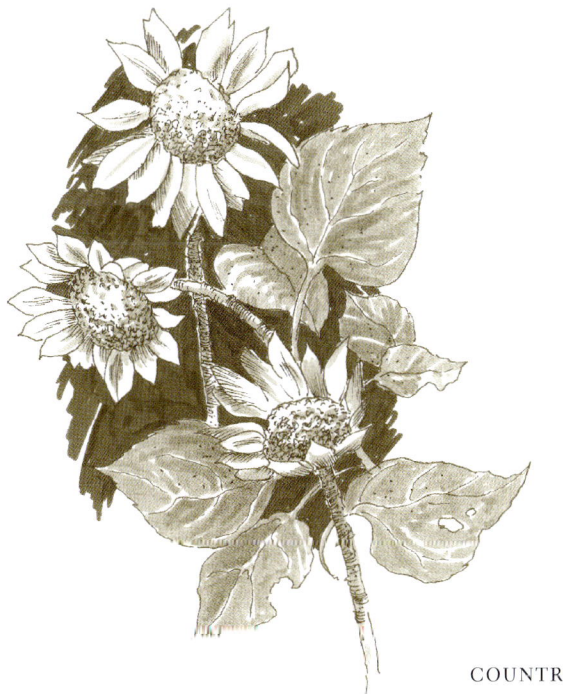

We drove out from Red Cloud to my grandfather's homestead one day in April. I was sitting on the hay in the bottom of a Studebaker wagon, holding on to the side of the wagon box to steady myself—the roads were mostly faint trails over the bunch grass in those days. The land was open range and there was almost no fencing. As we drove further and further out into the country, I felt a good deal as if we had come to the end of everything—it was a kind of erasure of personality.

INTERVIEW, AUGUST 10, 1913, F.H. SPECIAL CORRESPONDENCE OF
THE *PHILADELPHIA RECORD*. *WILLA CATHER IN PERSON: INTERVIEWS,
SPEECHES, AND LETTERS*, EDITED BY L. BRENT BOHLKE

Carl leaned forward and touched her arm, smiling,—"I even think I liked the old country better. This is all very splendid in its way, but there was something about this country when it was a wild old beast that has haunted me all these years."

O PIONEERS!

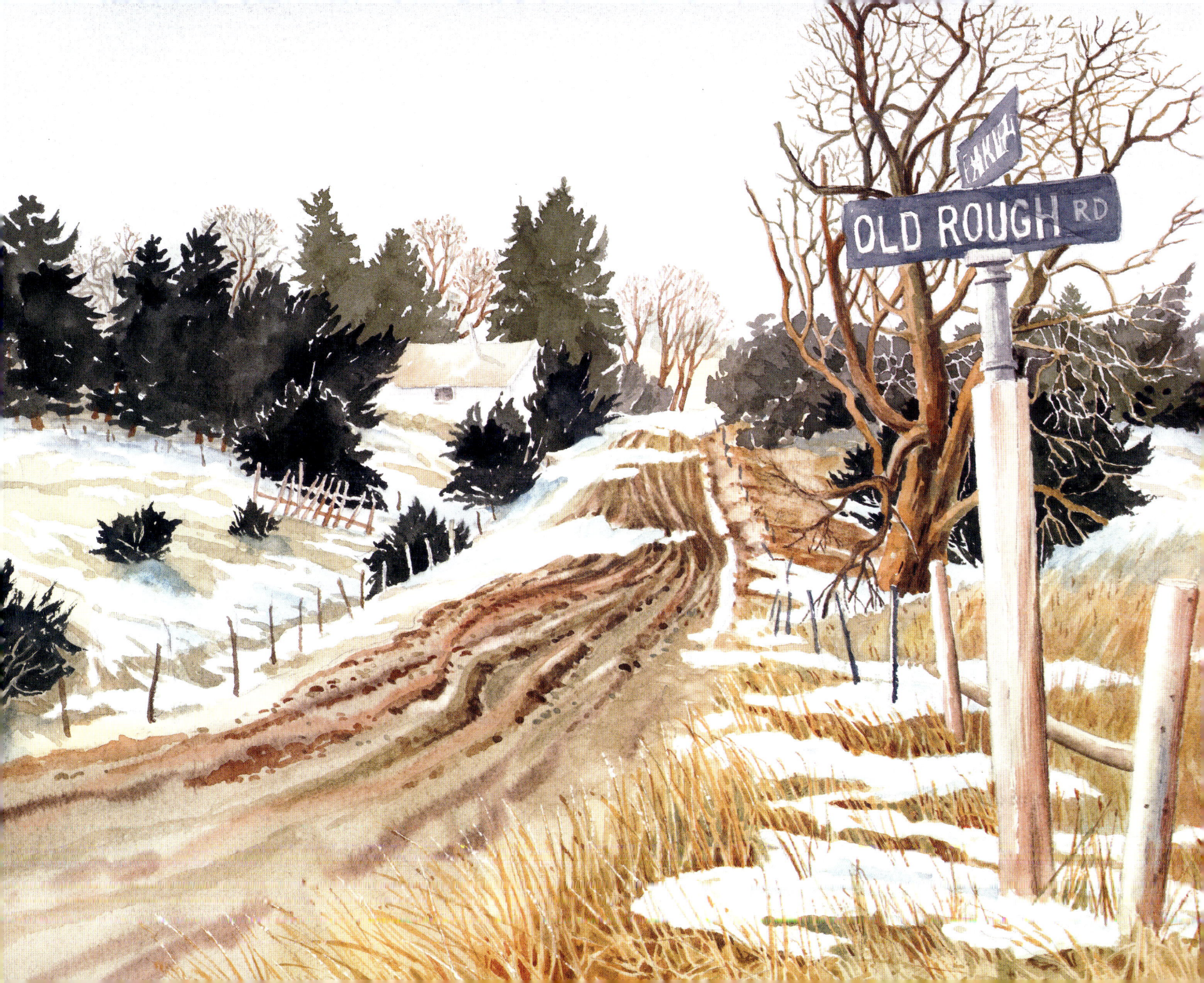

Winter lies too long in country towns; hangs on until it is stale and shabby, old and sullen. On the farm the weather was the great fact, and men's affairs went on underneath it, as the streams creep under the ice. But in Black Hawk the scene of human life was spread out shrunken and pinched, frozen down to the bare stalk.

By March the ice was rough and choppy, and the snow on the river bluffs was gray and mournful-looking. I was tired of school, tired of winter clothes, of the rutted streets, of the dirty drifts and the piles of cinders that had lain in the yards so long.   MY ÁNTONIA

My favorite manner of painting is called en plein air, which simply means painting outdoors on location. For most of my prairie pictures this was impossible either because of the weather or because it was very uncomfortable to set up in a corner of a field. I had to rely on quick sketches, color notes, and photo reference material to create the watercolor painting in my studio. I traveled as far as I could on this county road until blocked by this four-foot snow drift, the vestige of an earlier storm.

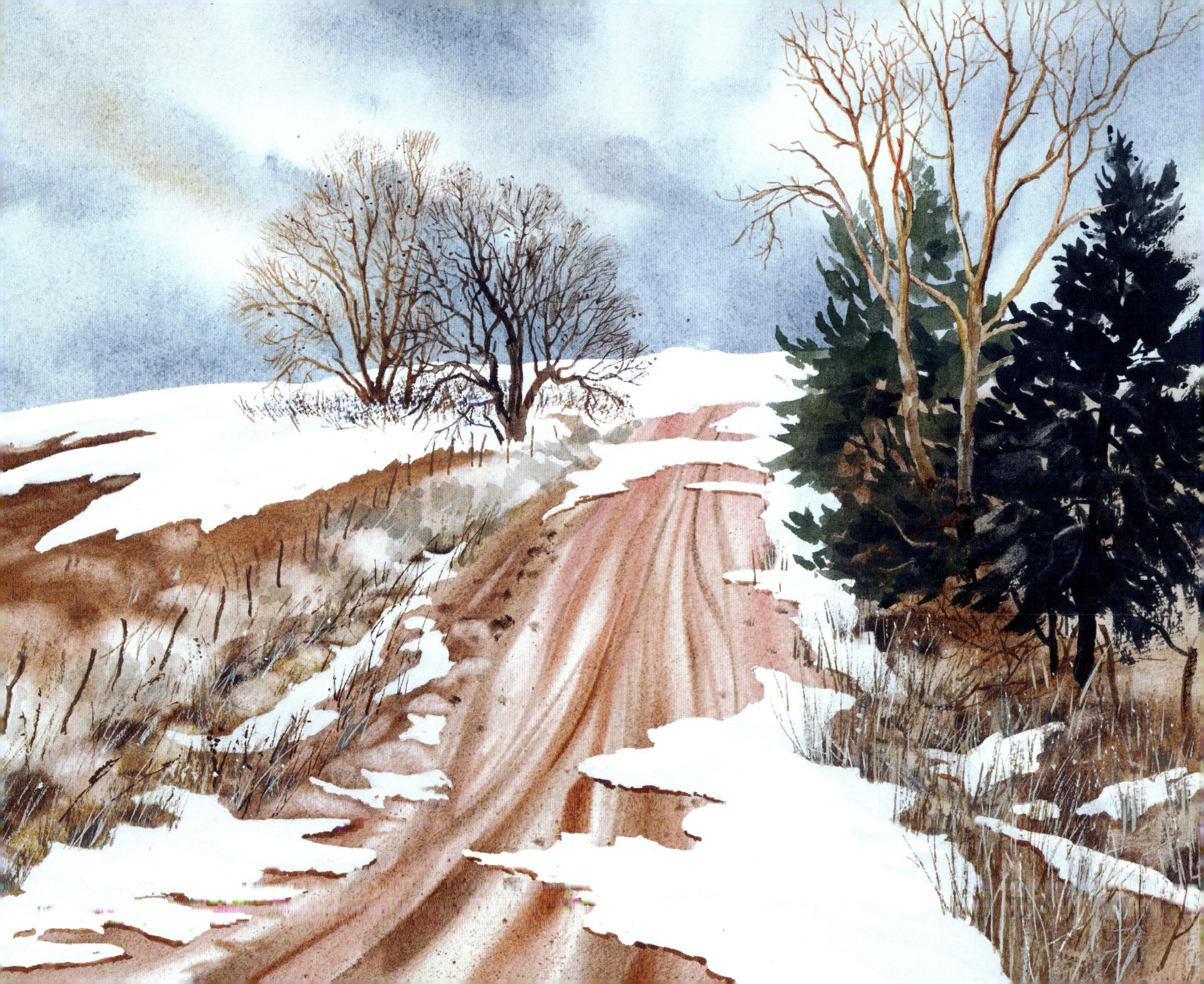

There were few days in the year when Wheeler did not drive off somewhere; to an auction sale, or a political convention, or a meeting of the Farmers' Telephone directors;—to see how his neighbours were getting on with their work, if there was nothing else to look after. He preferred his buckboard to a car because it was light, went easily over heavy or rough roads, and was so rickety that he never felt he must suggest his wife's accompanying him. Besides he could see the country better when he didn't have to keep his mind on the road. He had come to this part of Nebraska when the Indians and the buffalo were still about, remembered the grasshopper year and the big cyclone, had watched the farms emerge one by one from the great rolling page where once only the wind wrote its story. He had encouraged new settlers to take up homesteads, urged on courtships, lent young fellows the money to marry on, seen families grow and prosper; until he felt a little as if all this were his own enterprise. The changes, not only those the years made, but those the seasons made, were interesting to him.

ONE OF OURS

Men travel faster now, but I do not know if they go to better things.

DEATH COMES FOR THE ARCHBISHOP

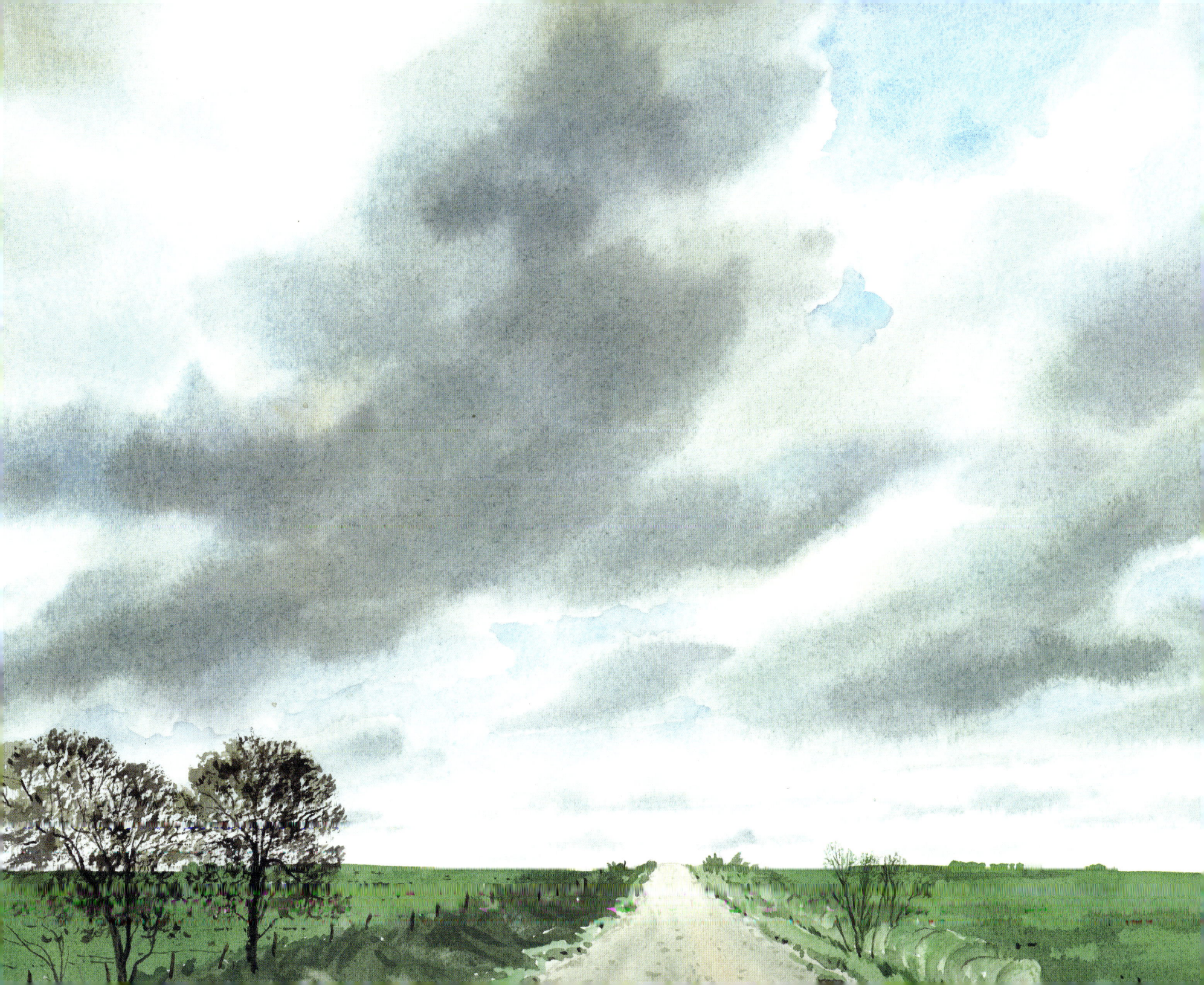

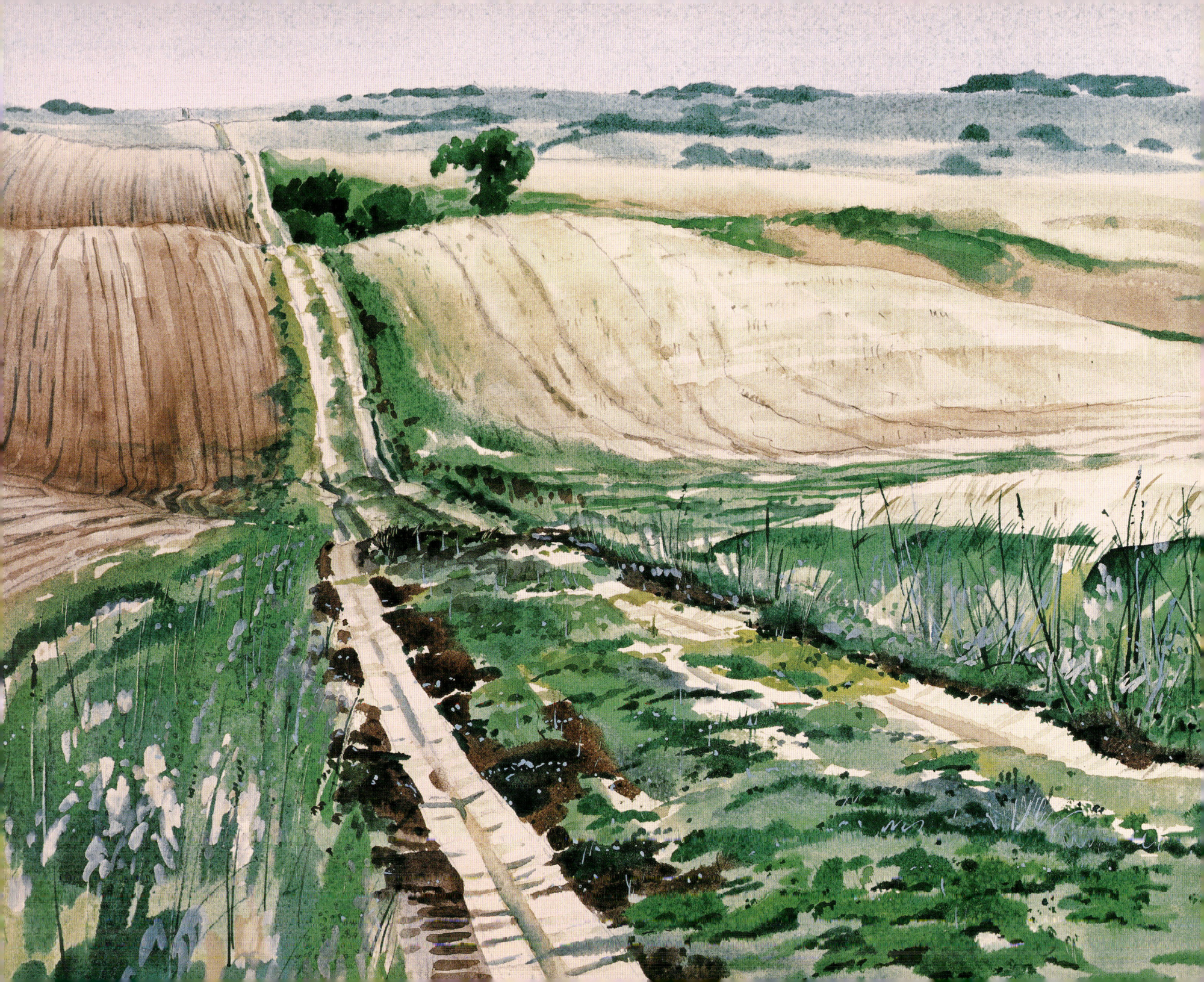

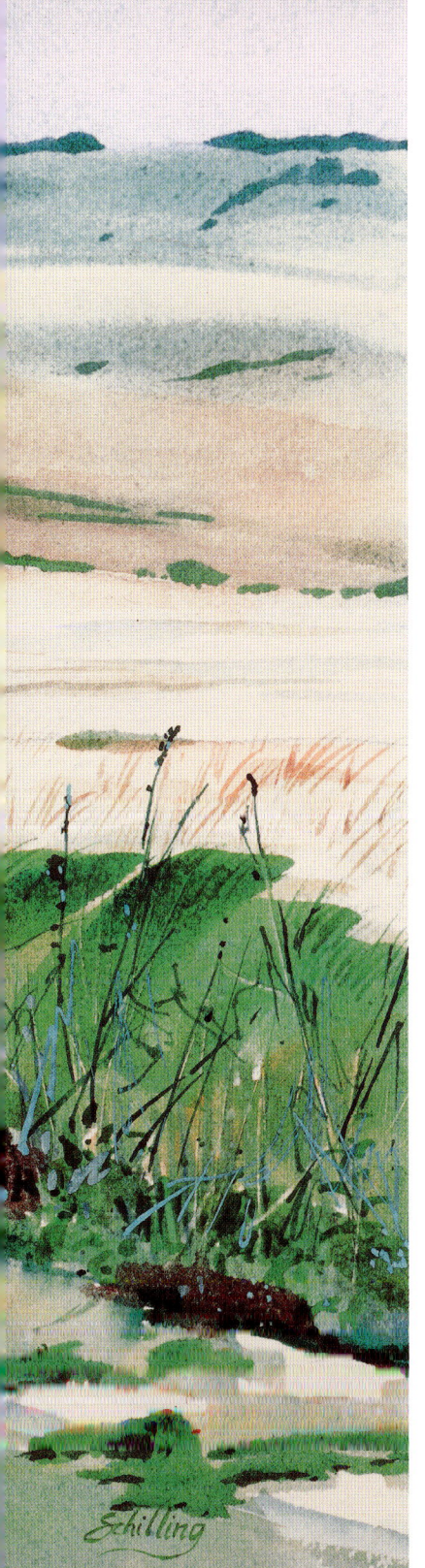

He rattled out of town and along the highway through a wonderfully rich stretch of country, the finest farms in the county. He admired this High Prairie, as it was called, and always liked to drive through it. "NEIGHBOUR ROSICKY"

As I looked about me I felt that the grass was the country, as the water is the sea. The red of the grass made all the great prairie the colour of wine-stains, or of certain seaweeds when they are first washed up. And there was so much motion in it; the whole country seemed, somehow, to be running. MY ÁNTONIA

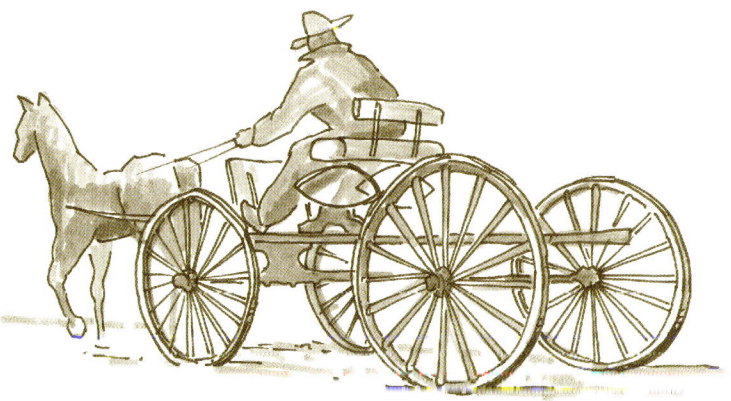

Every night Eric rode over to St. Anne, a little village in the heart of the French settlement, for the mail. As the road lay through the most attractive part of the Divide country, on several occasions Margaret Elliot and her brother had accompanied him. "ERIC HERMANNSON'S SOUL"

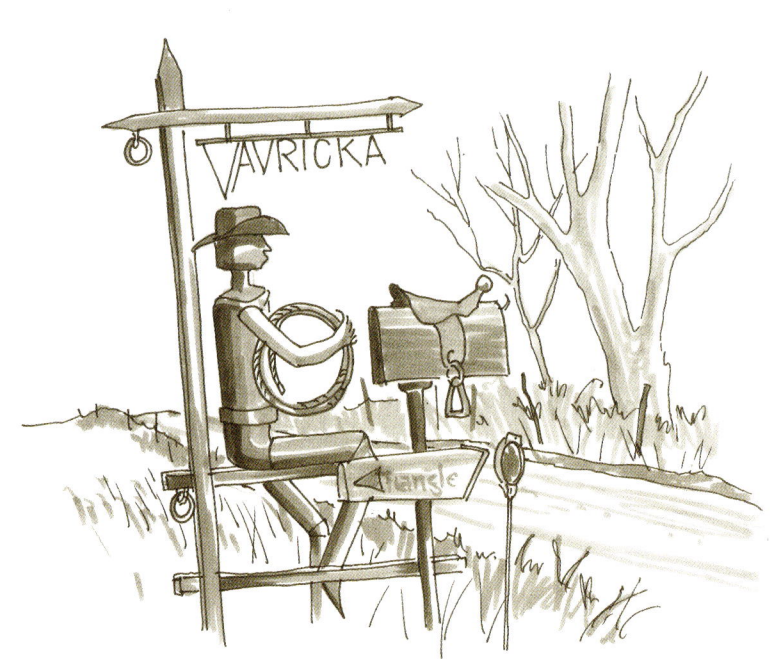

RFD, or Rural Free Delivery, began in the early 1900s and was a great largess to the country folks but a drain on the local merchants. They saw their sales suffer as most anything, even materials for a house, could now be purchased by mail from Sears, Roebuck and Co. or Montgomery Ward catalogs.

A PIPE-FITTED COWBOY

Certainly not everything was store-bought. Rural people expressed their creativity by making all kinds of mailboxes and holders for newspapers and packages. Some were made from any cast-off wood or iron pieces from the scrap heap behind the barn, and the craftsmen were limited only by imagination or skill.

The builder of this cowboy mailbox was probably, among other things, a talented blacksmith or pipe fitter.

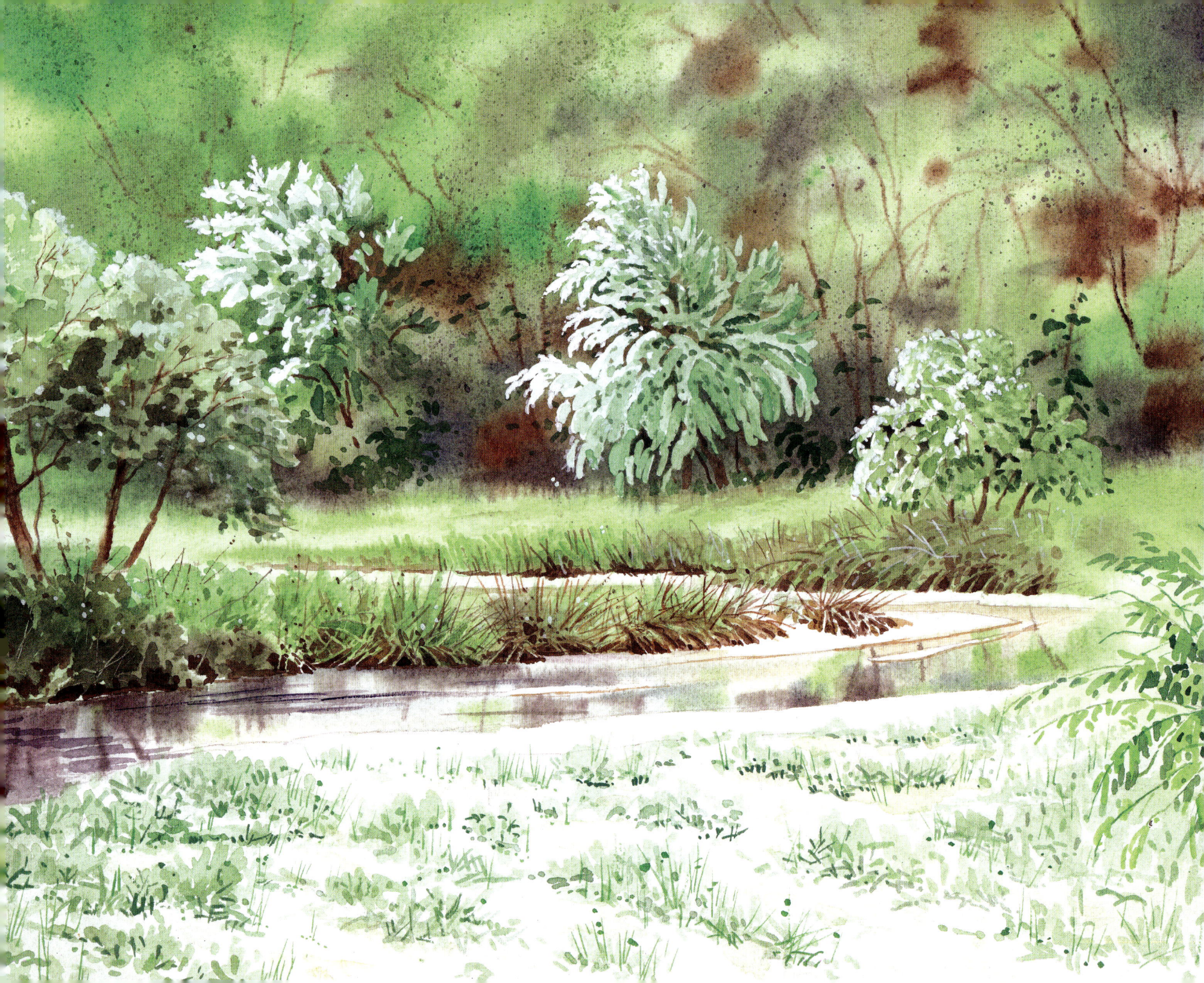

Waters of the Prairie

The sun popped up over the edge of the prairie like a broad, smiling face; the light poured across the close-cropped August pastures and the hilly, timbered windings of Lovely Creek,—a clear little stream with a sand bottom, that curled and twisted playfully about through the south section of the big Wheeler ranch. It was a fine day to go to the circus at Frankfort, a fine day to do anything; the sort of day that must, somehow, turn out well.

And, later in that year . . .

On the Sunday after Christmas Claude and Ernest were walking along the banks of Lovely Creek. They had been as far as Mr. Wheeler's timber claim and back. It was like an autumn afternoon, so warm that they left their overcoats on the limb of a crooked elm by the pasture fence. The fields and the bare tree-tops seemed to be swimming in light. A few brown leaves still clung to the bushy trees along the creek. In the upper pasture, more than a mile from the house, the boys found a bittersweet vine that wound about a little dogwood and covered it with scarlet berries. It was like finding a Christmas tree growing wild out of doors. ONE OF OURS

Of all the locations Cather described in her writings, I feel most connected here, most in touch with her sensitivity. As best I can tell, this watercolor painting is of the same place described in *One of Ours*. Over centuries this little creek has meandered through the dense canopy of box elders, ash, and elm branches, depositing fine white sand along its course. The water lazily flows clear in the summer and, on a cloudless day, reflects the cobalt blue sky and sunlight that steals through the tunnel of leaves and branches.

Alexandra sat down on the kitchen doorstep, while her mother was mixing the bread. It was a still, deep-breathing summer night, full of the smell of the hay fields. Sounds of laughter and splashing came up from the pasture, and when the moon rose rapidly above the bare rim of the prairie, the pond glittered like polished metal, and she could see the flash of white bodies as the boys ran about the edge, or jumped into the water. Alexandra watched the shimmering pool dreamily, but eventually her eyes went back to the sorghum patch south of the barn, where she was planning to make her new pig corral.

O PIONEERS!

Cather was a keen observer of light—the way that it played upon the land or reflected in the ponds, rivers, and streams of the prairie. In this excerpt, she describes the moonrise over Ivar's pond. My experience was different. The reflected light of the blue sky made the water of the pond appear cool and inviting.

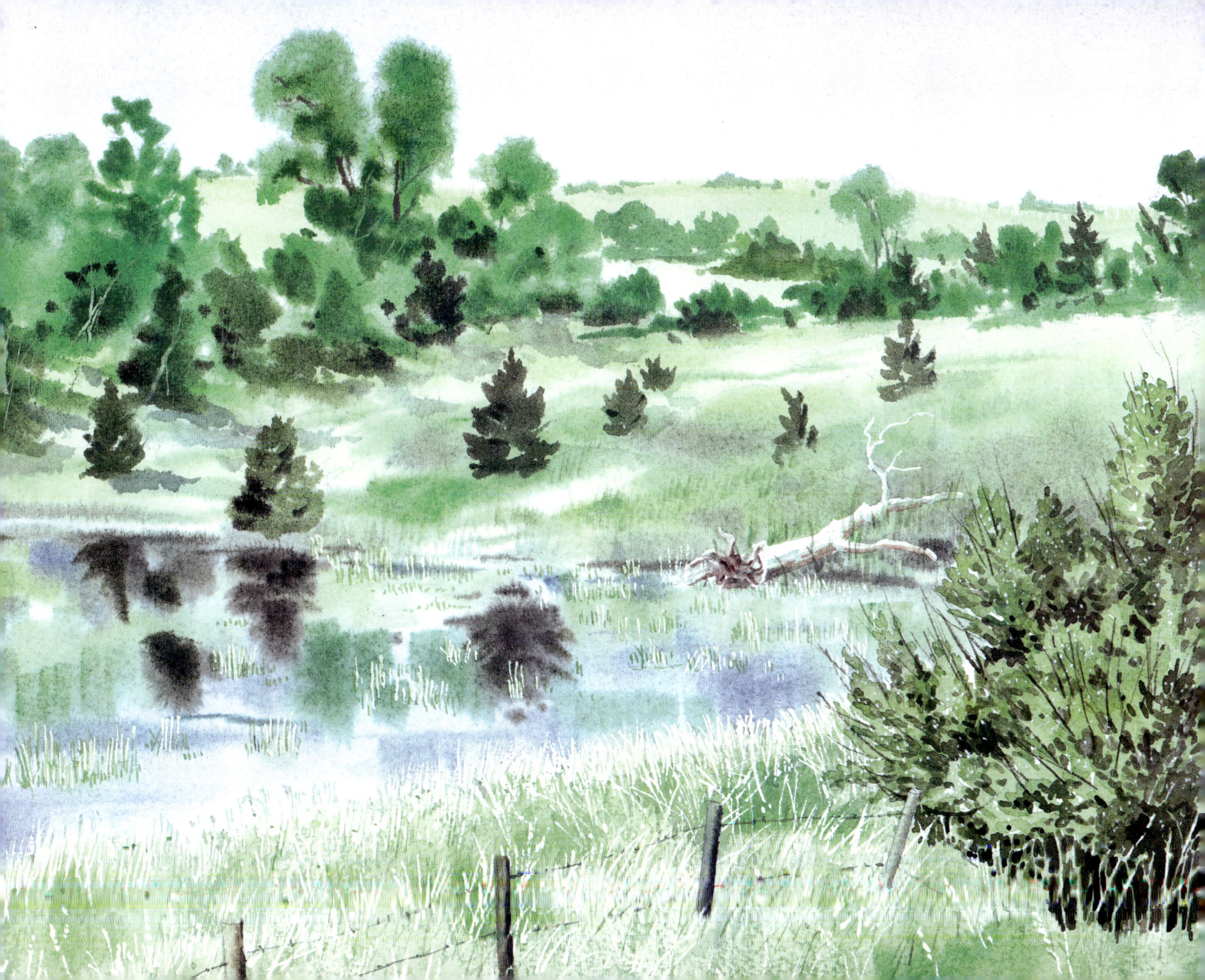

On a bright September morning in the year 1899 Miss Evangeline
Knightly was driving through the beautiful Nebraska land which lies
between the Platte River and the Kansas line. She drove slowly, for she
loved the country, and she held the reins loosely in the gloved hand.

"THE BEST YEARS"

The Little Blue River marks the unofficial northern
boundary of the Divide. Highway 281 passes over the
stream, and on my drive across Catherland on a cold
winter morning, I stopped to watch three wild turkeys
drink from the water hole and then scamper up the
ditch bank, disappearing into the woods. Frosty patterns
on partially thawed ice and watery reflections from
woods beyond created a beautiful winterscape that
morning and prompted this painting of the Little Blue.

The Blue River is historically important as a
navigational tool. After the Civil War, westward
immigrants left Independence, Missouri, on the
Oregon and California trails. Upon entering Nebraska
Territory they followed the Blue River north to reach
the Great Platte River Road, keeping to the river valleys
where water and grass for cattle were ample. I often
wondered why the European immigrants chose to settle
in Webster County. My guess is, some on the trail saw
the lush, tall grasslands and thought there was no need
to travel farther.

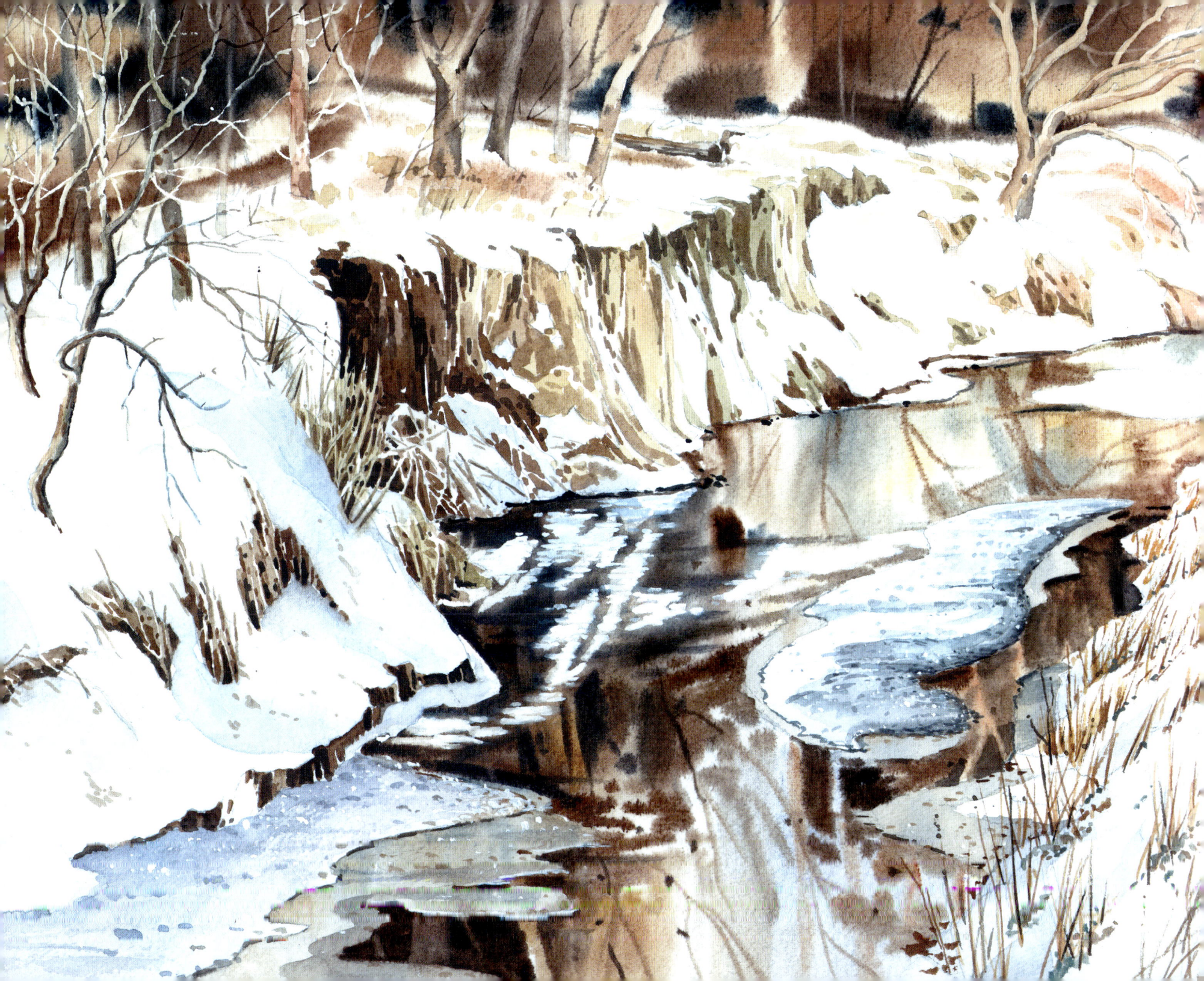

This stream traced artless loops and curves through the broad meadows that were half pasture land, half marsh. Any one but Captain Forrester would have drained the bottom land and made it into highly productive fields. But he had selected this place long ago because it looked beautiful to him, and he happened to like the way the creek wound through his pasture, with mint and joint-grass and twinkling willows along its banks.

A LOST LADY

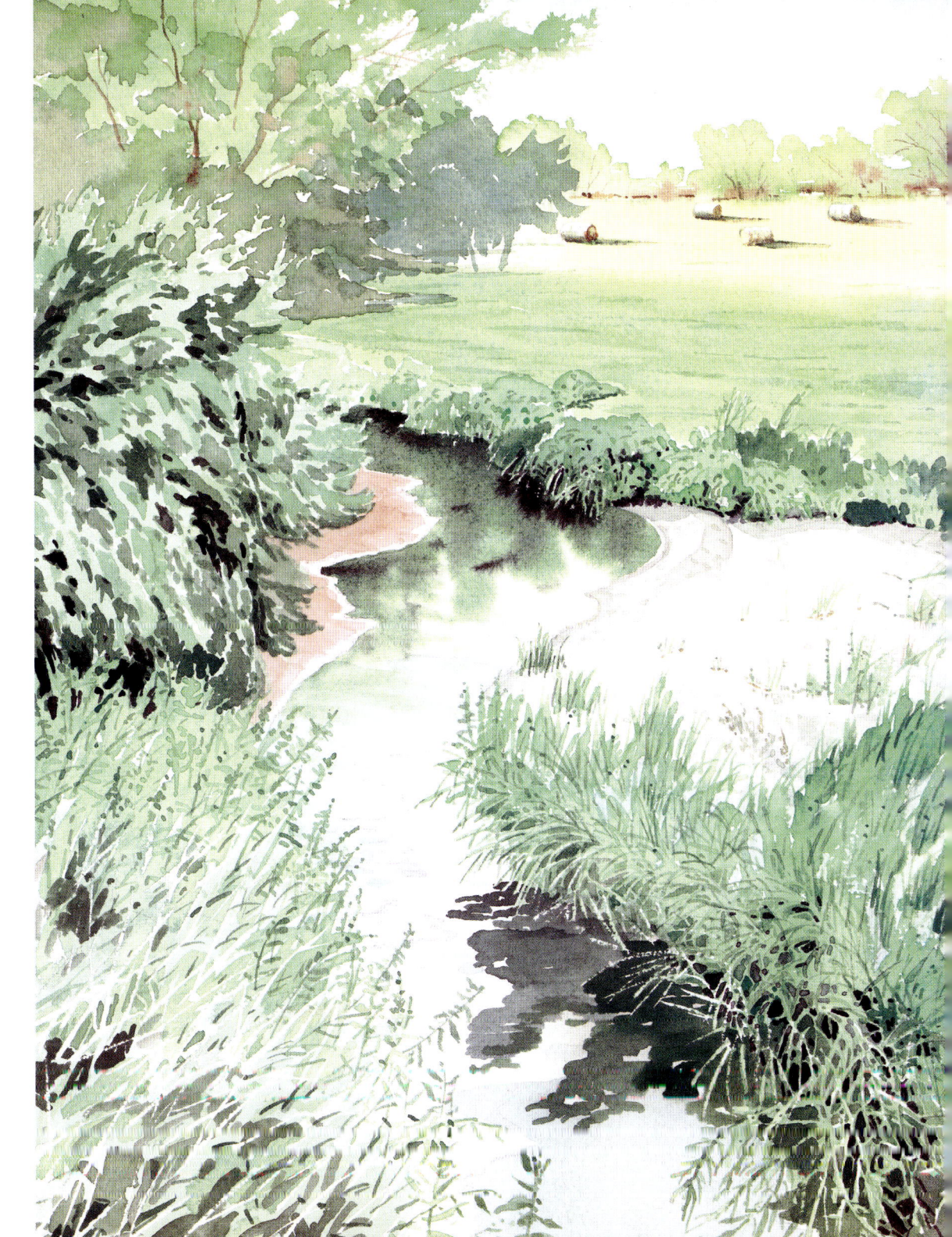

Located just a half mile north of Red Cloud, this was one of Cather's favorite playgrounds. It was here that she and her friends took picnic baskets and passed the day lingering in the mint-scented grass along watercress-lined banks of the creek.

We raced off toward Squaw Creek and did not stop until the ground itself stopped—fell away before us so abruptly that the next step would have been out into the tree-tops. We stood panting on the edge of the ravine, looking down at the trees and bushes that grew below us. *MY ÁNTONIA*

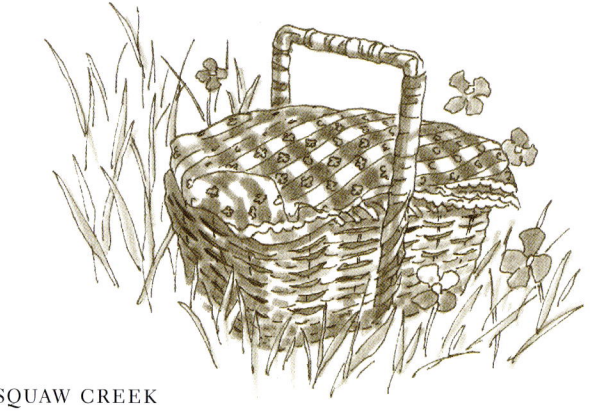

SQUAW CREEK

This creek is located two miles west of Red Cloud. Known as "Squaw Creek" in *My Ántonia*, "Norway Creek" in *O Pioneers!* and "Rattlesnake Creek" in "Eric Hermannson's Soul," it was often visited by Cather and her friends.

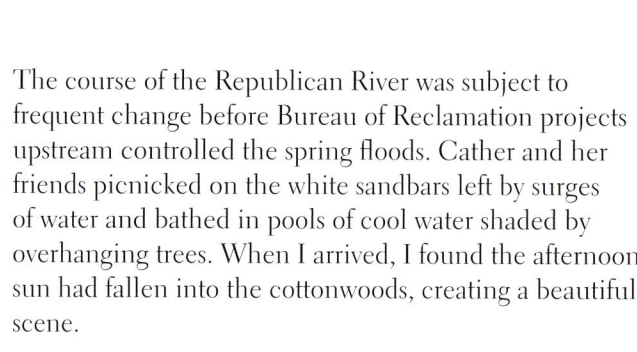

The course of the Republican River was subject to frequent change before Bureau of Reclamation projects upstream controlled the spring floods. Cather and her friends picnicked on the white sandbars left by surges of water and bathed in pools of cool water shaded by overhanging trees. When I arrived, I found the afternoon sun had fallen into the cottonwoods, creating a beautiful scene.

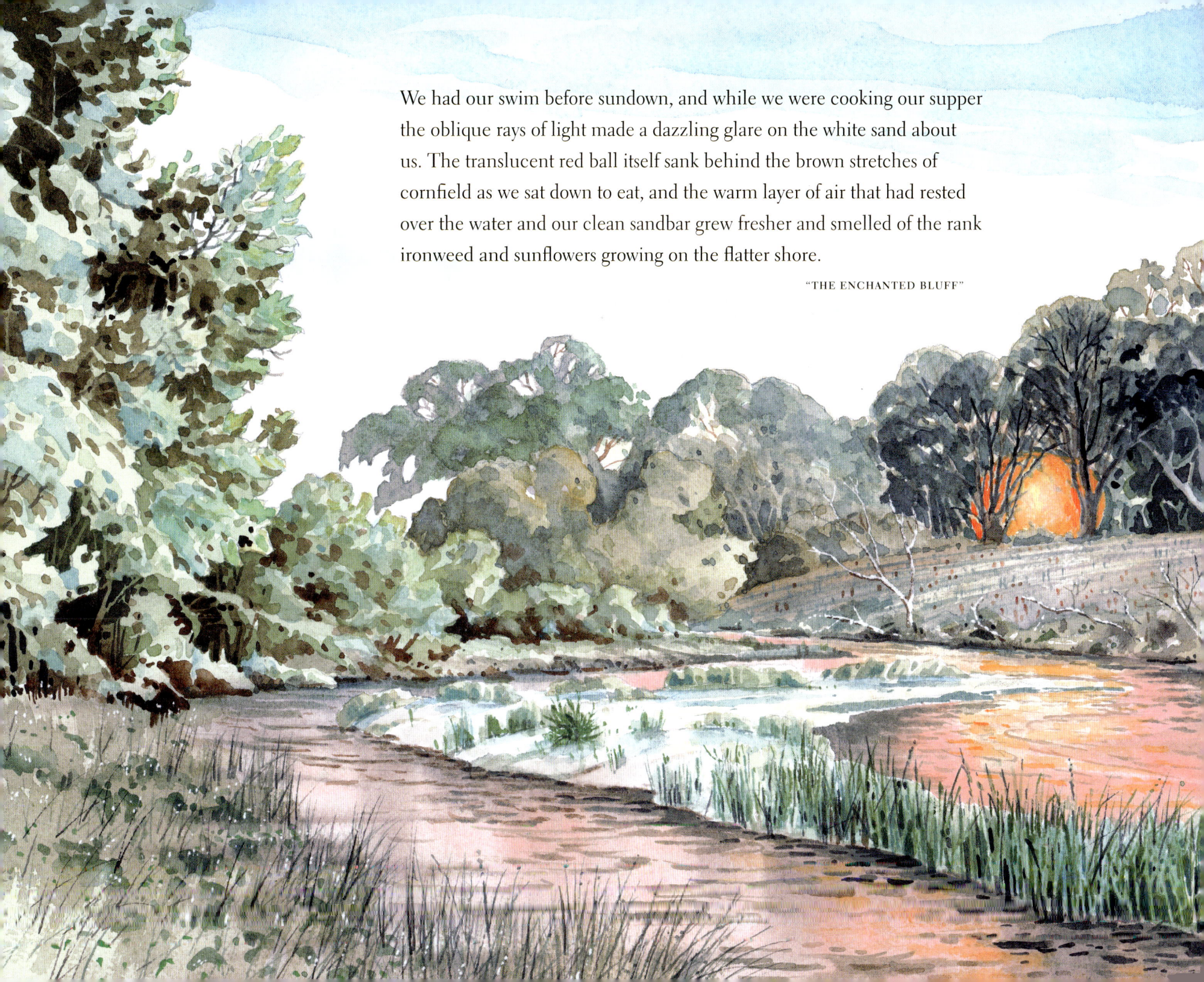

We had our swim before sundown, and while we were cooking our supper the oblique rays of light made a dazzling glare on the white sand about us. The translucent red ball itself sank behind the brown stretches of cornfield as we sat down to eat, and the warm layer of air that had rested over the water and our clean sandbar grew fresher and smelled of the rank ironweed and sunflowers growing on the flatter shore.

"THE ENCHANTED BLUFF"

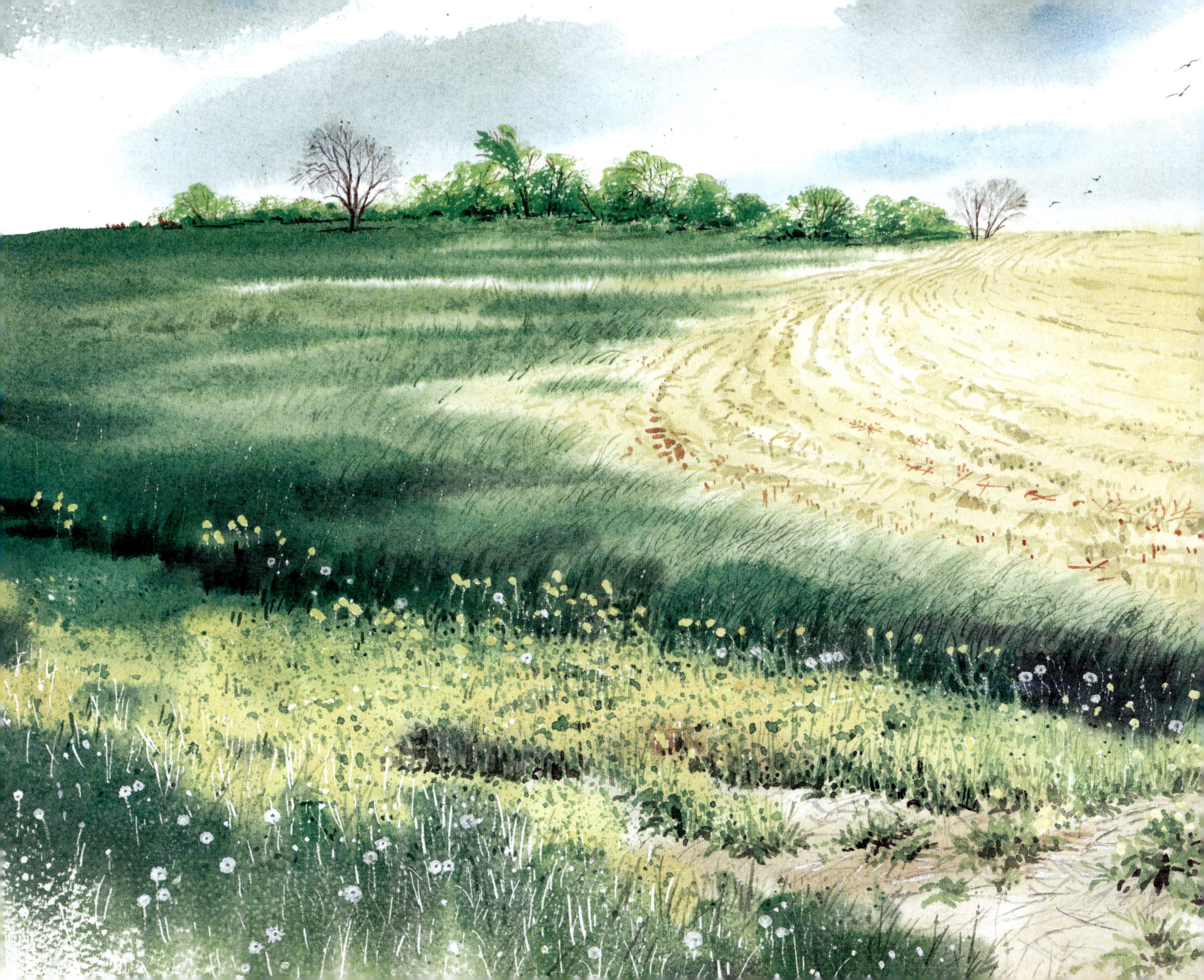

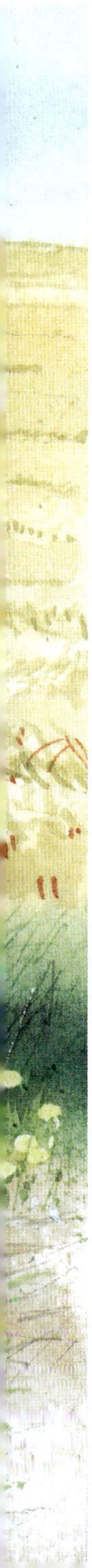

Seasons of the Prairie

Along the roadsides, from under the dead weeds and wisps of dried bluestem, the dandelions thrust up their clean, bright faces.

ONE OF OURS

There are few scenes more gratifying than a spring plowing in that country, where the furrows of a single field often lie a mile in length, and the brown earth, with such a strong, clean smell, and such a power of growth and fertility in it, yields itself eagerly to the plow; rolls away from the shear, not even dimming the brightness of the metal, with a soft, deep sigh of happiness. The wheat-cutting sometimes goes on all night as well as all day, and in good seasons there are scarcely men and horses enough to do the harvesting. The grain is so heavy that it bends toward the blade and cuts like velvet.

O PIONEERS!

Everywhere now there was the smell of burning grass. Our neighbours
burned off their pasture before the new grass made a start, so that the fresh
growth would not be mixed with the dead stand of last year. Those light,
swift fires, running about the country, seemed a part of the same kindling
that was in the air.   MY ÁNTONIA

Occasionally, farmers still burn off old growth. On this
day I watched the pale gray clouds of smoke drift for
miles in prairie skies.
   In earlier days without good fire-fighting resources,
a fire could easily get out of control and sweep over the
entire county. Even with great diligence, it was sometimes impossible for settlers to protect their property and
livestock from the devastation.

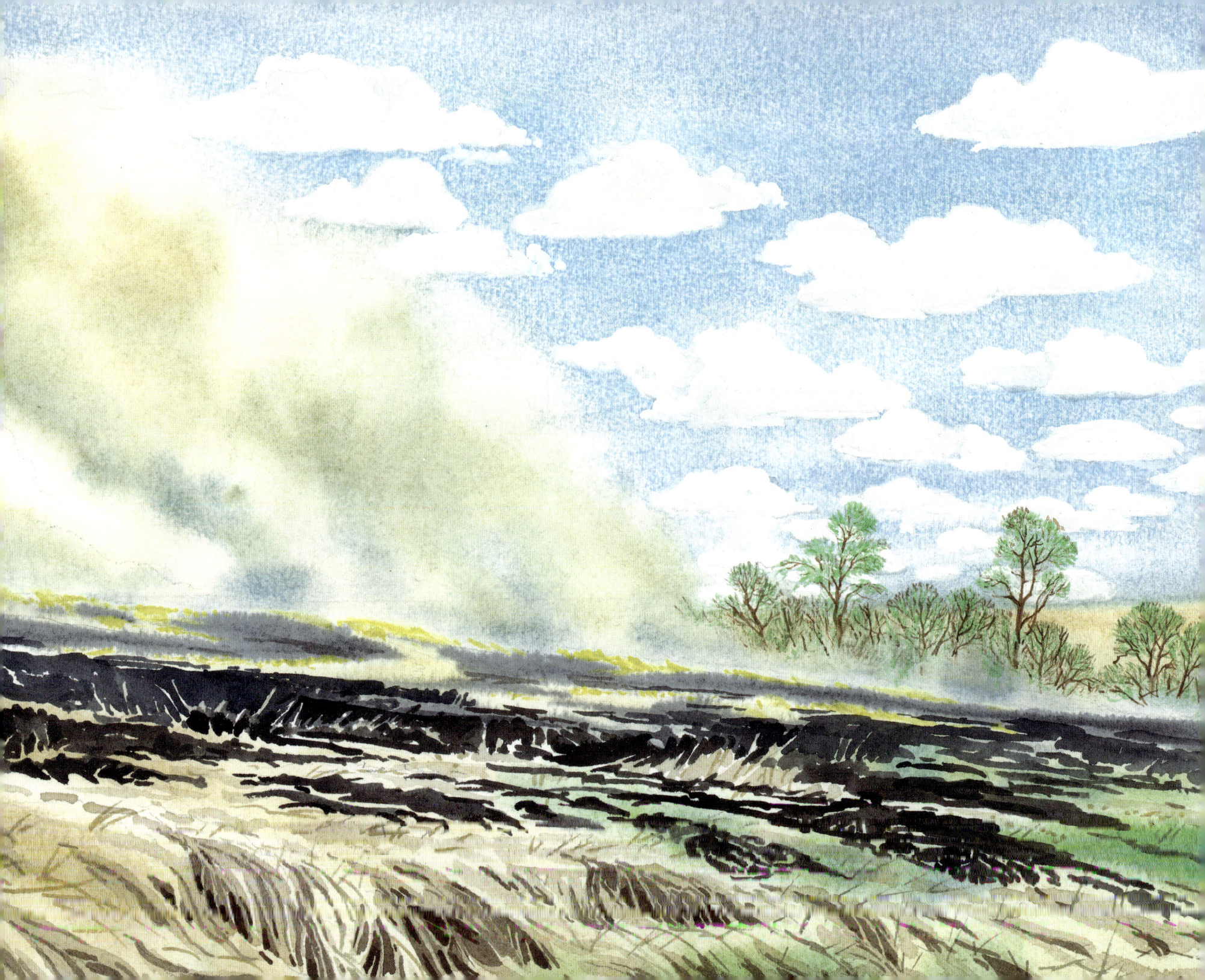

Spring came at last, and the Forrester place had never been so lovely. The
Captain spent long, happy days among his flowering shrubs, and his wife
used to say to visitors, "Yes, you can see Mr. Forrester in a moment; I will
send the English gardener to call him."   *A LOST LADY*

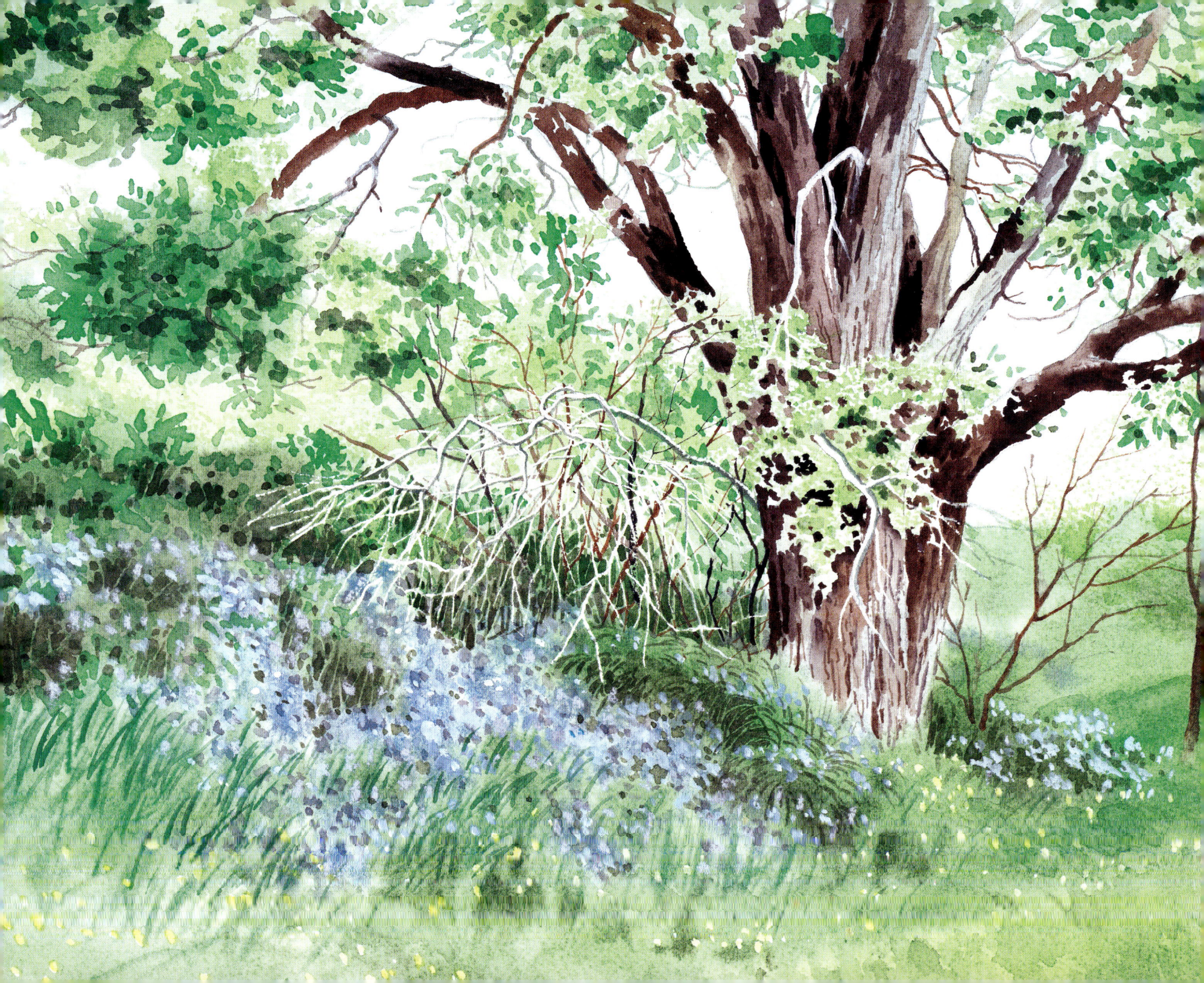

Back over the horseshoe-shaped gulch in which the town is built the sky
was glorious with red splotches of sunset cloud just above the horizon.
The big trees on the bluffs were tossing their arms restlessly in the breeze
that blew up the river, and across on the level plains of the Missouri
side the lights of the farm houses began to glow through the soft humid
atmosphere of the April night. The smell of burning grass was everywhere,
and the very air tasted of spring.   "A RESURRECTION"

It was springtime, and the early morning sunlight played
on the white trunks of the old cottonwoods near the river.
These trees bear the scars of their struggle to survive,
their hides skinned by lightning and violent weather. To
the West, a new storm hung a dark blue curtain behind
the forest. I followed the game trail through the woods,
stopping here and there to study how the new growth of
spring grass was knitted into the dead grass from last season.

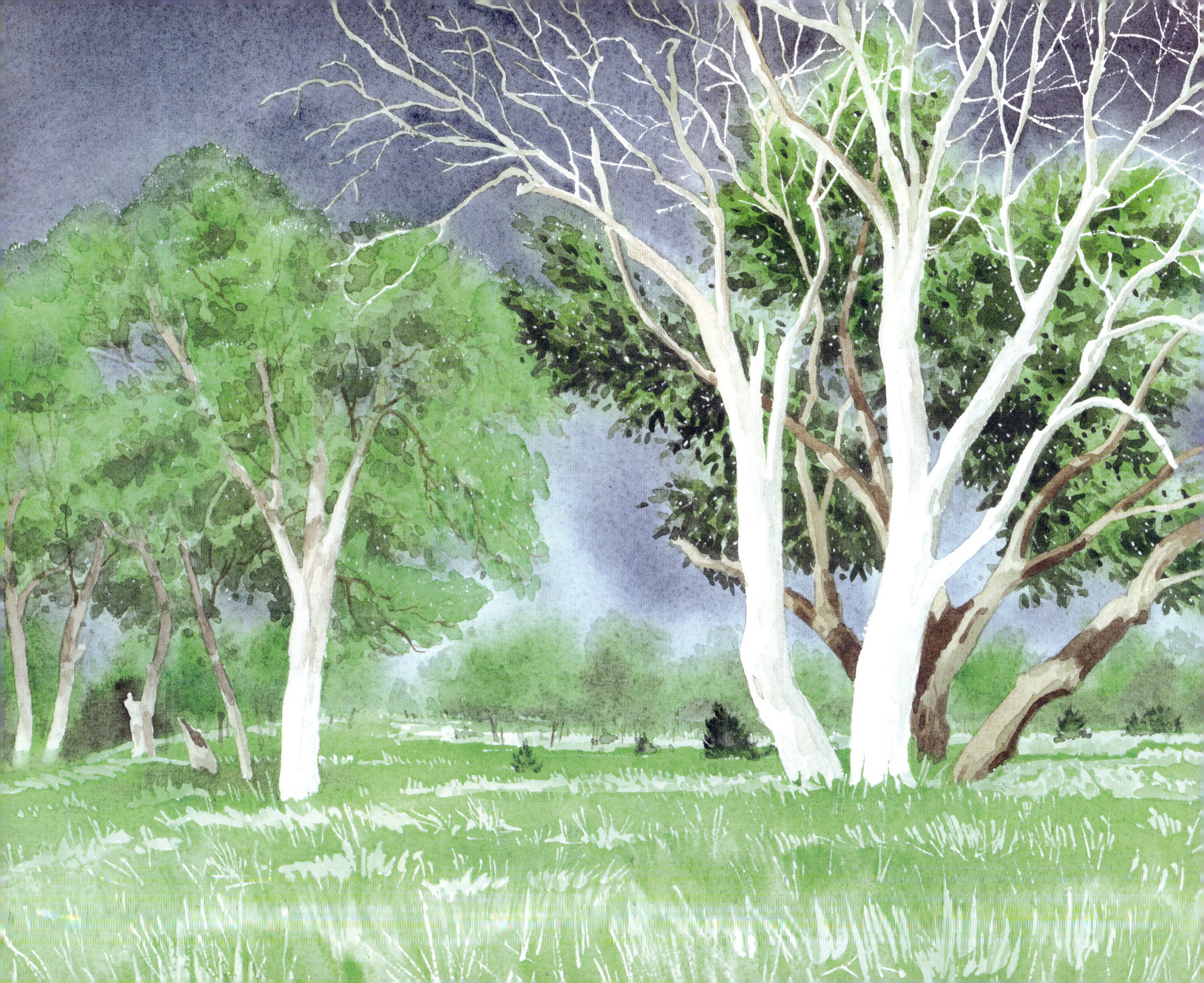

'And it was Summer, beautiful Summer!' . . .
It was in the summer that one really lived. . . .
With the warm weather came freedom for
everybody.   *THE SONG OF THE LARK*

O! the world was full of the summer time,
And the year was always June,
When we two played together
In the days that were done too soon.

EXCERPT FROM "THE WAY OF THE WORLD,"
WILLA CATHER, *THE HOME MONTHLY* 6 (APRIL 1898)

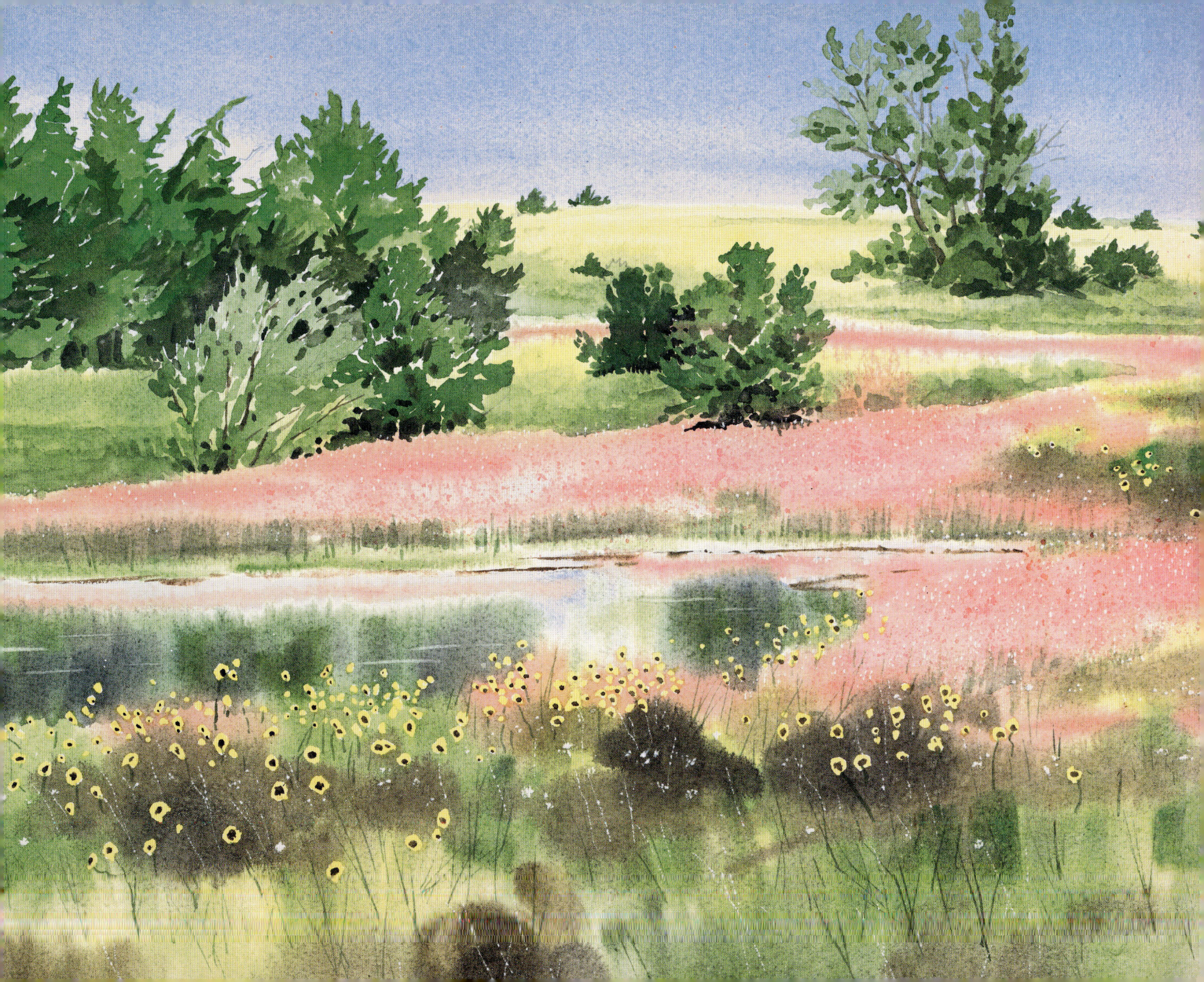

The sky was burning with the soft pink and silver of a cloudless summer dawn. The heavy, bowed grasses splashed him to the knees. All over the marsh, snow-on-the-mountain, globed with dew, made cool sheets of silver, and the swamp milkweed spread its flat, raspberry-coloured clusters. There was an almost religious purity about the fresh morning air, the tender sky, the grass and flowers with the sheen of early dew upon them. There was in all living things something limpid and joyous—like the wet morning call of the birds, flying up though the unstained atmosphere.

A LOST LADY

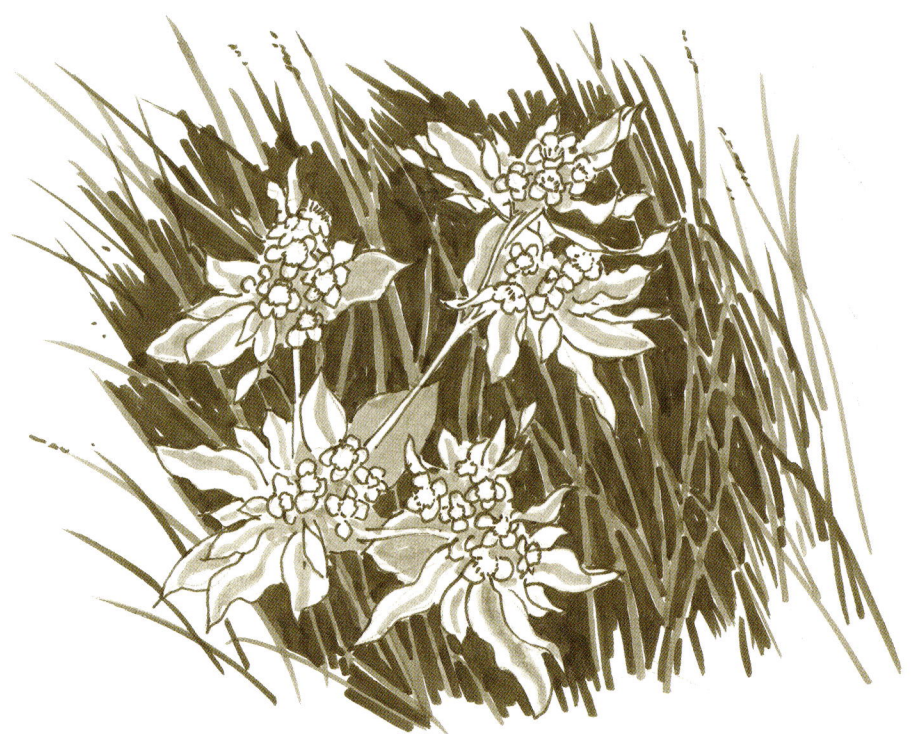

SNOW-ON-THE-MOUNTAIN BLOOMS

People seem to either love or hate snow-on-the-mountain. Though very beautiful, especially when the pale green and white bracts and blooms are examined closely, the plant is very toxic and has caused severe reactions in some individuals. If the stem is broken a milky white sap extrudes from the break.

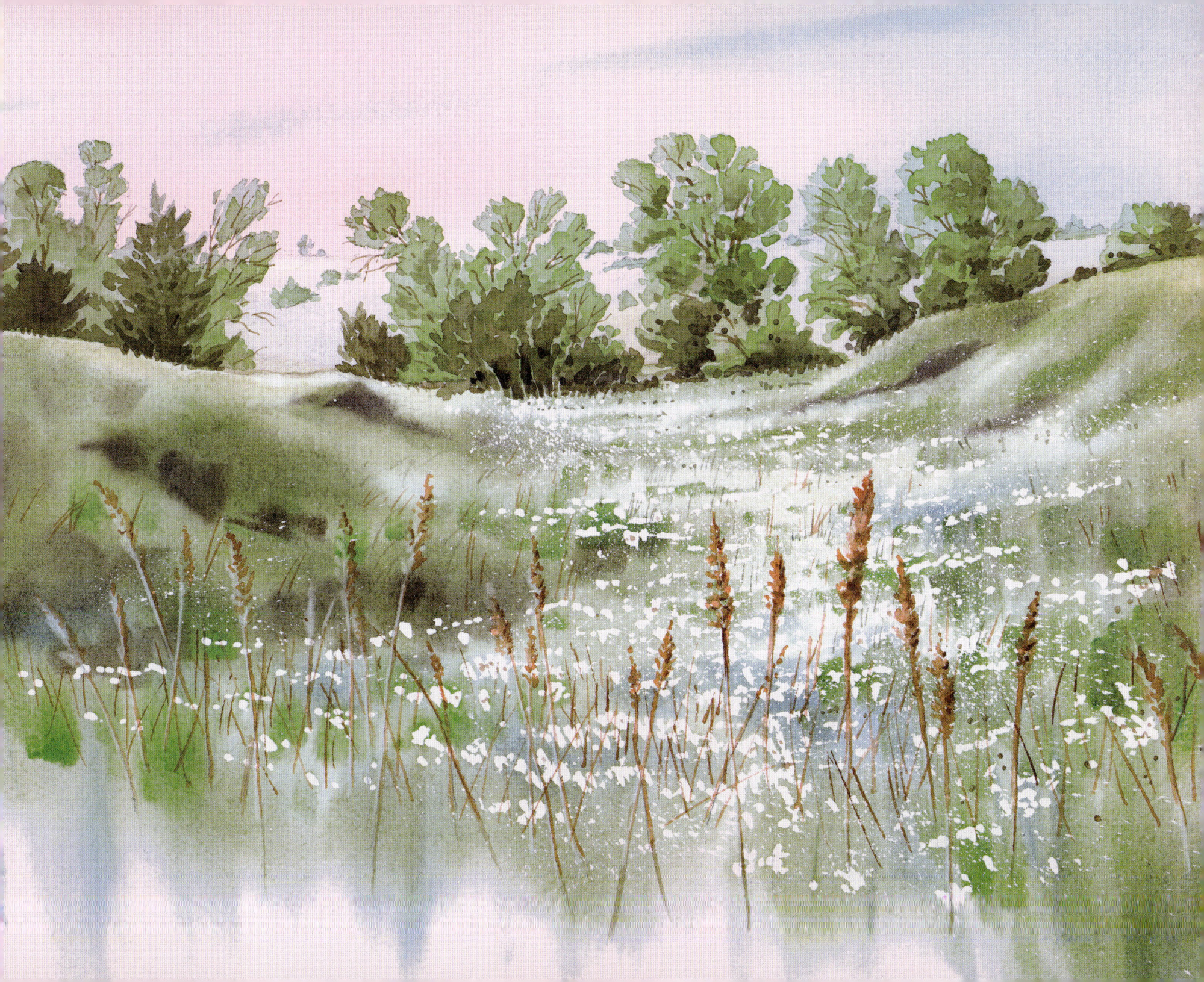

I took a long walk north of the town, out into the pastures where the land was so rough that it had never been ploughed up, and the long red grass of early times still grew shaggy over the draws and hillocks. Out there I felt at home again.

MY ÁNTONIA

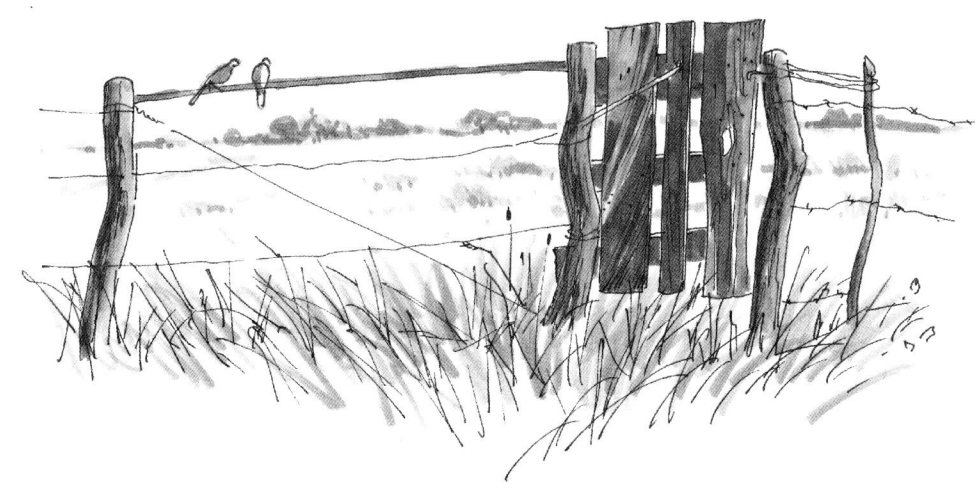

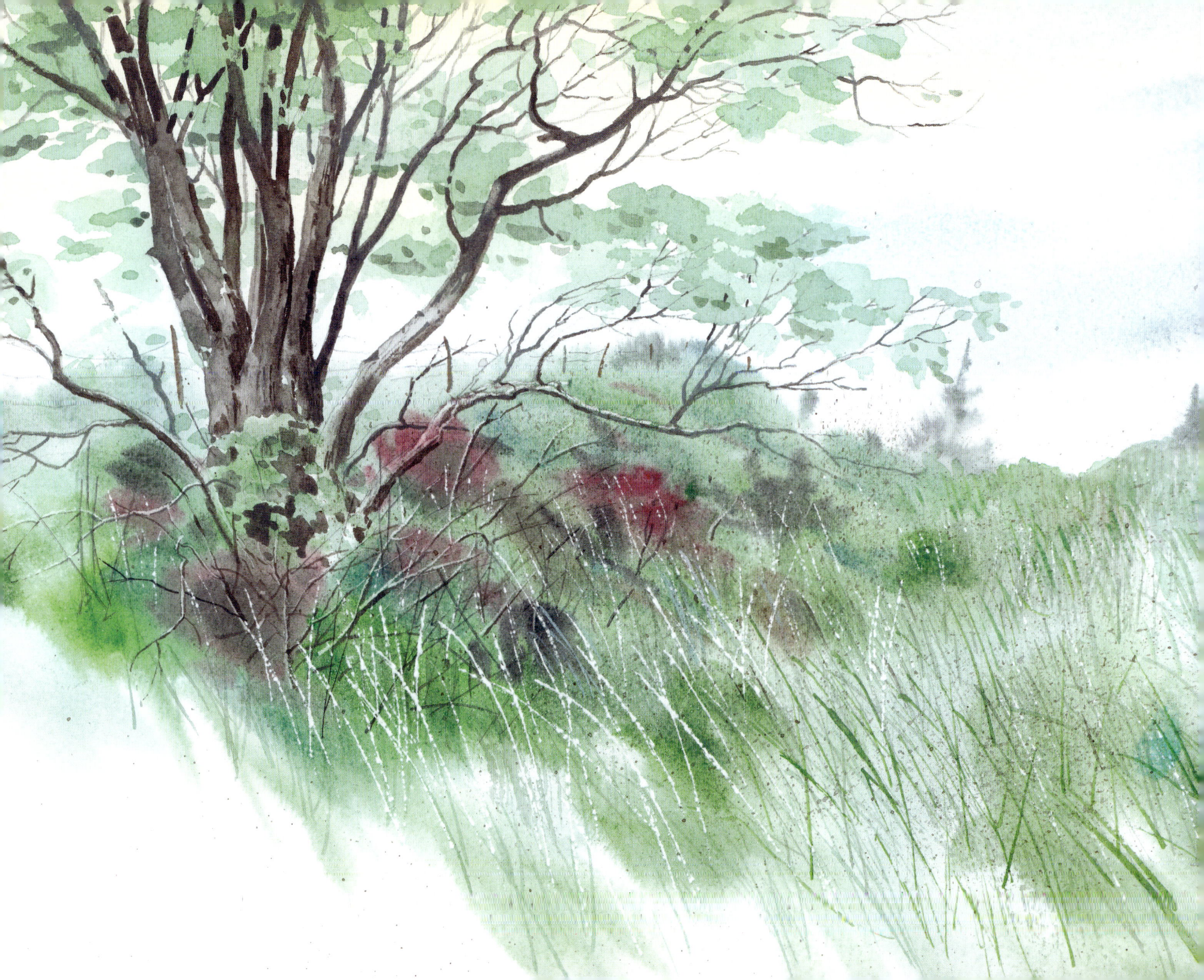

The weather was dry and intensely hot for several weeks, and then, at the end of July, thunder-storms and torrential rains broke upon the Sweet Water valley. The river burst out of its banks, all the creeks were up, and the stubble of Ivy Peters' wheat fields lay under water.   A LOST LADY

Summer rains are usually short-lived, and if the sun comes out later, it seems as though the whole country had been washed and scrubbed. Rain puddles collect in the hollows, reflecting blue sky after storm clouds drift away.

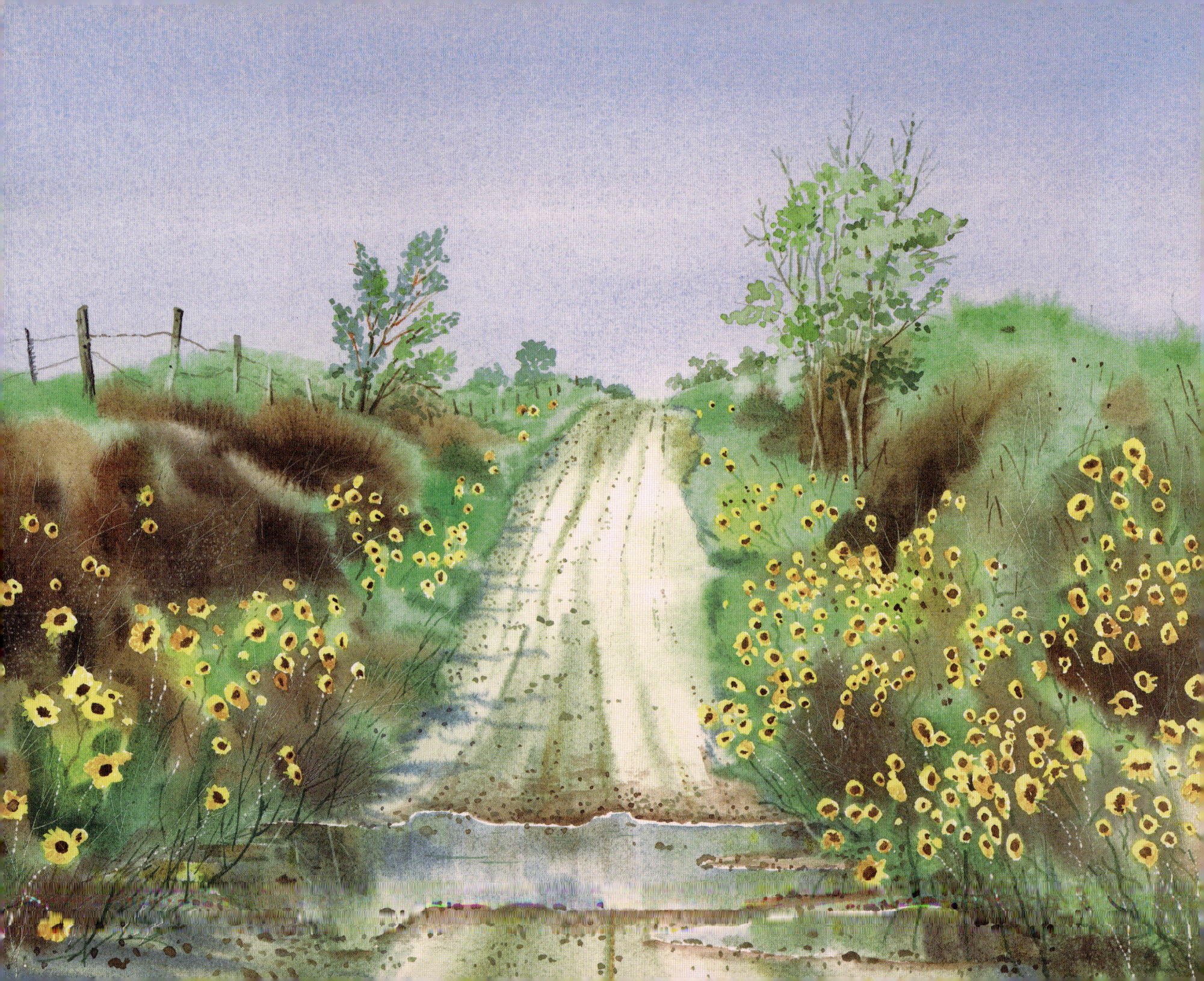

The land was growing rougher; I was told that we were approaching Squaw Creek, which cut up the west half of the Shimerdas' place and made the land of little value for farming. Soon we could see the broken, grassy clay cliffs which indicted the windings of the stream, and the glittering tops of the cottonwoods and ash trees that grew down in the ravine. Some of the cottonwoods had already turned, and the yellow leaves and shining white bark made them look like the gold and silver trees in fairy tales.

MY ÁNTONIA

Umber and gold leaves drip through the air on this warm autumn day as from the alchemist's melting pot. When conditions are right, cottonwood leaves lose chlorophyll, producing beautiful colors before winds scatter them among the grasses. This old cottonwood sentinel shows scars of previous battles with wind and weather. When I choose a subject to paint, I look for this kind of character.

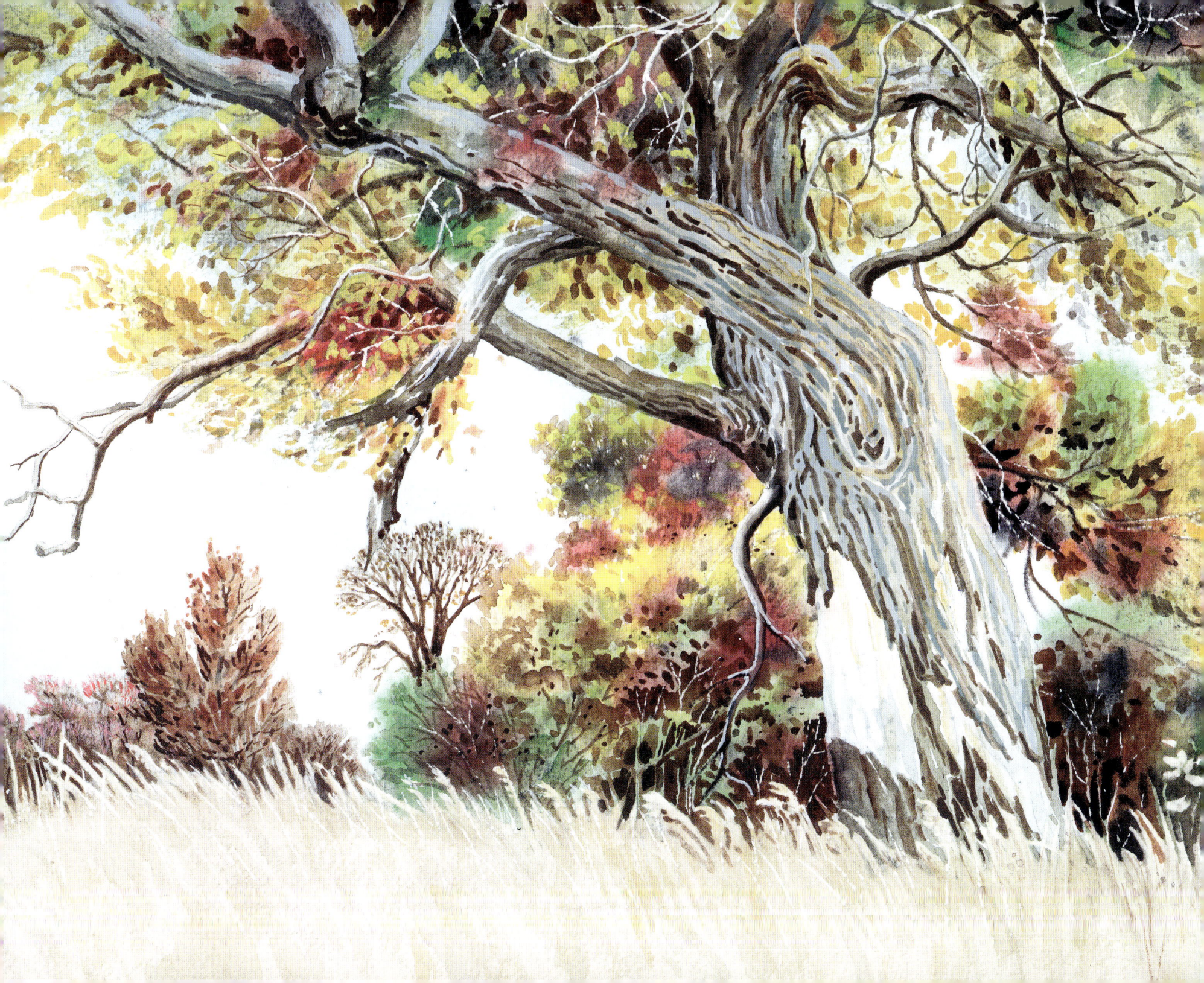

Toward evening the clouds banked up in the western sky, and with the night a violent storm set in, one of those drenching rains that always come too late in that country, after a barren summer has waned into a fruitless autumn. For some reason he felt indisposed to go to bed. He sat watching the lightning from the window and listening to the swollen Soloman, that tore between its muddy banks with a sullen roar, as though it resented this intrusion upon its accustomed calm and indolence. Once he thought he saw a light flash from one of the bluffs across the river, but on going to the door all was dark. At last he regretfully put out his lamp and went to bed.

"EL DORADO: A KANSAS RECESSIONAL," WILLA SIBERT
CATHER, *NEW ENGLAND MAGAZINE*, JUNE 1901

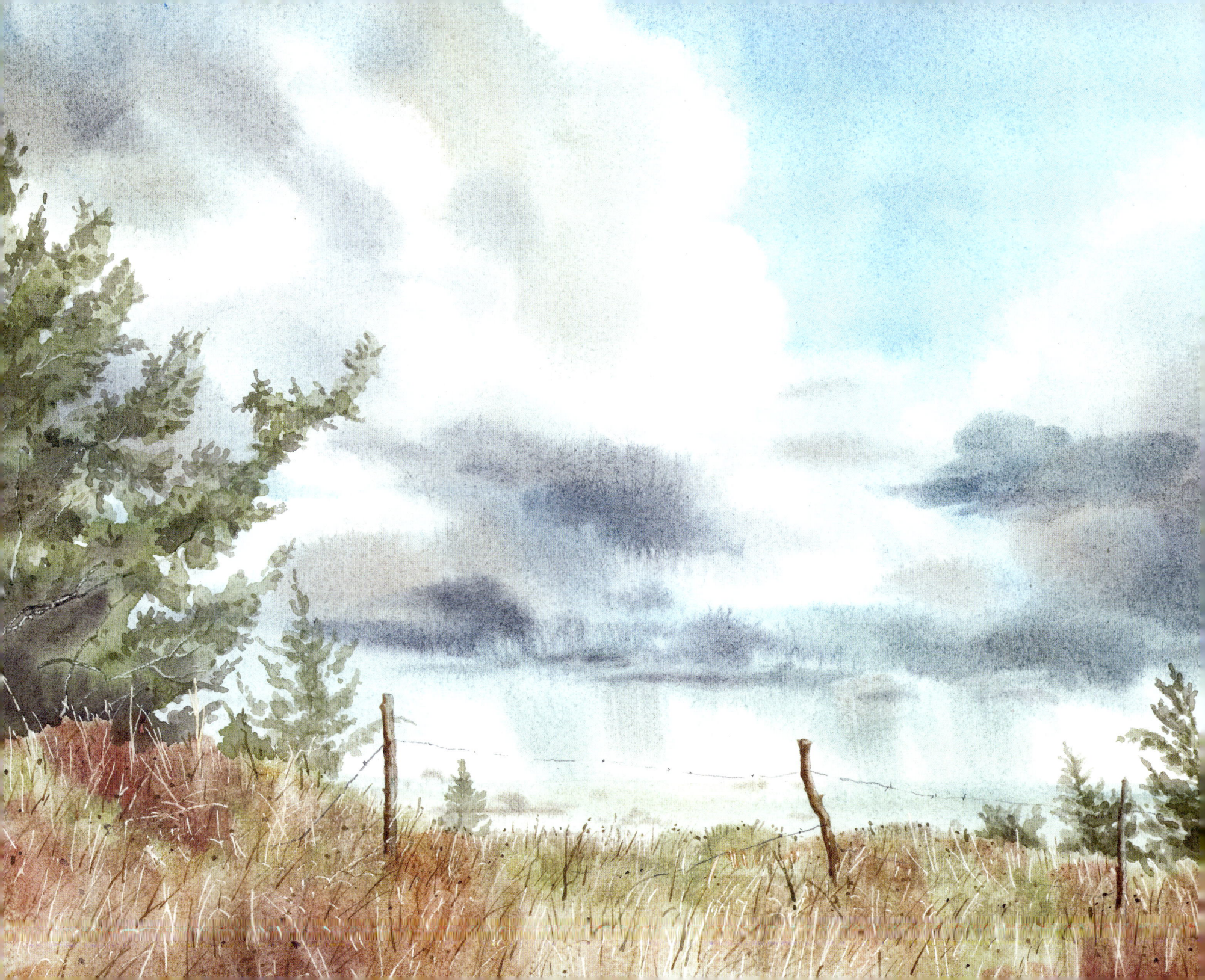

The afternoon sun was behind them, throwing over the pasture and the harvested, resting fields that wonderful light, so yellow that it is actually orange.

"THE BEST YEARS"

As far as we could see, the miles of copper-red grass were drenched in sunlight that was stronger and fiercer than at any other time of the day. The blond cornfields were red gold, the haystacks turned rosy and threw long shadows. The whole prairie was like the bush that burned with fire and not consumed.

MY ÁNTONIA

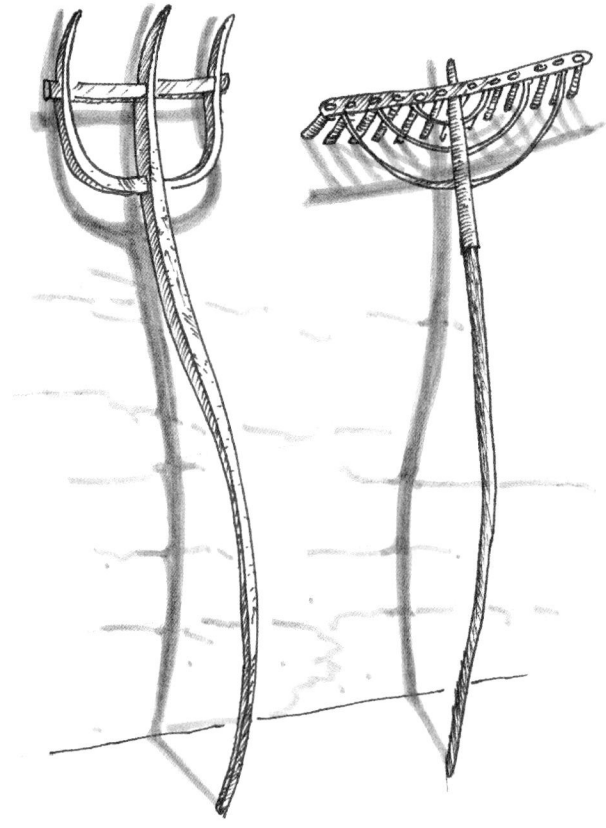

It was one of those glorious, golden days of autumn. I was energized by the beauty of this hay field in its final cutting. It had been a good year, and many bales of hay would be laid up for the long winter.

My best work happens when I am emotionally involved with my subject. I was inspired by the early afternoon sunlight playing in the grass and on rolls of bailed hay.

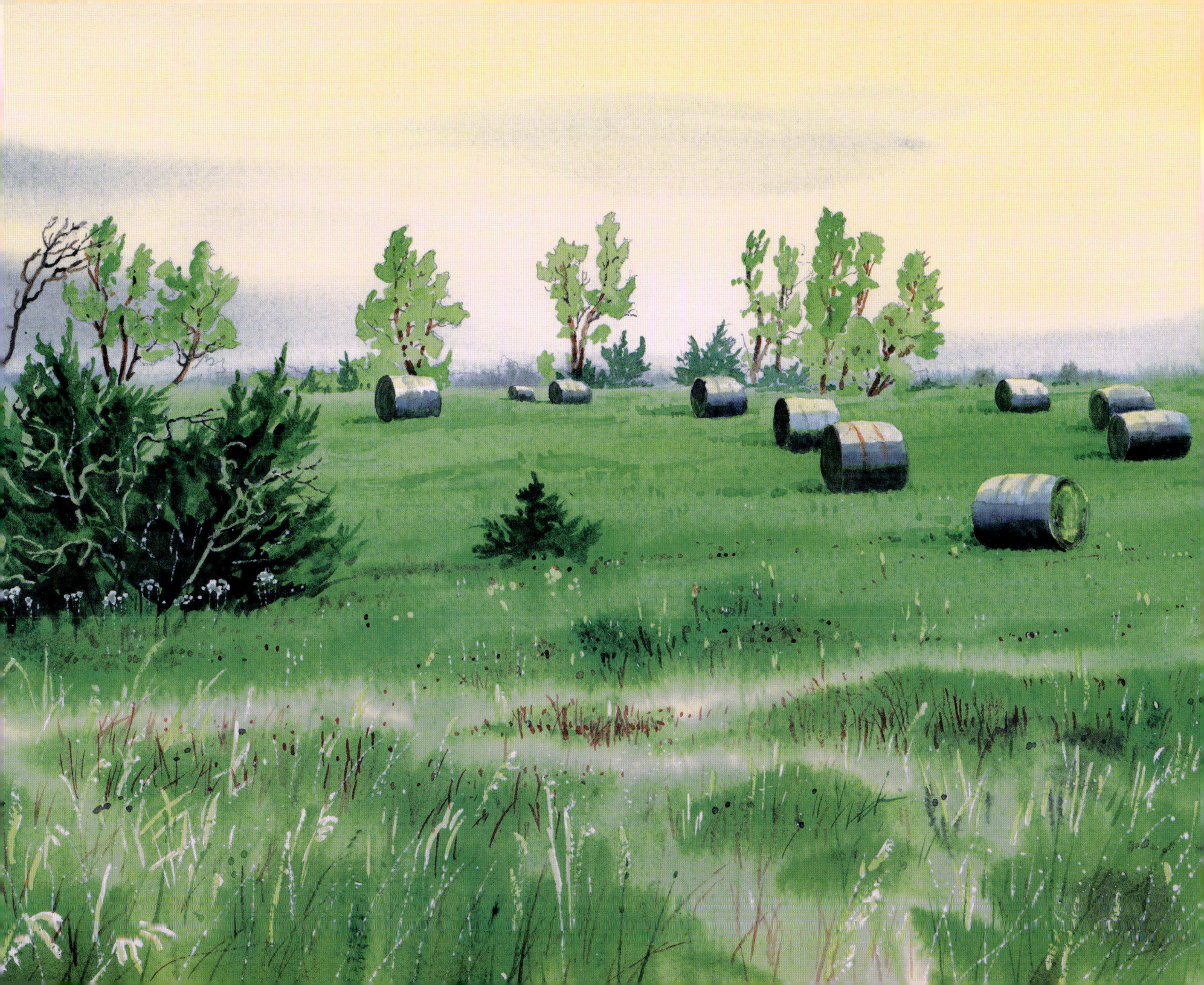

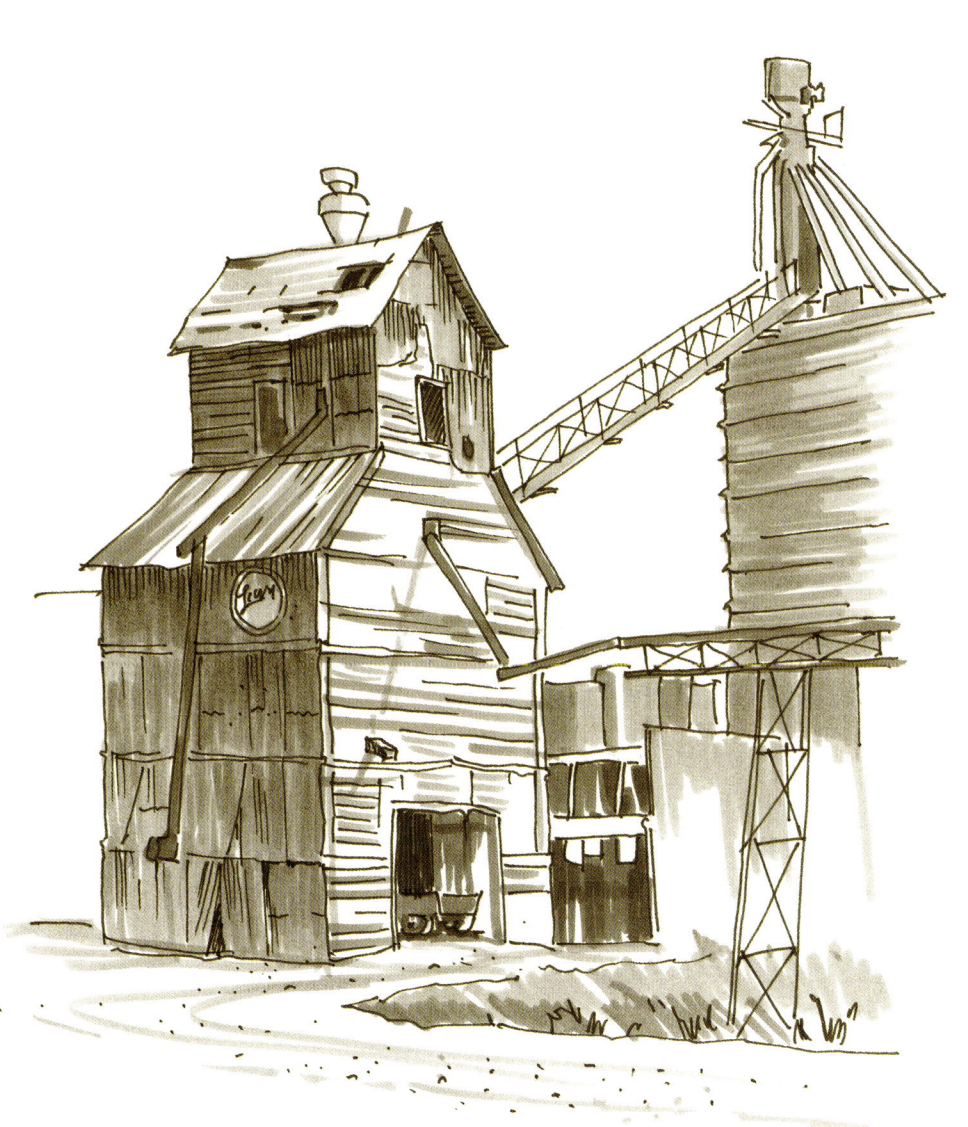

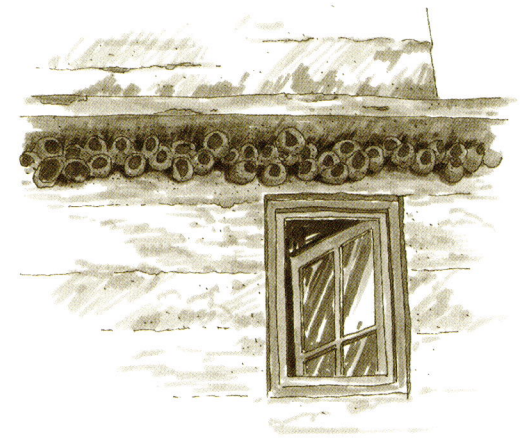

According to the Webster County Museum, the railroads situated towns roughly eight miles apart. This distance, they believed, best served the railroad's interests. A farmer could haul a wagonload of grain eight miles to a market and be home for evening chores.

Thus, grain elevators were one reason for small towns to exist. Here wealth from the neighboring countryside was gathered and stored.

The main street was a deeply rutted road, now frozen hard, which ran from the squat red railway station and the grain "elevator" at the north end of the town to the lumber yard and the horse pond at the south end.   *O PIONEERS!*

This grain elevator, believed to have been constructed in 1878, still stands south of Red Cloud on Webster Street and may have been the elevator that Cather imagined as she invented the town of Hanover for *O Pioneers!*

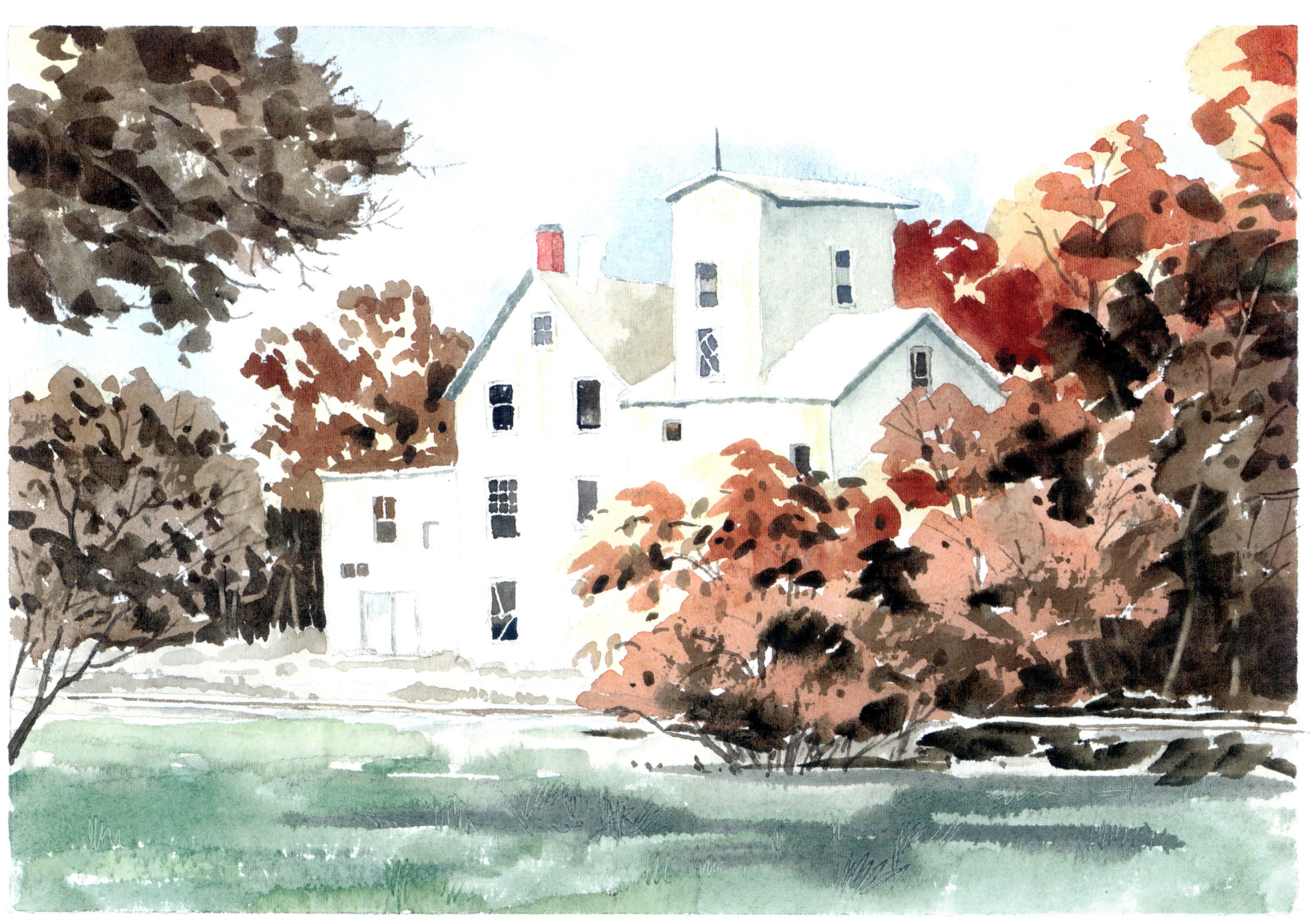

I can remember exactly how the country looked to me as I walked beside my grandmother along the faint wagon-tracks on that early September morning. Perhaps the glide of long railway travel was still with me, for more than anything else I felt motion in the landscape; in the fresh, easy-blowing morning wind, and in the earth itself, as if the shaggy grass were a sort of loose hide, and underneath it herds of wild buffalo were galloping, galloping . . .   MY ÁNTONIA

I went out on a September morning, motivated by these words, to get a feeling for the autumn heat, the wind that swept the dry grass on the prairie, and the sounds of insects and snapping grasshoppers. The overgrown trail reminded me of the one that Jim Burden and his grandmother might have walked.

I chose to paint this windblown hill that rose on an earthen bench above the Republican River valley, where old wagon tracks disappeared into the sea of grass. As I often do, I began this painting using a wet-in-wet technique. The entire sheet of heavy watercolor paper was first saturated with water. When the paper lost its glistening surface, I began dropping pigments of raw sienna, burnt umber, and naples yellow onto the damp surface for the land and added various shades of blue to create the sky. Then, when the paper was thoroughly dry, I added the river valley and completed some of the detail in the foreground.

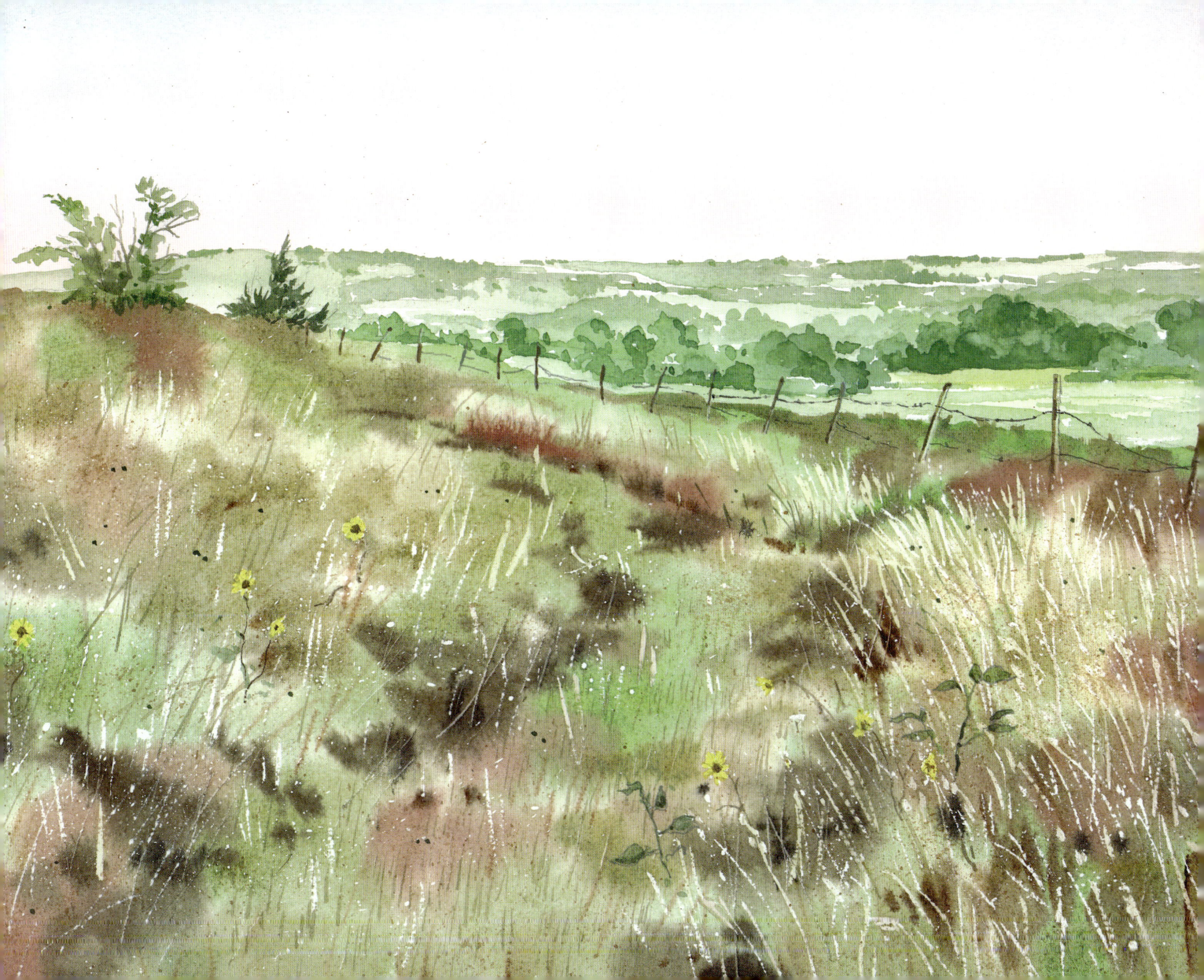

I wanted to walk straight on through the red grass and over the edge of the world, which could not be very far away. The light air about me told me that the world ended here: only the ground and sun and sky were left, and if one went a little farther there would be only sun and sky, and one would float off into them, like the tawny hawks which sailed over our heads making slow shadows on the grass.   MY ÁNTONIA

Red grass is not as ubiquitous today as it was in pioneer times, since much of the land is under cultivation. Red grass is of the bluestem variety and is sometimes referred to as "bunch grass." As summer wanes into autumn, the grasses dry and take on a reddish cast.

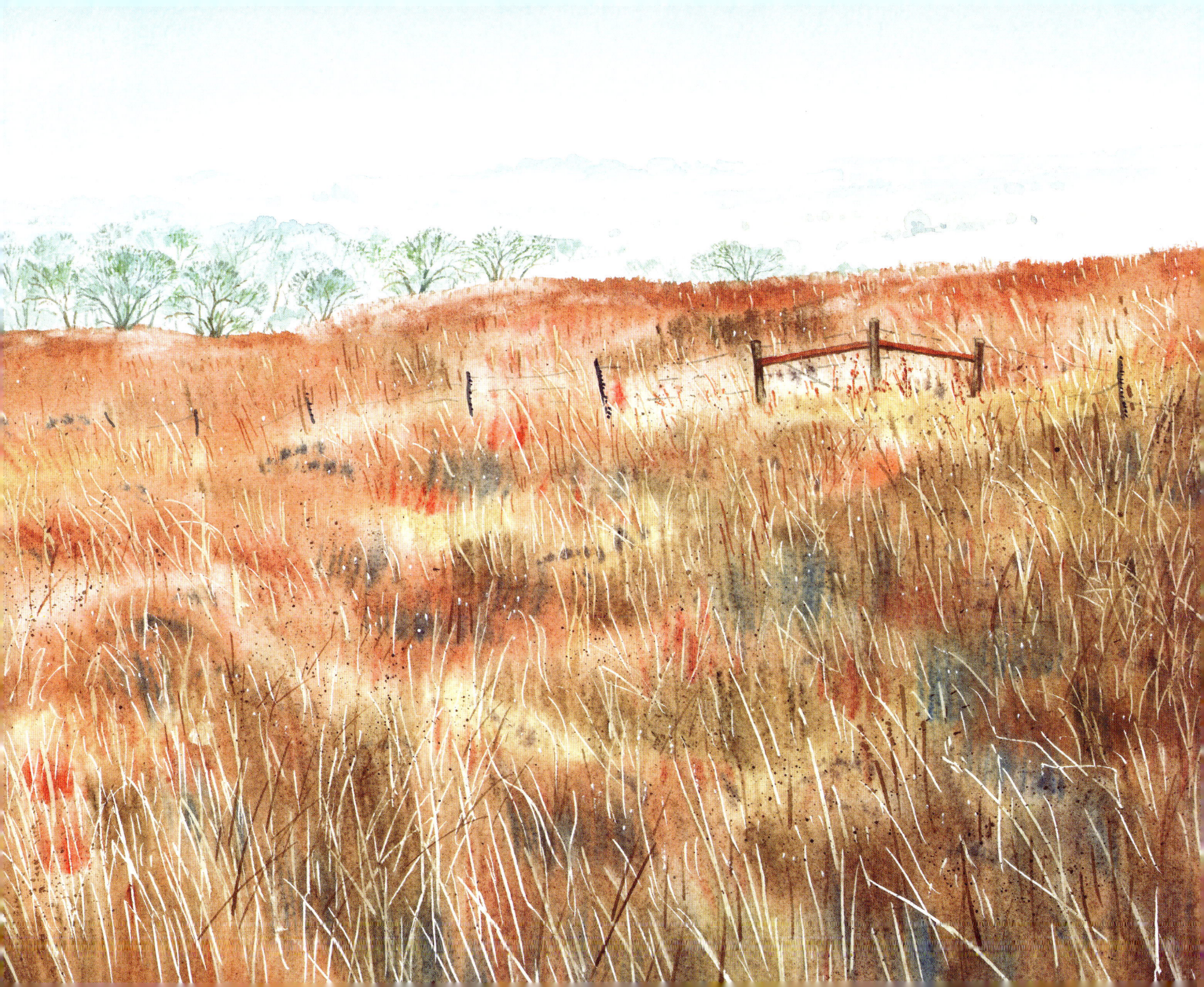

The first snowfall came early in December. I remember how the world looked from our sitting-room window as I dressed behind the stove that morning: the low sky was like a sheet of metal; the blond cornfields had faded out into ghostliness at last; the little pond was frozen under its stiff willow bushes. Big white flakes were whirling over everything and disappearing in the red grass.

MY ÁNTONIA

Winter solstice. Nights seem endless and days are short, gray, and gloomy. The land seems imprisoned in what feels to be a permanent ice age. Wind swirls around the corncrib, sculpting long, drifting tails, and the only color in the landscape is from a few sad corn stalks piercing their snowy blanket.

Still, I like to paint these scenes, which are not necessarily beautiful but express the bleakness of midwinter days. Many who live here do so in expectancy, filled with hope knowing that winter can often end abruptly.

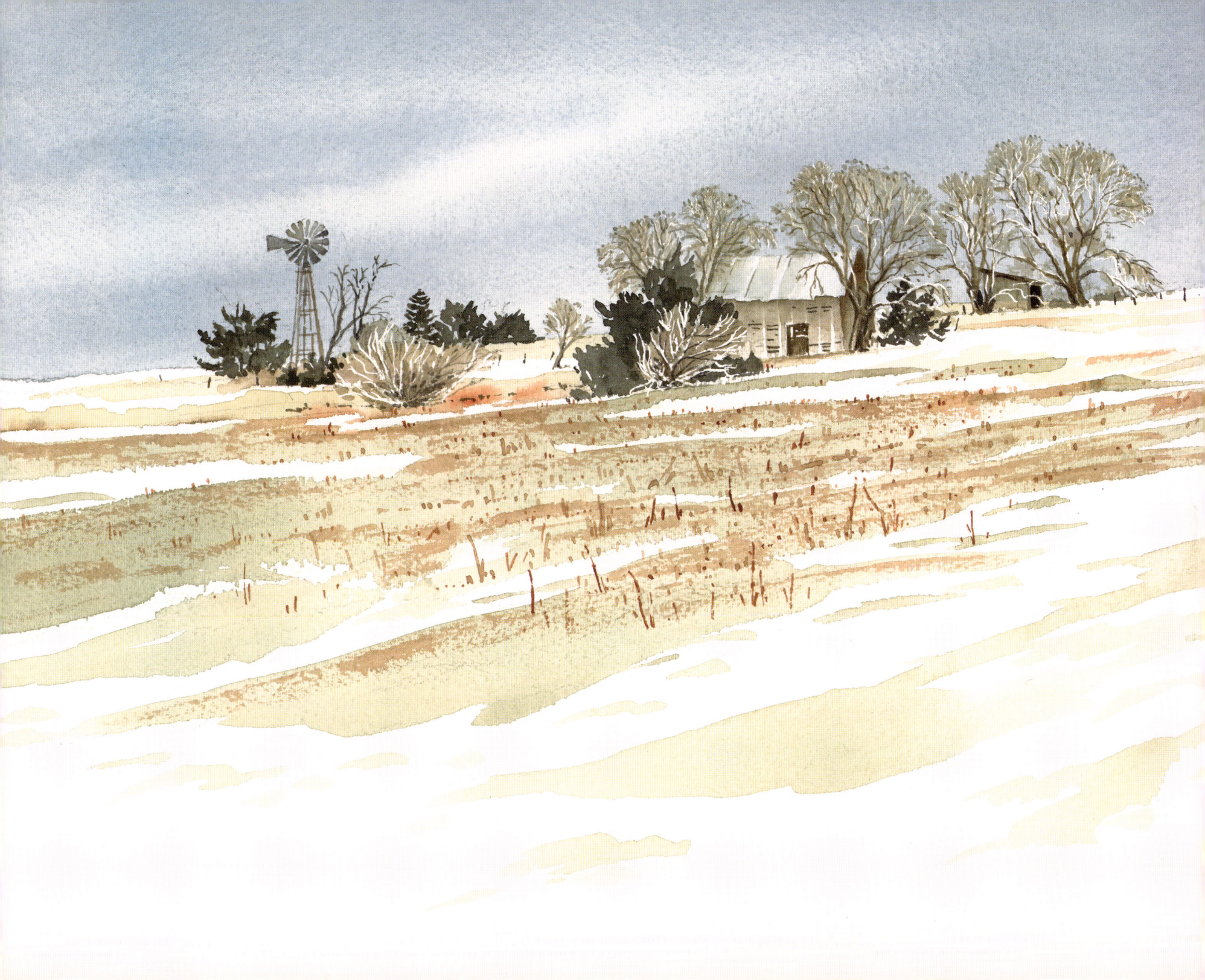

Lucy found the walking bad enough. The roads had been rutted during the thaw, and afterwards the deep cuts made by the wagon-wheels had frozen hard. Yesterday's snowfall had packed into them. Her foot kept catching in the walls of the ruts. On either side of the wheel-tracks the mud had frozen in jagged ridges, rough and sharp like mushroom coral. Since yesterday few countrymen had been abroad, and the horses' hoofs had not yet broken down these frozen incrustations. Lucy couldn't remember that her feet had ever got so cold when she was walking; but this was not walking, really, it was plodding, and breaking through.

LUCY GAYHEART

Ridges of brown earth protrude above the snow-filled ruts created by a hapless driver after one of autumn's hard rains. The roads are frozen now and easier to travel, but I am the first one over this road today. The temperature is fifteen degrees, but with wind and humidity, the chill factor is somewhere between "miserable" and "bone-snapping" cold. Come spring, these ruts fill with snow-melt and become a morass of slippery, gooey clay gumbo, causing many a frightened driver to slowly slide from the crown of the road into the barrow pit. I have visions of those early settlers who found their wagon wheels axel-deep in mud. Only a good team of horses could extract them from the roadside ditch.

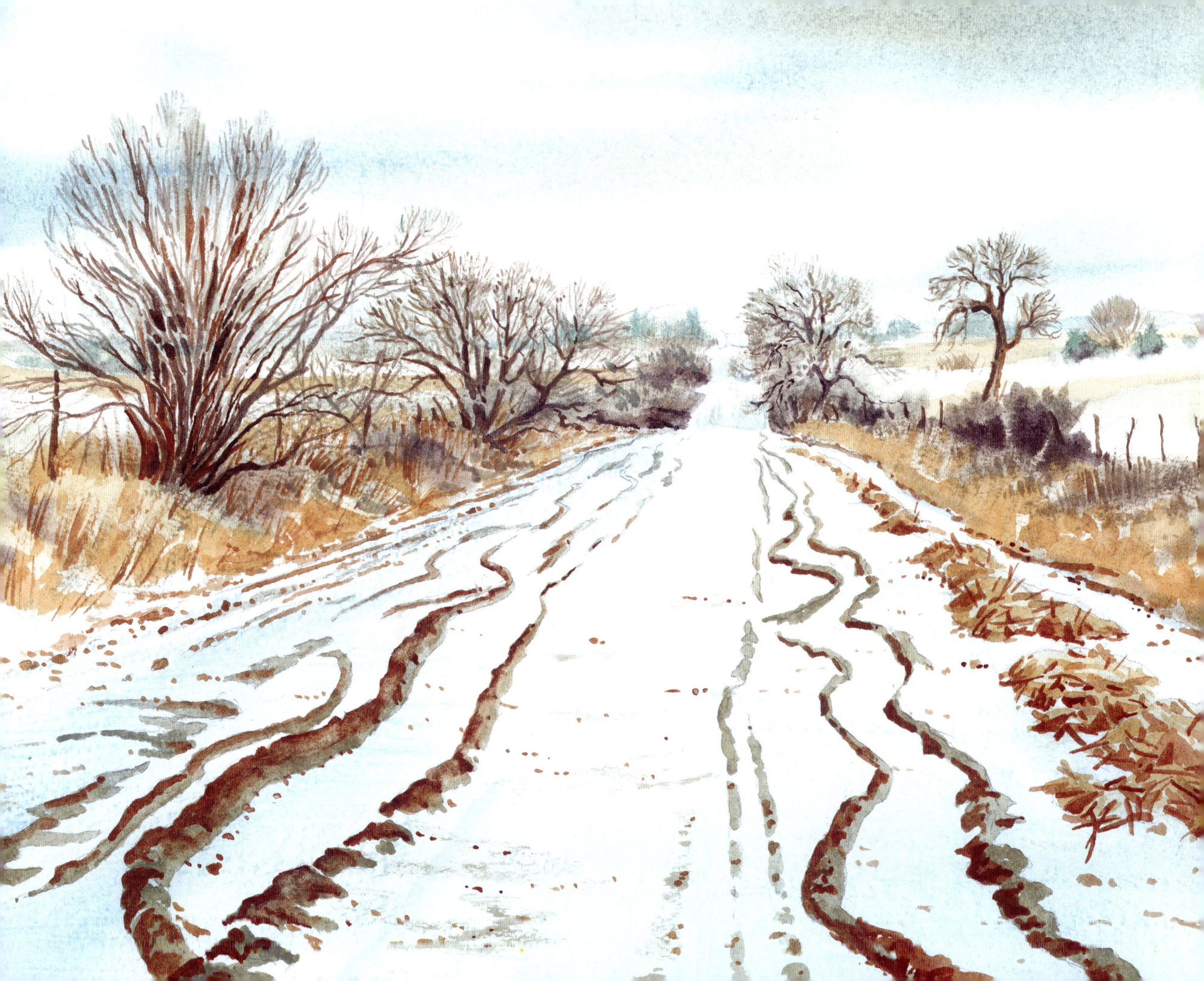

The sky was brilliantly blue, and the sunlight on the glittering white
stretches of prairie was almost blinding. As Ántonia said, the whole world
was changed by the snow; we kept looking in vain for familiar landmarks.
The deep arroyo through which Squaw Creek wound was now only a cleft
between snowdrifts—very blue when one looked down into it.

MY ÁNTONIA

The arroyos and barrow pits give up their caches of snow
reluctantly to the lengthening days and sunshine. Scenes
in which warm, tawny grasses are enveloped in snow are
some of my favorite painting subjects. The blue sky is in
striking opposition to the warmer tones of the earth, and
the white of the paper is left for snow, producing strong
contrasts of colors and values. Long shadows in snow
scenes interest me because they produce action lines and
because objects are almost perpendicular to their cast
shadows, adding yet another dimension to the design.

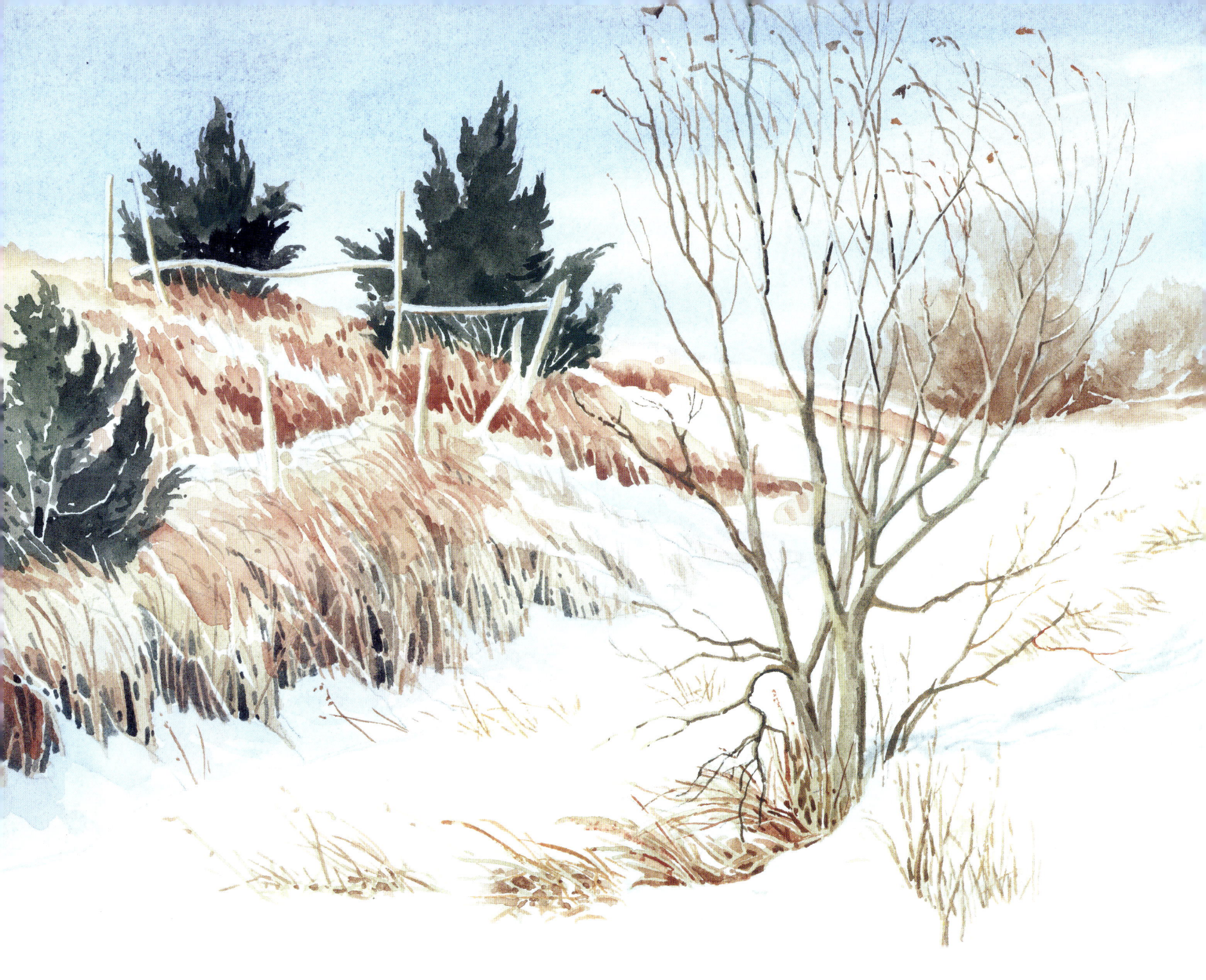

The little town behind them had vanished as if it had never been, had fallen behind the swell of the prairie, and the stern frozen country received them into its bosom. The homesteads were few and far apart; here and there a windmill gaunt against the sky, a sod house crouching in a hollow. But the great fact was the land itself, which seemed to overwhelm the little beginnings of human society that struggled in its sombre wastes. It was from facing this vast hardness that the boy's mouth had become so bitter; because he felt that men were too weak to make any mark here, that the land wanted to be let alone, to preserve its own fierce strength, its peculiar, savage kind of beauty, its uninterrupted mournfulness.   *O PIONEERS!*

I enjoy painting winterscapes, particularly because of the nuance they require when it comes to color. The subtle pastel shades of the sky and soft clouds are juxtaposed with the clean snow, patches of tawny grass, thistles, and thickets that accent the flat prairie. Raw sienna, white, and cerulean blue are beautiful together. If you study the colors of winter on the prairie, you will actually find more colors on the warm rather than the cool scale. Skies and clouds are often the warm shades of cerulean blue and Davy's gray rather than the cool cobalt blue skies of summer.

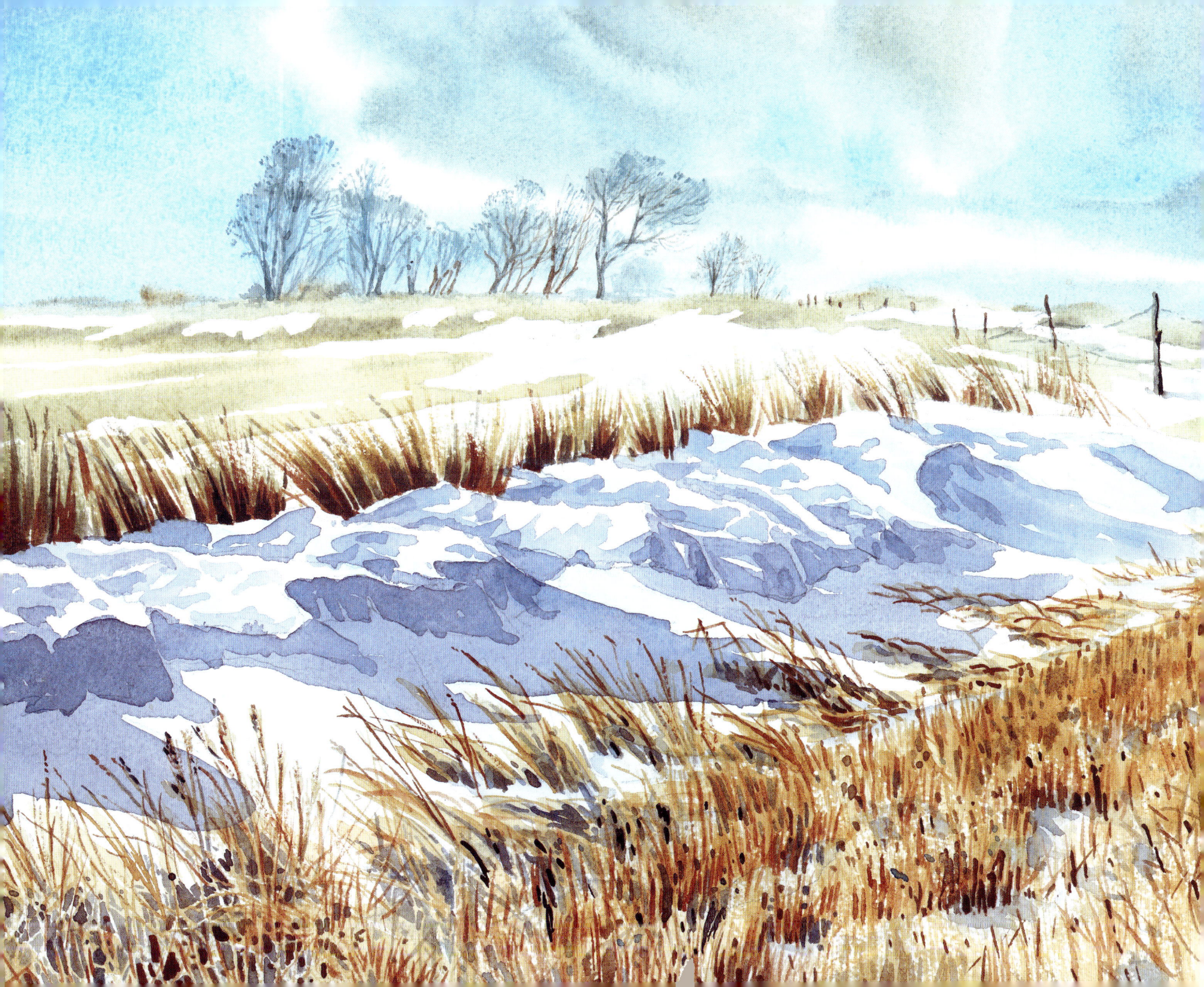

She began to notice things about the country that she had never taken much heed of before. She believed she was bidding the country good-bye this winter, and that made her eye more searching. One thing she watched for, every afternoon. Long before sunset an unaccountable pink glow appeared in the eastern sky, about half-way between the zenith and the horizon. It was not a cloud, it had not the depth of a reflection: it was thin and bright like the colour on a postcard. On sunny afternoons it was sure to be there, a pink rouge on the hard blue cheek of the sky. From her window she could watch this colour come above the tall, wide-spreading cottonwood trees of the town park, where her father led the band concerts in summer.

LUCY GAYHEART

The catalyst for this painting was the beauty of the sky above the eastern outskirts of the town of Red Cloud that reminded me of a scene in *Lucy Gayheart* in which Cather keenly describes the nuance of color of a winter sky. It is in her expert descriptions that I connect with Cather's artistic muse through her perceptive eyes.

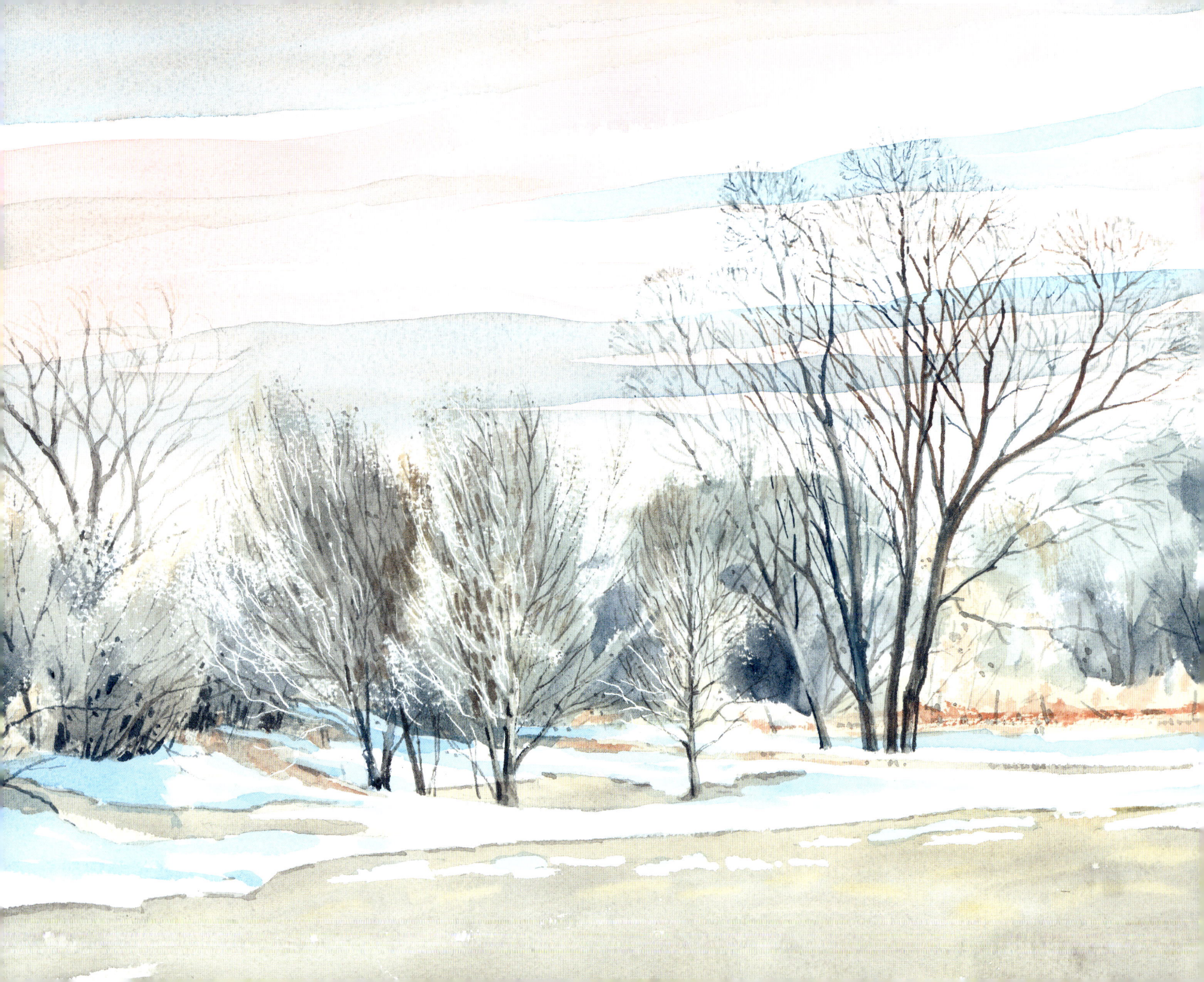

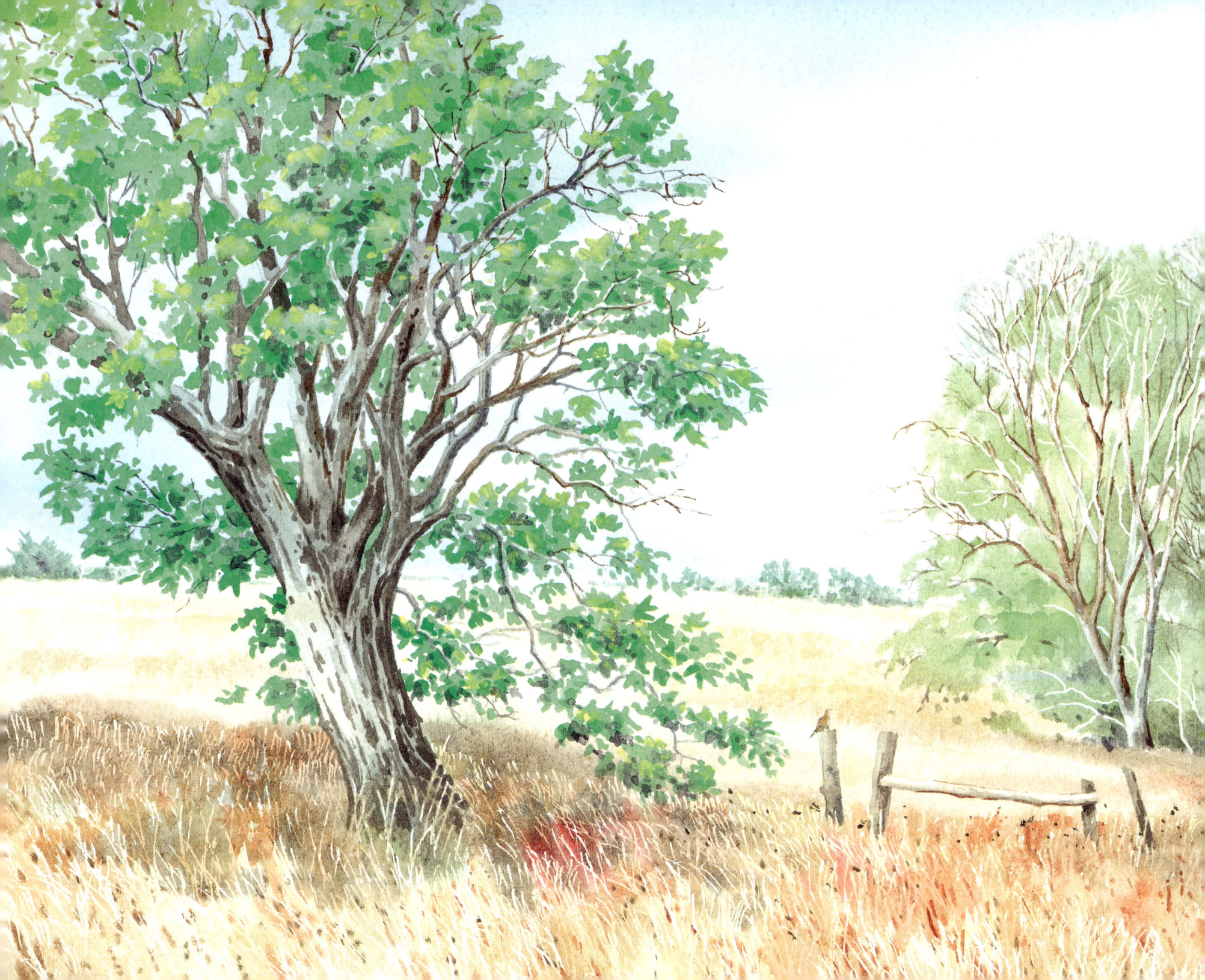

Trees

It was the custom for the mowers to have their dinner in the field. The scythes were left beside the swath last cut, and the hands gathered in the shade under a wide-spreading maple tree. In every hayfield one big tree was left for that purpose. It was always called "the mowers' tree."

SAPPHIRA AND THE SLAVE GIRL

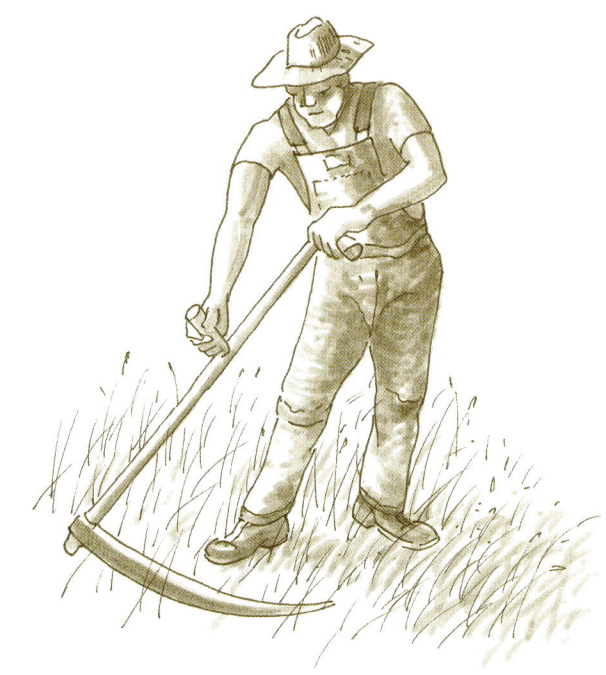

In this painting, the farmers and their hired hands have left the shade of the mowers' tree, leaving only a meadowlark on a fence post to sing its song. One might ask why people are not represented in my paintings. I found the prairie to be a rather lonesome place with few workers in the fields. These days, when seasonal work is done, it is mechanized and often solitary.

Sometimes I went south to visit our German neighbours and to admire their catalpa grove, or to see the big elm tree that grew up out of a deep crack in the earth and had a hawk's nest in its branches.

MY ÁNTONIA

There are a number of catalpa trees in the town of Red Cloud. You can easily identify them by their large, heart-shaped leaves; white blossoms in springtime; and hanging, elongated fruit that resembles bean pods in the summer.

A tall catalpa tree is truly a beautiful sight. I have observed this particular one for several years. There was a time, though, when it was near death. During some very dry years it sprouted very few leaves, and I thought that it would not survive. I admired this tree for its patient and enduring character, powerful trunk, and heavy branches.

Happily, the rains returned and soon the tree was full of large, beautiful white blossoms. It was a tall tree, but now it grew even higher and its uppermost branches seemed to brush passing clouds. I visited the tree this spring and paused to sketch its magnificent lower branches, leaves, and blossoms. My old friend greeted me as always. We both had endured another year.

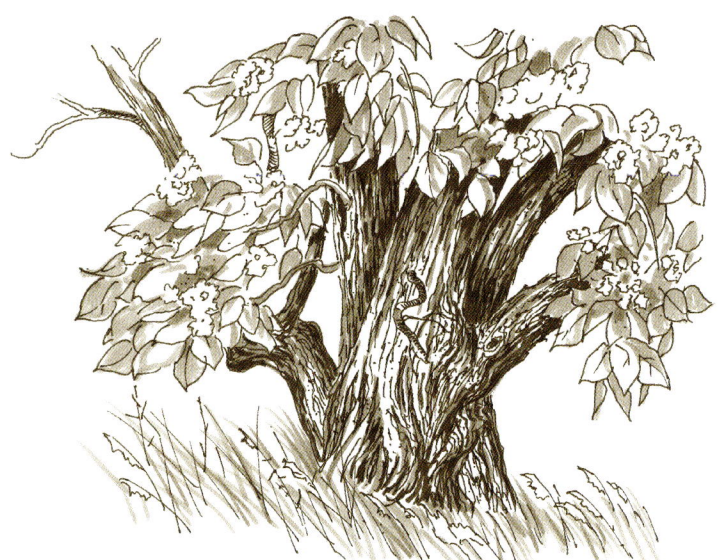

. . . like a tree firmly planted by streams of water, which yields its fruit in its season and its leaf does not wither.

PSALM 1:3

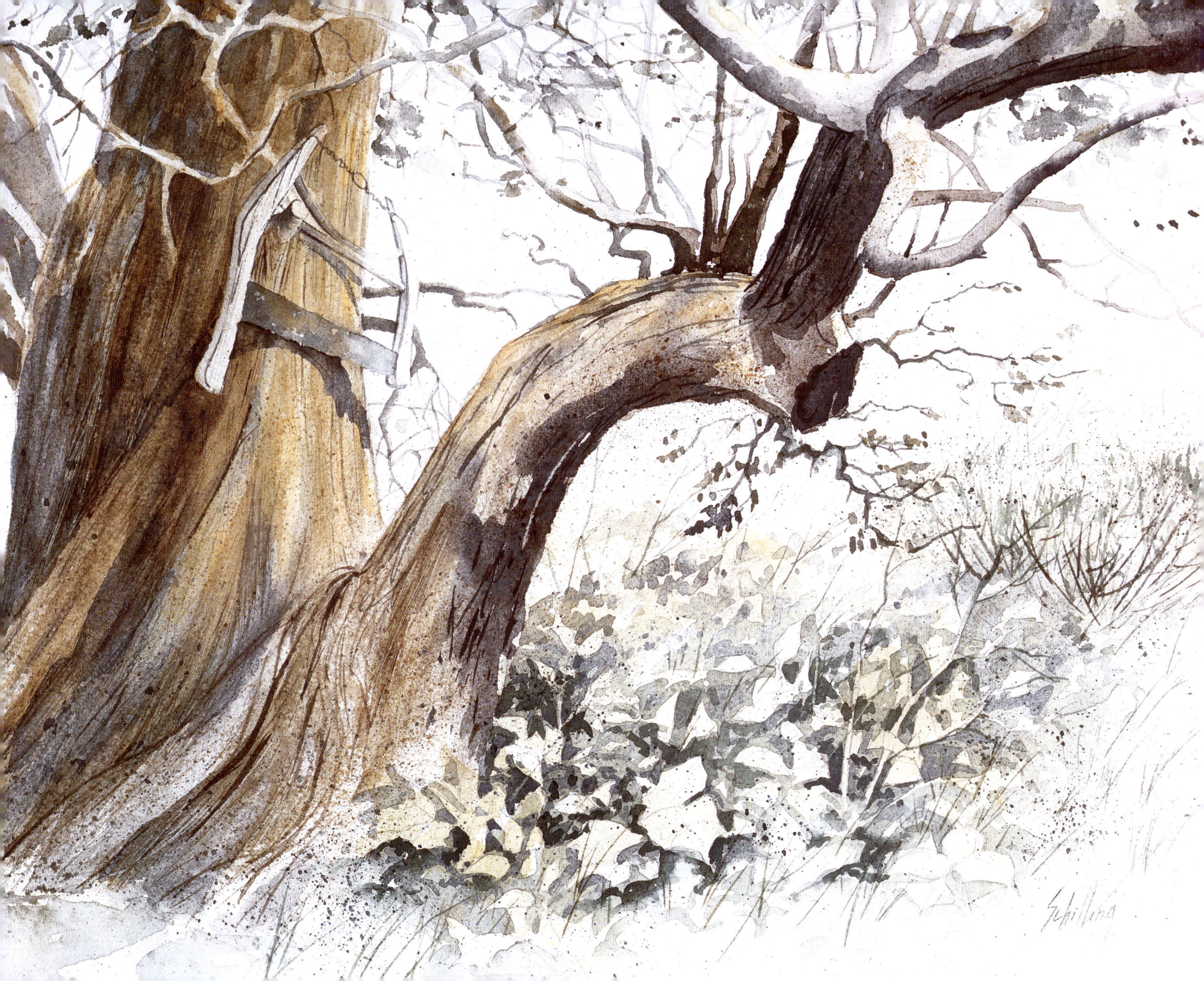

Trees were so rare in the country, and they had to make such a hard fight to grow, that we used to feel anxious about them, and visit them as if they were persons. It must have been the scarcity of detail in that tawny landscape that made detail so precious.   MY ÁNTONIA

Trees were scarce one hundred years ago on the prairie. They are still rare on the Divide, but closer to water, survival is more certain. A splendid forest guards both shores of the Republican River, which snakes through the bottomland and is home to whitetail deer and wild turkeys.

A SOGGY AUTUMN DAY

Inavale is a river town west of Red Cloud. I went there on a drizzly day in search of the school where my mother taught after graduating from high school. Only a few determined individuals cling to this settlement, where unpainted houses fell into disrepair long ago. Many vacant houses are surrounded by jettisoned, broken farm implements; worn-out tires; and some cast-off building supplies.

I drove through the unpaved, puddled streets of town looking for the old school building. I thought that it might have been torn down when at last I saw a large thicket of cottonwood and elm trees that might be hiding a structure. I walked into the overgrowth and parted some of the tree limbs to find a red brick schoolhouse. It was a square, two-story building with a white double door in the center. Above the door lintel were the large numbers "1922," the year my mother started teaching school here. Behind the schoolhouse was a field of tall grass, tree saplings, and some ancient cottonwood trees. This was the setting for my painting.

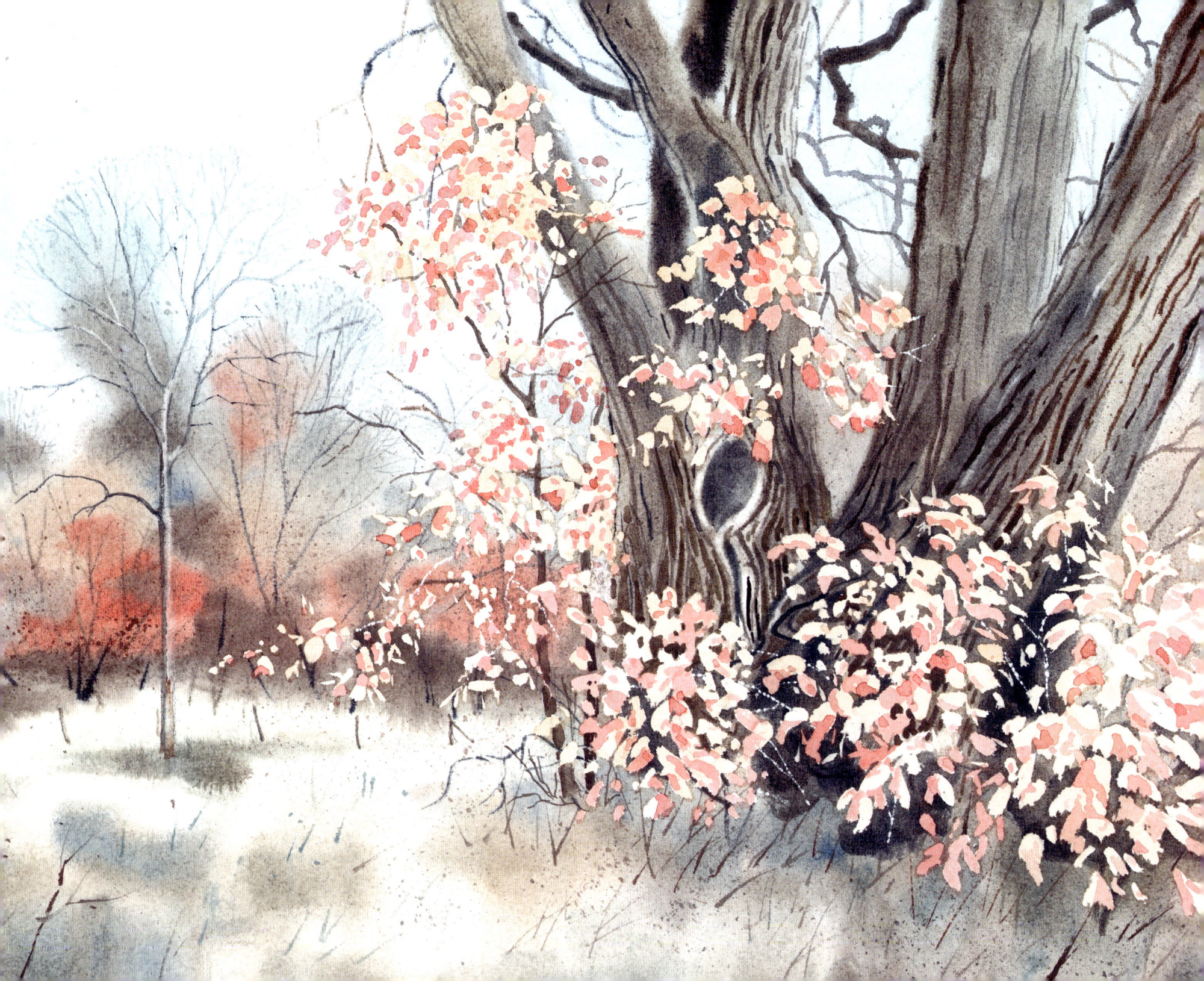

I like trees because they seem more resigned to the way they have to live than other things do. I feel as if this tree knows everything I ever think of when I sit here. When I come back to it, I never have to remind it of anything; I begin just where I left off.   *O PIONEERS!*

Trees, like people, reveal their true character during times of adversity and stress.

Some trees are weaker than others and succumb to less stress. The willow does not live long and is susceptible to infestation and broken limbs caused by early and late snowstorms. On the other hand, there is the cottonwood. Though the cottonwood does not enjoy the winter like the cedar and pine that seem to rejoice in the blowing snow, the older cottonwoods have weathered many years of freezing sleet, lightning, and windstorms. Their broken limbs have split and now touch the earth or appear as broken, stubby appendages. Still, when spring arrives they put on leafy coats that often hide their imperfections.

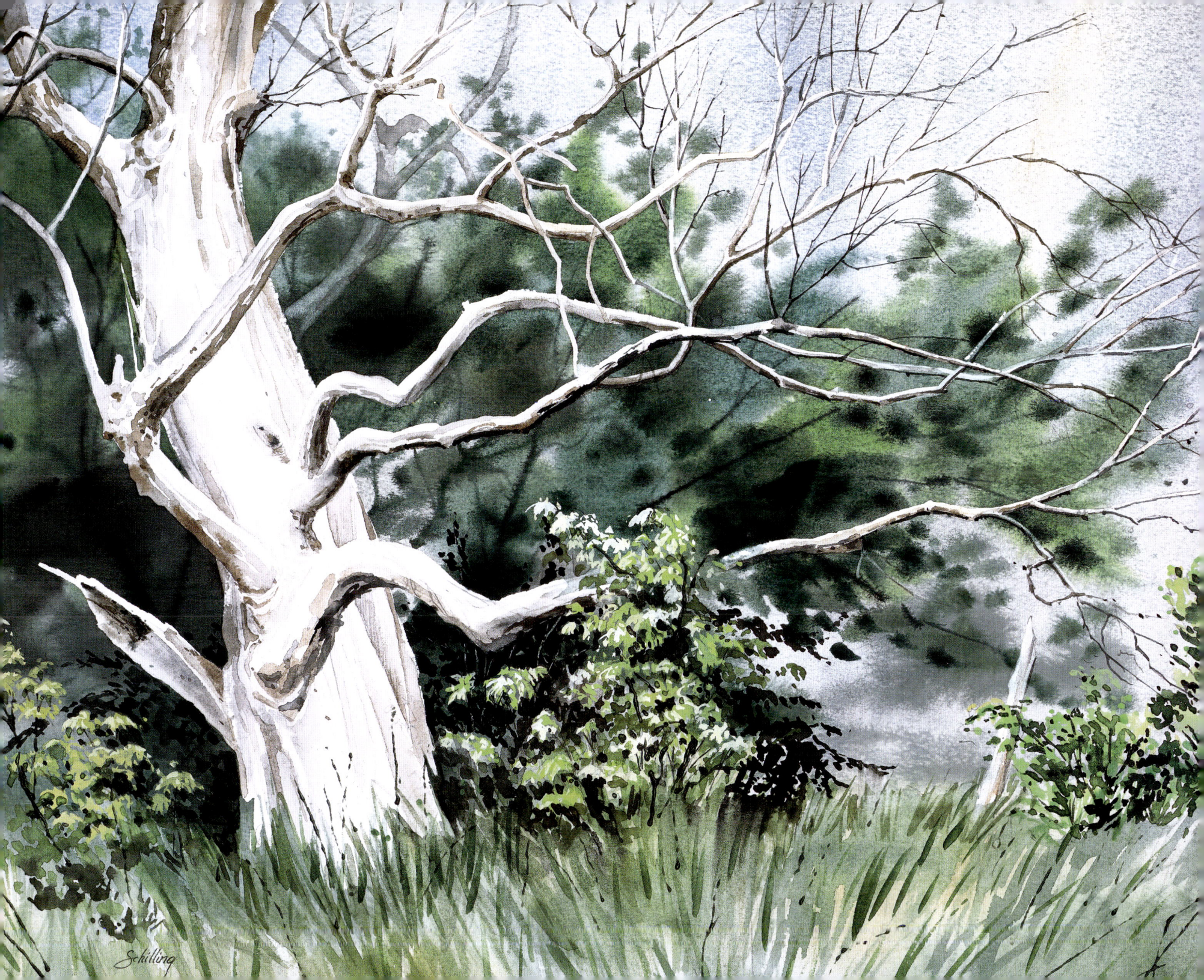

The Forrester place, as every one called it, was not at all remarkable . . .
Stripped of its vines and denuded of its shrubbery, the house would probably
have been ugly enough. It stood close into a fine cottonwood grove that
threw sheltering arms to left and right and grew all down the hillside behind
it. . . . To approach Captain Forrester's property, you had first to get over a
wide, sandy creek which flowed along the eastern edge of town. Crossing
this by footbridge or the ford, you entered the Captain's private lane
bordered by Lombardy poplars, with wide meadows lying on either side.

A LOST LADY

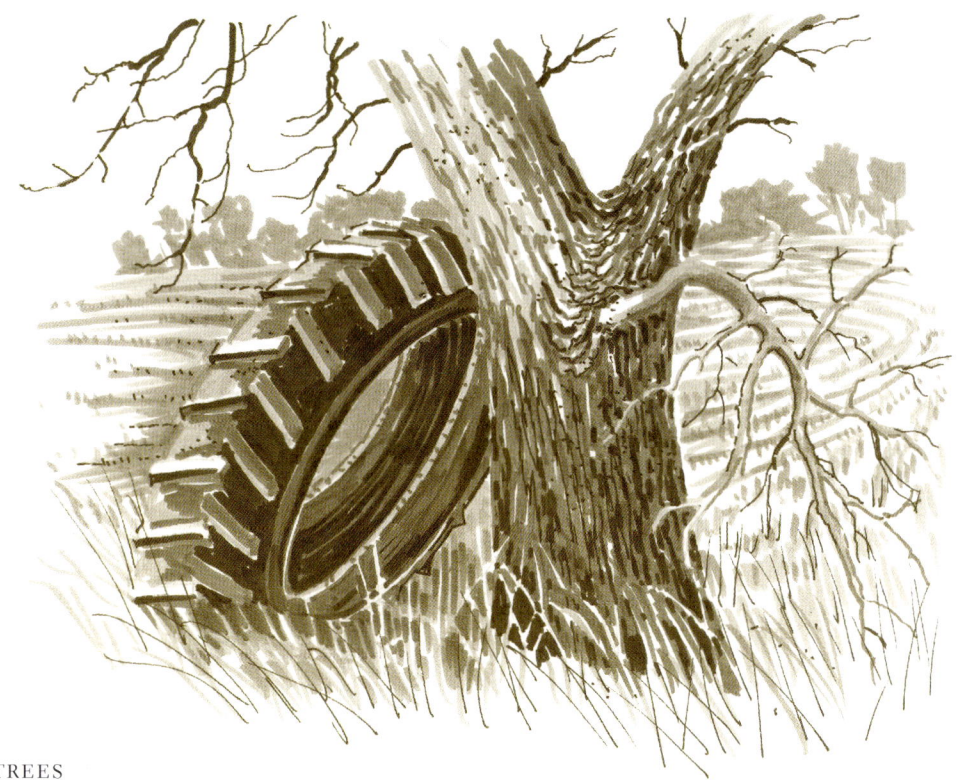

It was a rainy day in early autumn. The knoll in the
middle of the picture was the setting for the Forrester
home in *A Lost Lady*. The Lombardy poplars that
bordered the lane up to the house are long gone, but the
knoll is now covered with tall cottonwoods. The property,
which burned down in 1920, actually belonged to Silas
Garber, the model for Captain Forrester.

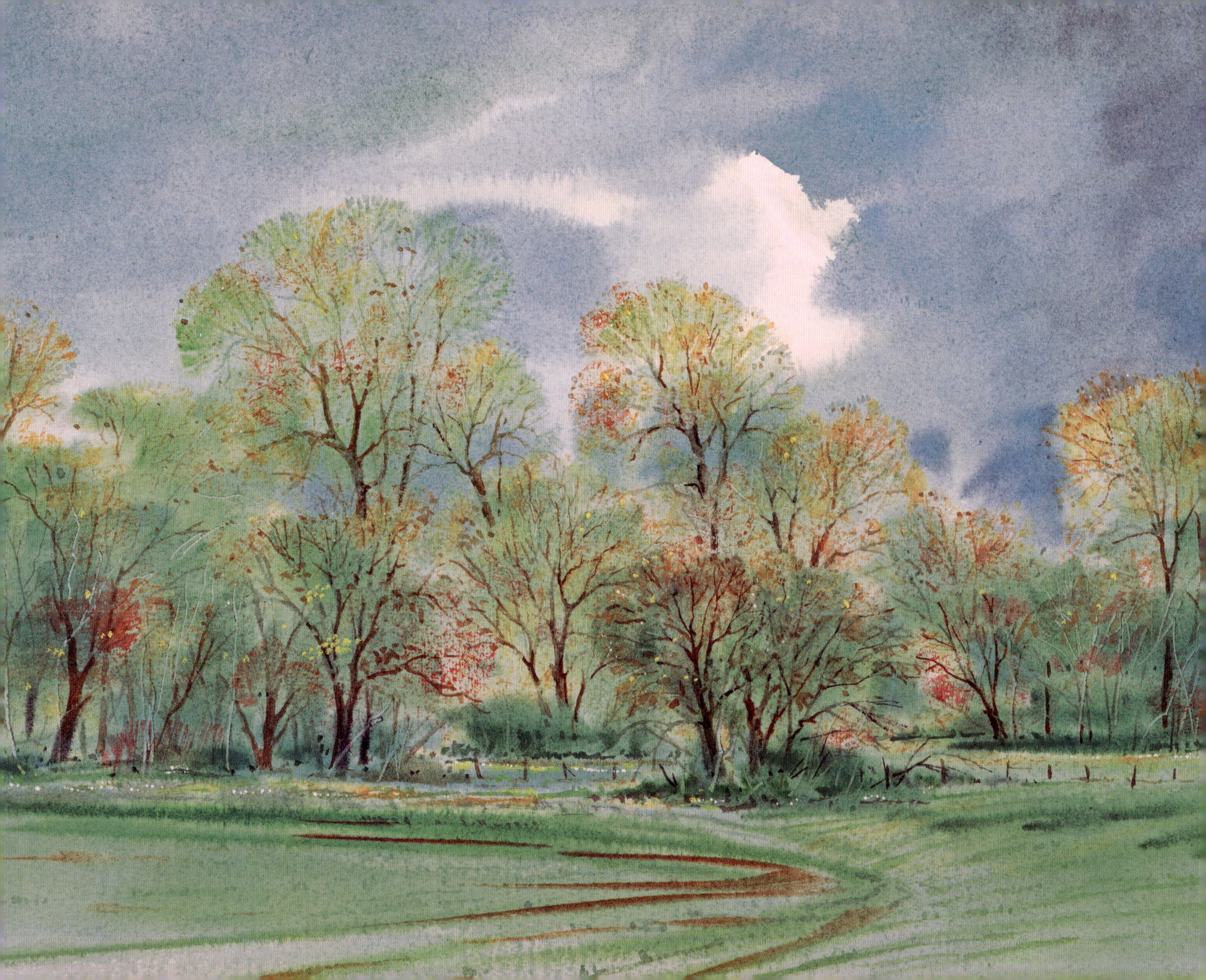

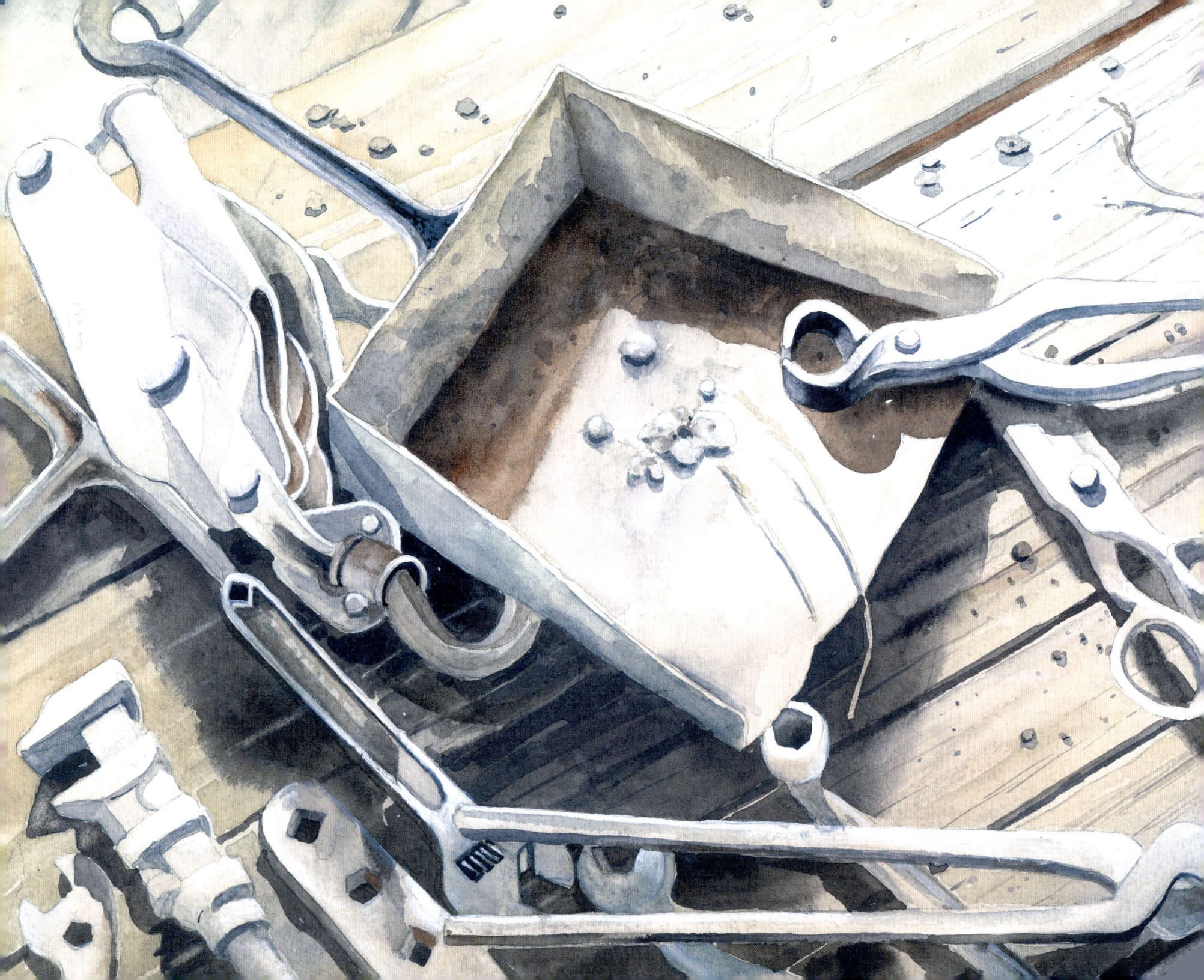

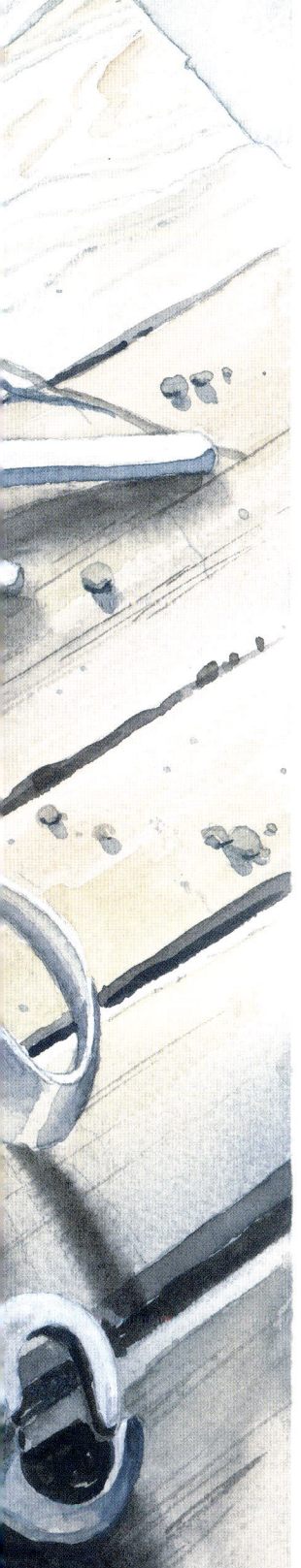

Art in Unexpected Places

A blacksmith's tools lay on a table bathed in light from the small broken window on the west side of the century-old barn. Covered by dust but otherwise just as the smithy might have left them, the forging implements—long-handled tongs, wrenches, a coal scoop, block and tackle—were artfully but casually placed on the wooden bench as though he had set them down at the end of a weary day. "Art, it seems to be, should simplify," wrote Cather in "On the Art of Fiction," and that simplicity, she felt, did not diminish beauty or significance. Though uncomplicated, her words were carefully chosen and measured in every description. Likewise, the smithy chose his tools with skill and fueled his fire to the proper temperature. The smithy's creations were strong in design and powerful in utility. Forged under fire and hammer, he crafted hitches, hinges, hooks, hasps, and replaced the broken forks of a hundred hay rakes. Cather respected the artisan's skill and wrote stories of human character—perseverance, malleability, strength, endurance—qualities that were tested and then solidified by the land.

The tools were just the composition I needed for a watercolor painting. The wooden table was covered with a blanket of grayish tan dust. I wanted my painting to show some of the character that lay beneath the dust—the rust and bluish black color of the tempered steel.

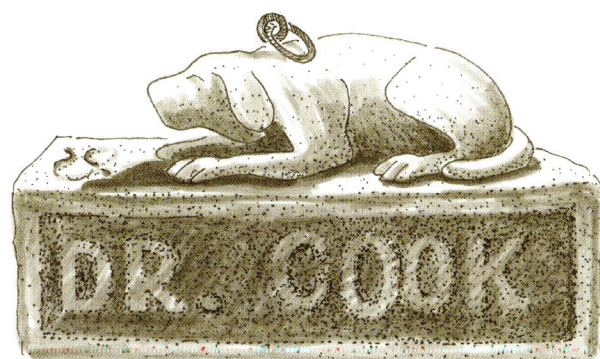

DR. COOK'S TIE-UP

A stone carver created this unique hitch for Dr. Cook. The sculptor has done other works of art that can be found in the Red Cloud Cemetery.

103

She was convinced that the great thing was *desire* in art, that a desire to express ourselves be a clear compelling thing that must out, whether it be a poem, a painting, a novel, a symphony, or a piece of sculpture.

MILDRED R. BENNETT, *THE WORLD OF WILLA CATHER*

I stood on the bank of the Republican River near the bridge abutment thinking of Cather's characters who played and picnicked on sandbars on summer evenings. When I turned to climb the embankment, I saw a mural of brightly painted graffiti on the underside of the bridge. Names were spray painted with brilliant colors, outlined in blue or black, names like "Buck" and "Melanie—Class of 2006." Many names had faded with time and were now overlaid with those of a younger generation. The lettering required skill, but what amazed me was the ingenuity that was required to create this art on the underbelly of a bridge. If Cather were alive today, would she think of this as art? If so, she might have held the ladder for her artist friends.

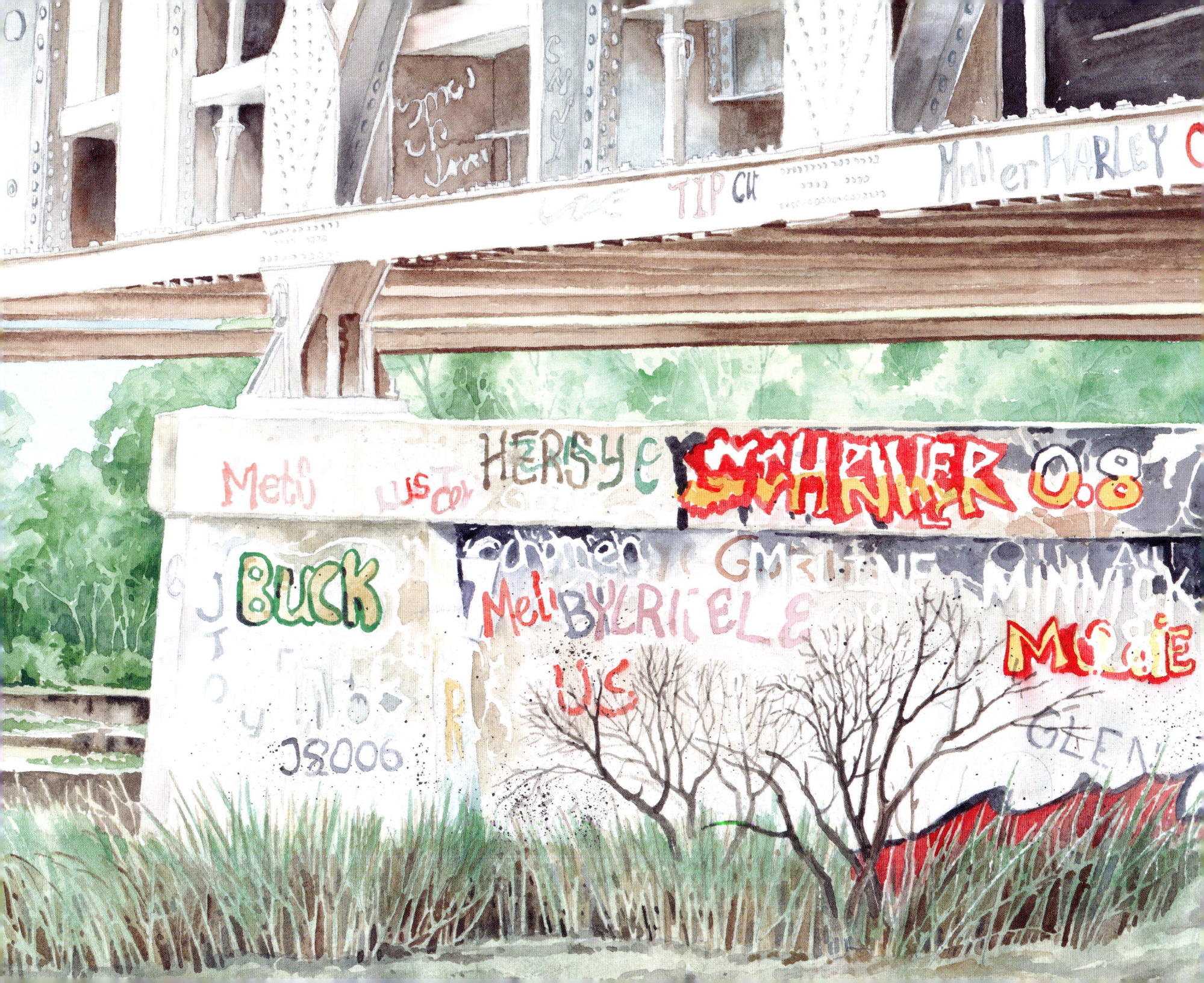

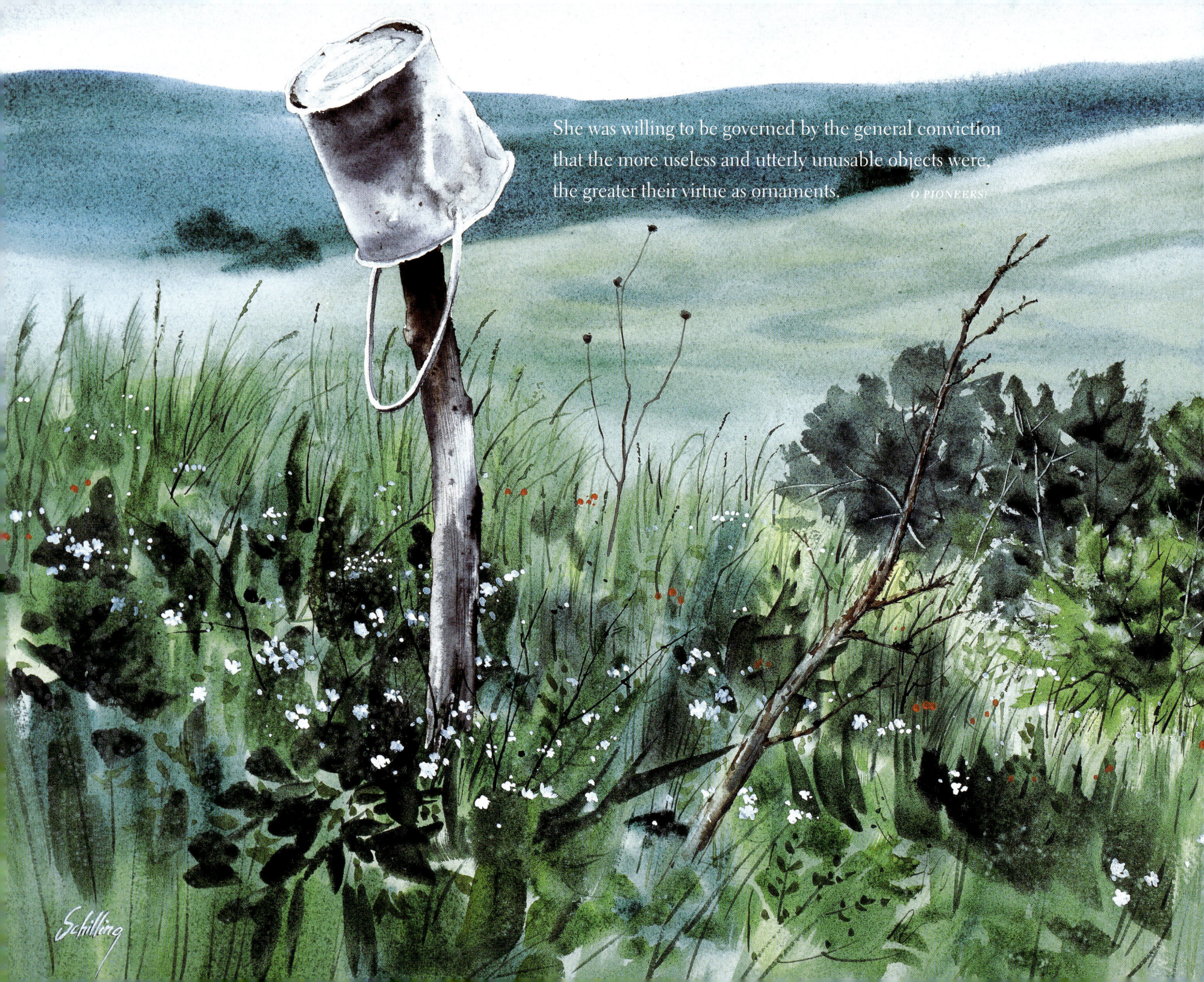

She was willing to be governed by the general conviction
that the more useless and utterly unusable objects were,
the greater their virtue as ornaments. *O PIONEERS!*

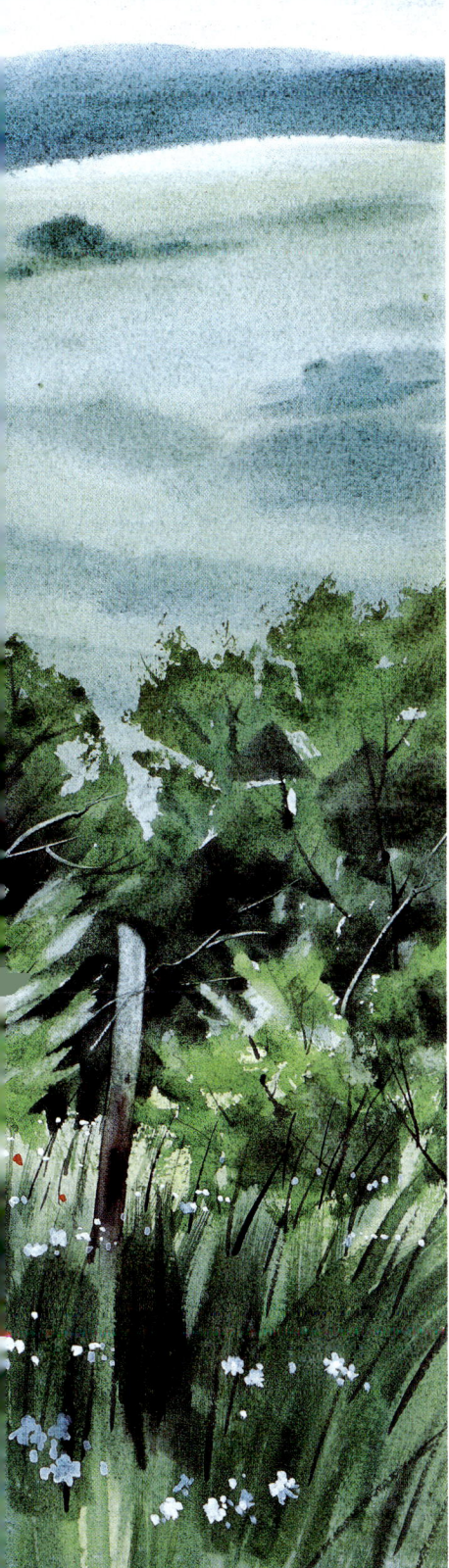

South of town on the memorial prairie, untouched by a sodbuster's plow, I found a curious sight. A bucket had been thrown over the end of a fence post. Had this been placed as a notice of lost and found, or was it a totally useless decoration?

COWBOY ART

I turned my car north and headed into the Divide. The soil was good here and cornfields stretched as far as the eye could see. A row of fence posts caught my eye. A cowboy boot covered the top of each fencepost. Some had rotted from storms and days of scorching sun while others, placed more recently, were well intact. I was reminded of the cast-off art of which Cather spoke. Here was evidence of a farmer's expression of creativity with a sense of humor—a fence row of worn-out boots lined up like Andy Warhol's tomato soup cans.

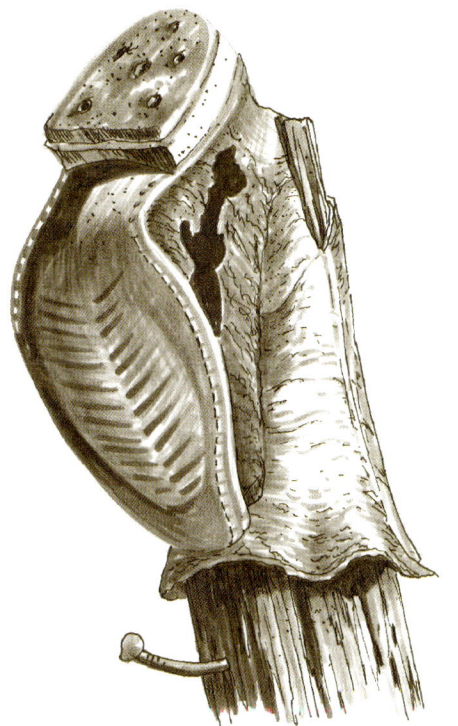

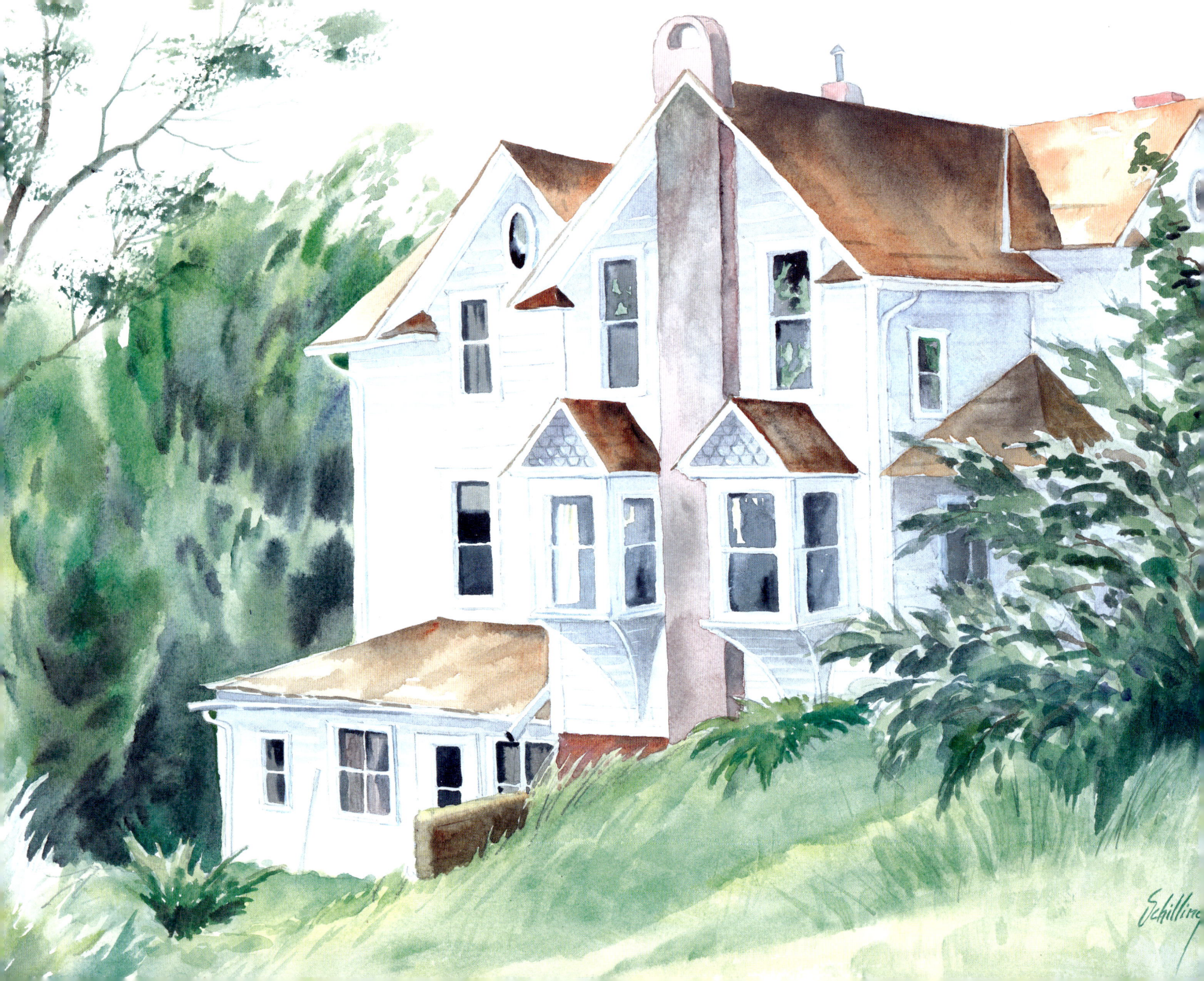

Homes and Prairie Towns

He crept down two flights of stairs, feeling his way in the dusk, his red hair standing up in peaks, like a cock's comb. He went through the kitchen into the adjoining washroom, which held two porcelain stands with running water. Everybody had washed before going to bed, apparently, and the bowls were ringed with a dark sediment which the hard, alkaline water had not dissolved. Shutting the door on this disorder, he turned back to the kitchen.

ONE OF OURS

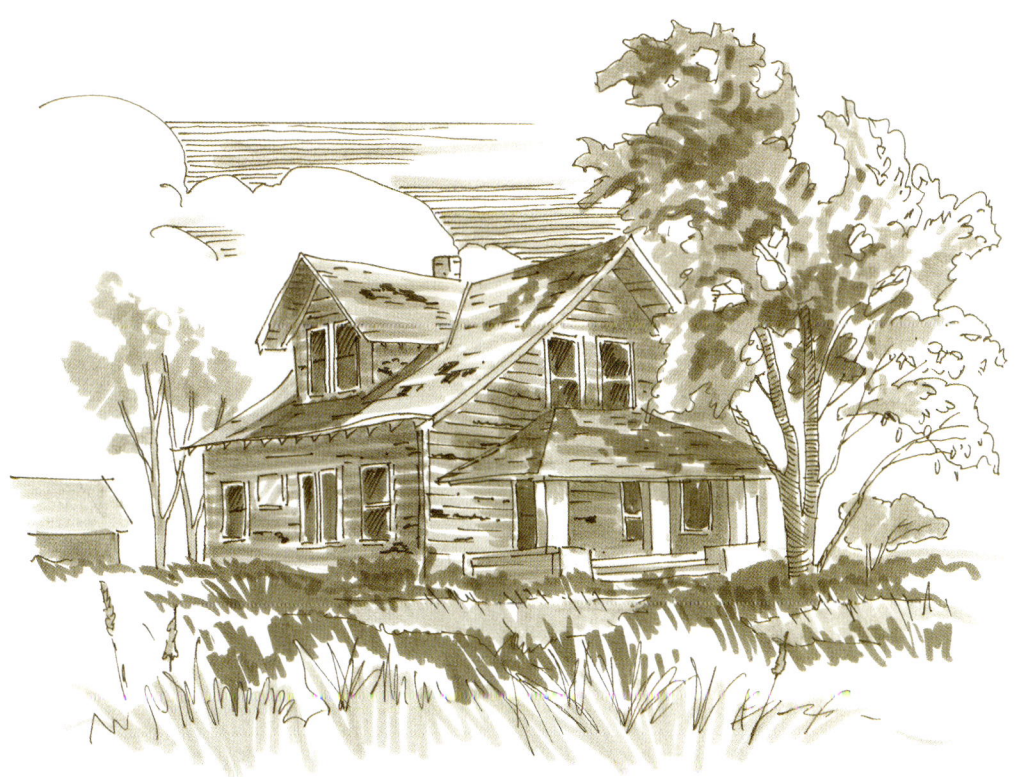

C. P. Cather was Willa's cousin and the prototype for her character Claude Wheeler. The kitchen was found on the lowest level of George Cather's large home, and like the kitchen in *One of Ours* and many kitchens today, it was where family members gathered, made plans, and conducted casual discourse over cups of strong coffee.

THE GEORGE CATHER HOMESTEAD

When George Cather arrived in Nebraska from Virginia, there was very little to break the prairie winds. This was his homestead before moving to Bladen.

There was nothing but land: not a country at all, but the material out of which countries are made.

MY ÁNTONIA

They turned into another street and saw before them lighted windows; a low story-and-a-half house, with a wing built on at the right and a kitchen addition at the back, everything a little on the slant—roofs, windows, and doors. *THE SONG OF THE LARK*

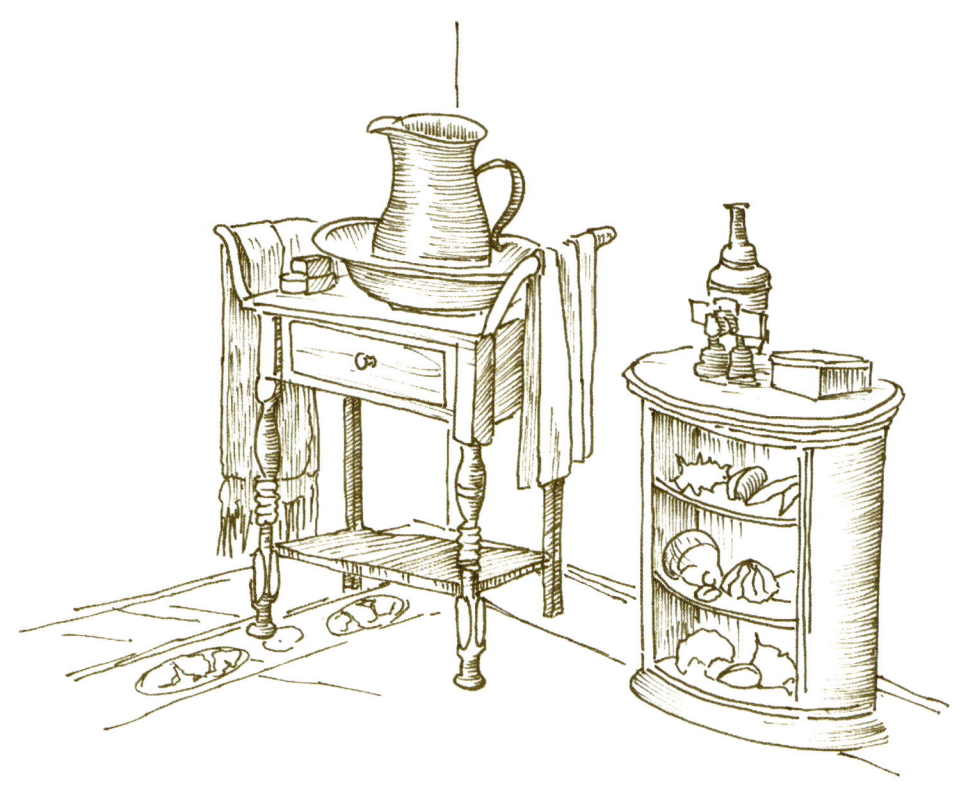

WILLA'S CHILDHOOD BEDROOM

. . . her pupils paid her twenty-five cents a lesson—to fit up a little room for herself upstairs in the half-story. It was the end room of the wing, and was not plastered, but was snugly lined with soft pine. The ceiling was so low that a grown person could reach it with the palm of the hand, and it sloped down on either side. There was only one window, but it was a double one and went to the floor. *THE SONG OF THE LARK*

Young Willa was privileged to have her own bedroom in the attic floor of the home on Cedar Street, while her four brothers shared the open space beneath the rafters. She purchased rose-patterned wallpaper with the money she earned working at the drug store and hung the paper herself. She did well since it still decorates the room today.

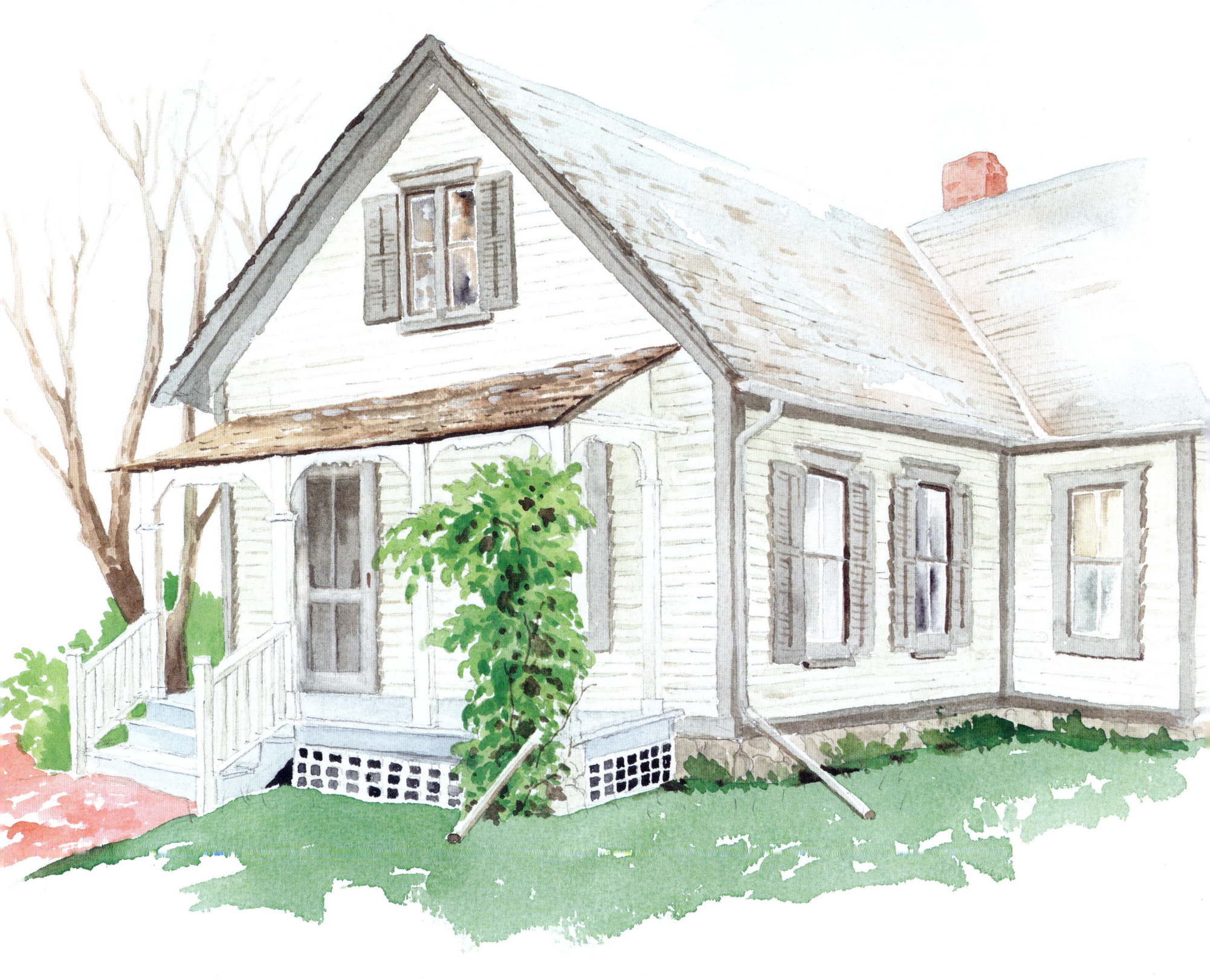

Even in American cities, which seem so much alike, where people seem all to be living the same lives, striving for the same things, thinking the same thoughts, there are still individuals a little out of tune with the times—there are still survivals of a past more loosely woven, there are disconcerting beginnings of a future yet unforeseen.   "UNCLE VALENTINE"

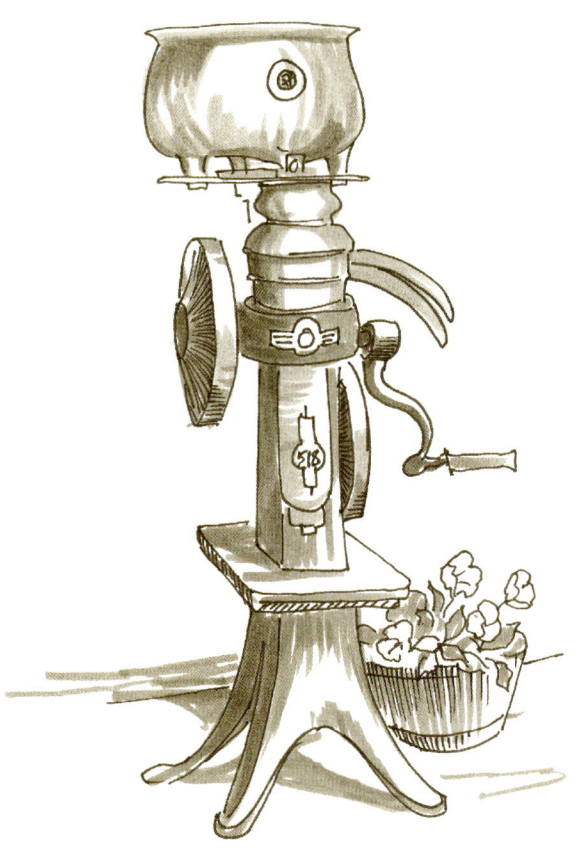

THE CREAM SEPARATOR

Mrs. Wheeler's pale eyes twinkled. "Mahailey and I will never be quite up-to-date, Ralph. We're old-fashioned, and I don't know but you'd better let us be. I could see the advantage of a separator if we milked half-a-dozen cows. It's a very ingenious machine. But it's a great deal more work to scald it and fit it together than it was to take care of the milk in the old way."

ONE OF OURS

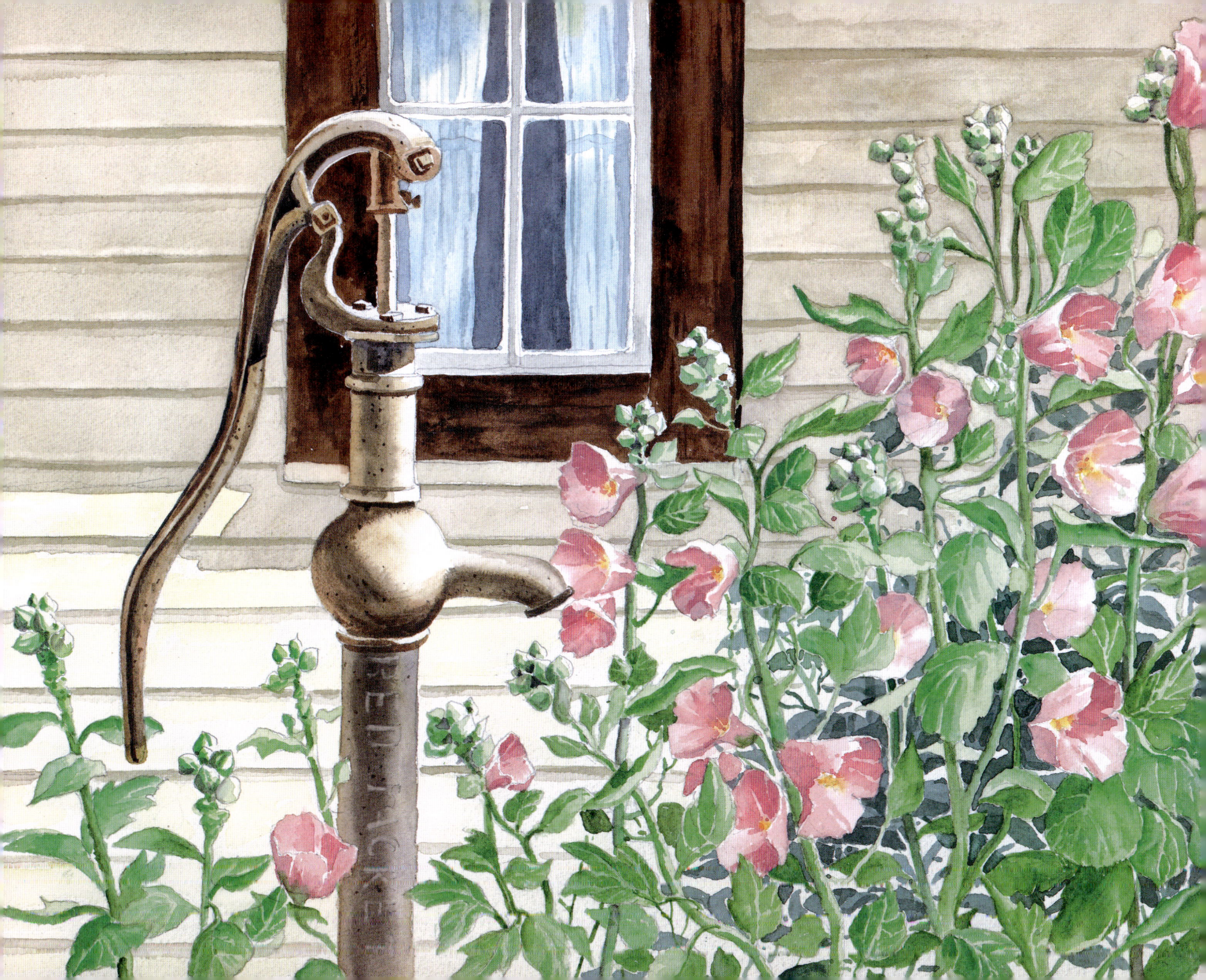

Nobody can paint the sun, or sunlight. He can only paint the tricks that shadows play with it, or what it does to forms. He cannot even paint those relations of light and shade—he can only paint some emotion they give him.

"LIGHT ON ADOBE WALLS"

This painting is of the Cather family home, known today as Cather's Retreat. Charles and Virginia Cather moved here in 1904 from their rented home on Third Avenue and Cedar Street. By this time, young Willa had left Red Cloud to follow her career in the East, though she continued to spend her summers and a few holidays in her parents' home. She was given the sunny south-facing bedroom on the second floor.

It was a cold February morning, yet the sun shone brightly on the walls of the Cather home, casting long shadows across the lawn. The scene immediately reminded me of her words regarding light in her essay, "Light on Adobe Walls." As an artist I must agree with Cather. I cannot paint the sunshine any more than I can paint the wind. I can only paint the effects of these natural occurrences. At times an artist may manipulate color to cause a visual sensory response where a writer is privileged to simply use words. The house is white, but rarely is anything truly white. There are subtle colors that reflect onto a white surface from things nearby. Judicious placement of a light yellow tint in a white wall provides brilliance and sometimes warmth. In a summer scene, I may choose to paint a sky of transparent blue over a wash of transparent yellow. It says to the viewer, "This is a hot day."

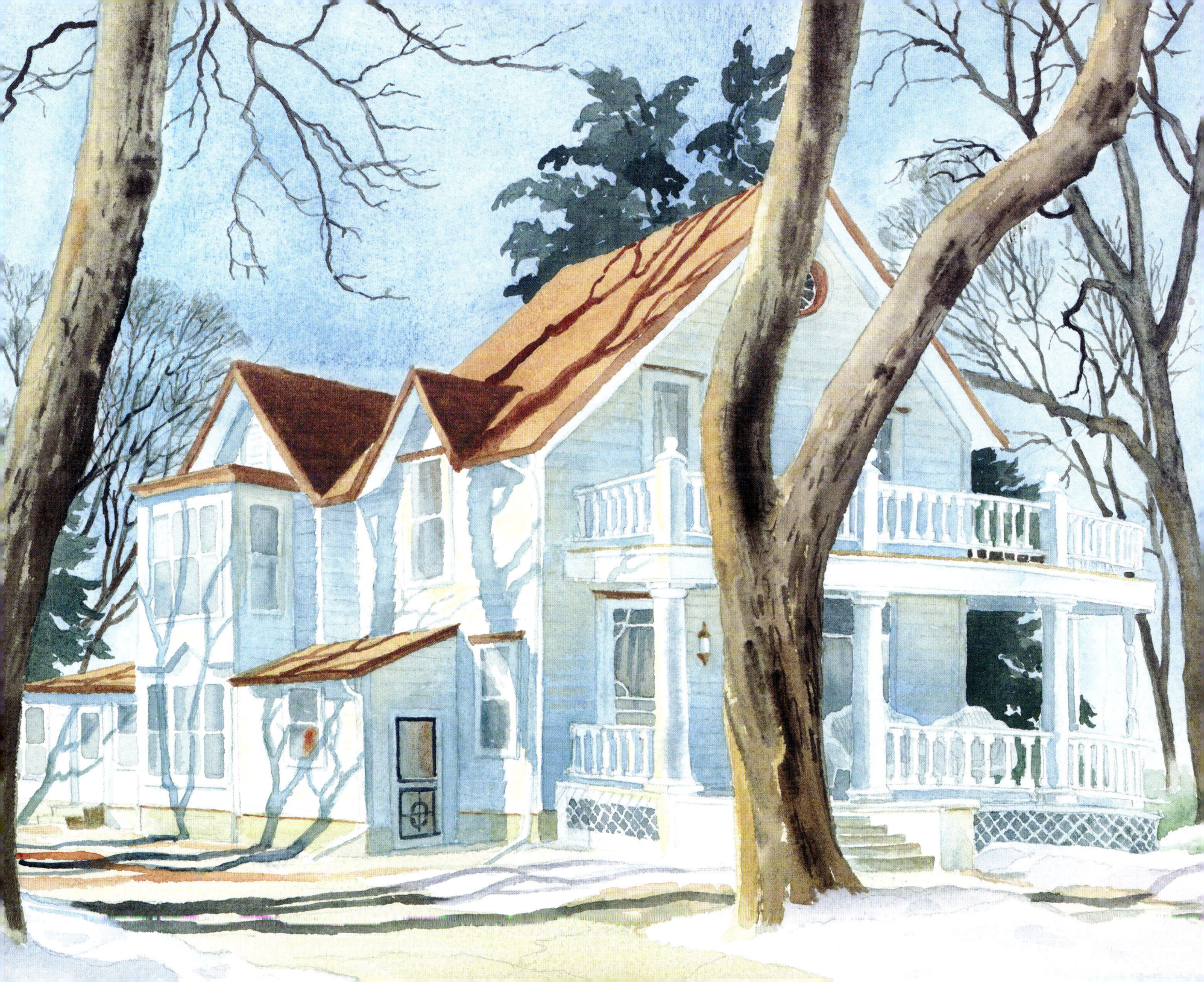

WILLA'S ROOM IN HER PARENT'S HOME

Today, the room in the second Cather home looks as though it was awaiting one of her summer visits. The white, ornamental, iron bed is neatly covered with a quilted cover. On a mirrored dressing table, her parents peer from within a hinged picture frame, and a comfortable chair in the opposite corner completes the simple furnishings. The second-story room looks over a street lamp that lights the quiet intersection below, and during the day the room is flooded with sunshine from east- and south-facing windows.

It was a long train trip from New York to Red Cloud and consequently her visits were extended. Her carefully chosen clothes were packed in a large trunk, which also served as a wardrobe chest and extra table in her closet-less bedroom.

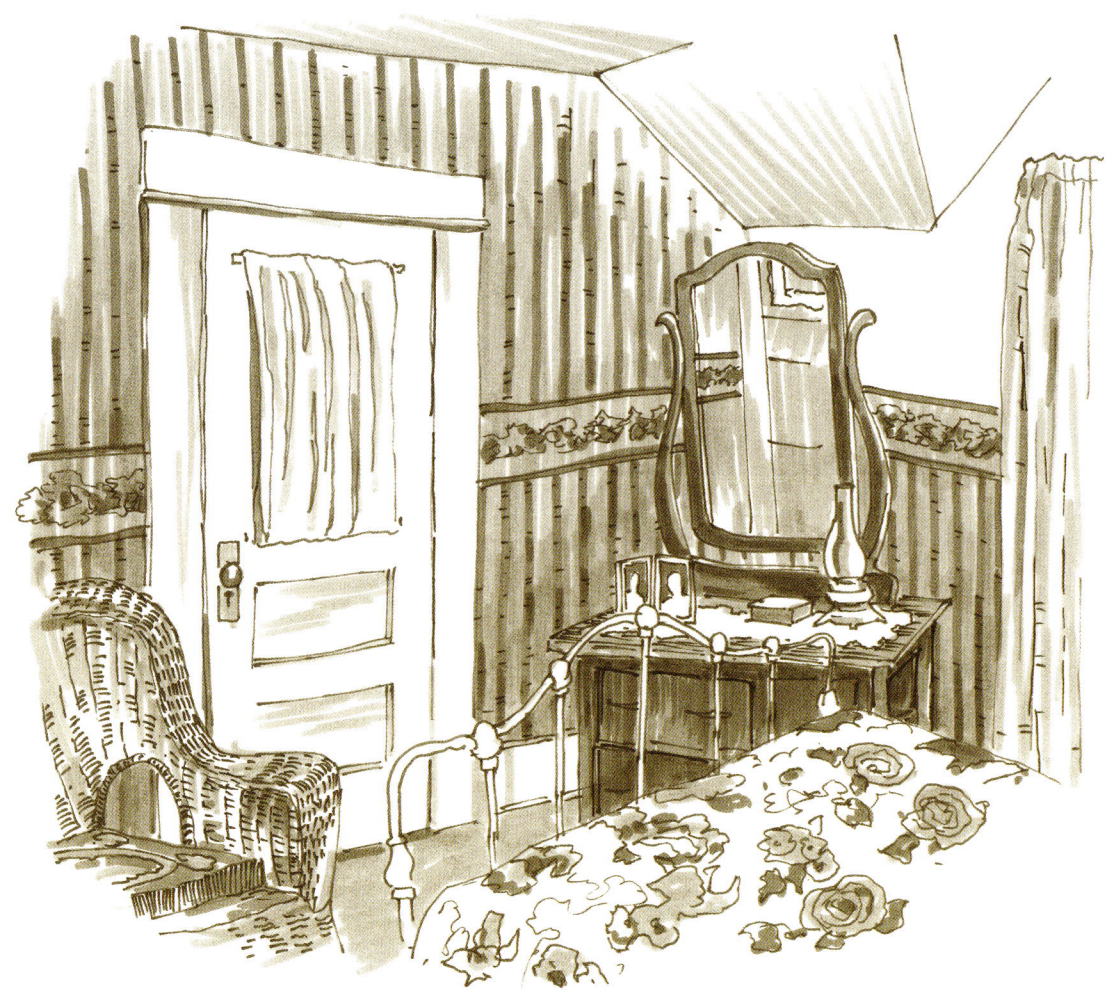

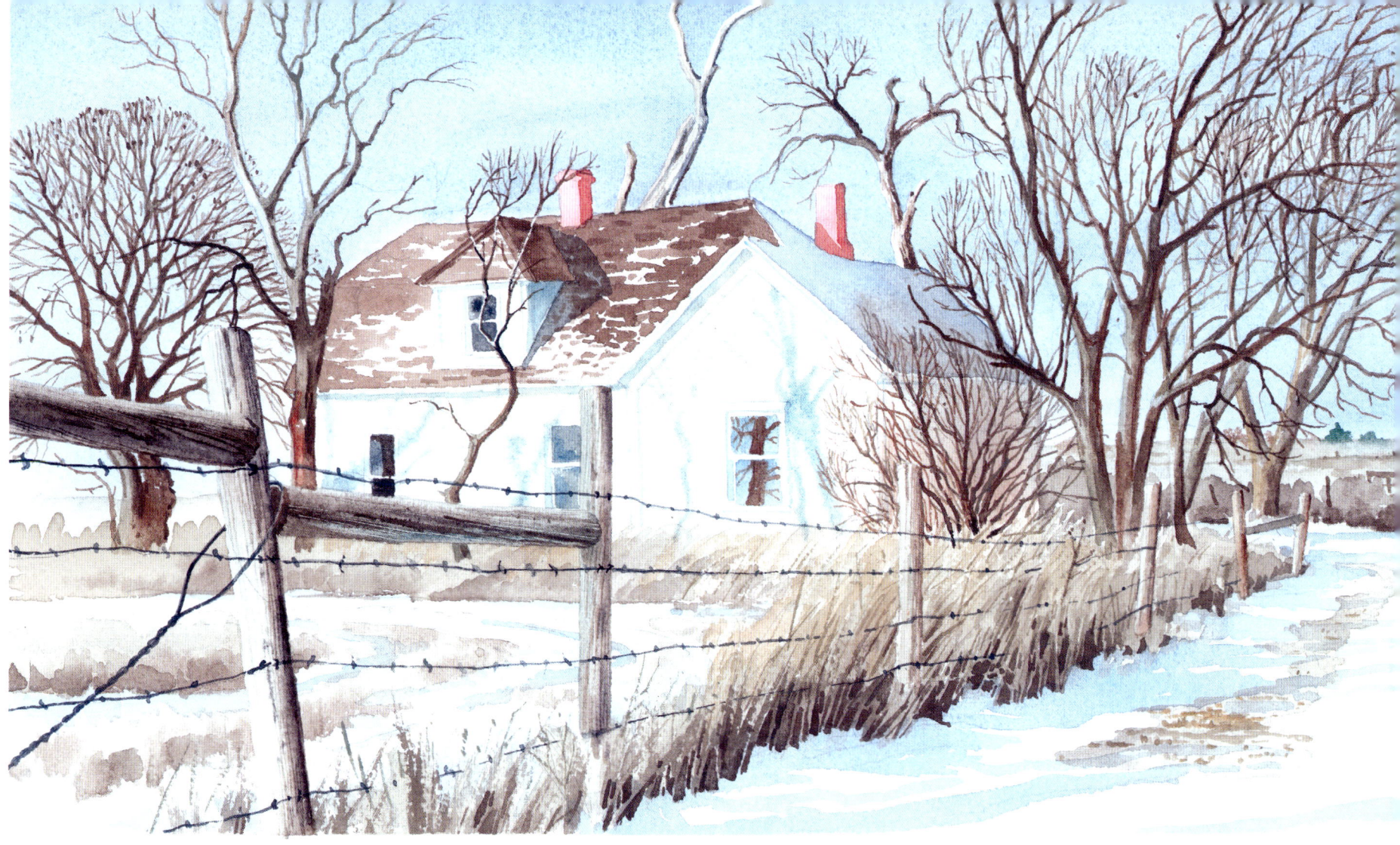

Annie Sadilek Pavelka of Bladen was the model for Ántonia Shimerda Cuzak. This painting is of the Pavelka homestead, the inspiration for Ántonia Cuzak's home in *My Ántonia*.

Jim Burden visits Ántonia and her family near the end of Cather's story. Ántonia speaks without regret of her life and her family:

No, I never got down-hearted. Anton's a good man, and I loved my children and always believed they would turn out well. I belong on a farm. I'm never lonesome here like I used to be in town. . . . And I don't mind work a bit, if I don't have to put up with sadness. *MY ÁNTONIA*

. . . in farmhouses, somehow, life comes and goes by the back door. The roof was so steep that the eaves were not much above the forest of tall hollyhocks, now brown and in seed. Through July, Ántonia said, the house was buried in them; the Bohemians, I remembered, always planted hollyhocks. The front yard was enclosed by a thorny locust hedge, and at the gate grew two silvery, mothlike trees of the mimosa family.

MY ÁNTONIA

A large stone kept the back screen door from swinging in the gusty wind. I moved it aside and turned the brass doorknob. To my surprise the door did not resist but opened with a jingling of a loose windowpane. I treaded between glass shards and fallen plaster that littered the wood floor. Shreds of wrinkled and faded old newspapers lay beneath the broken window. Nothing had been left behind but a cabinet hanging askew from the kitchen wall.

How I wished these walls could speak. I listened for the voices of those who had lived here—for their laughter or their cries of sadness. But only the wind answered back, whistling through the window frames and loose siding. Two pigeons flew from their roost—the only signs of life.

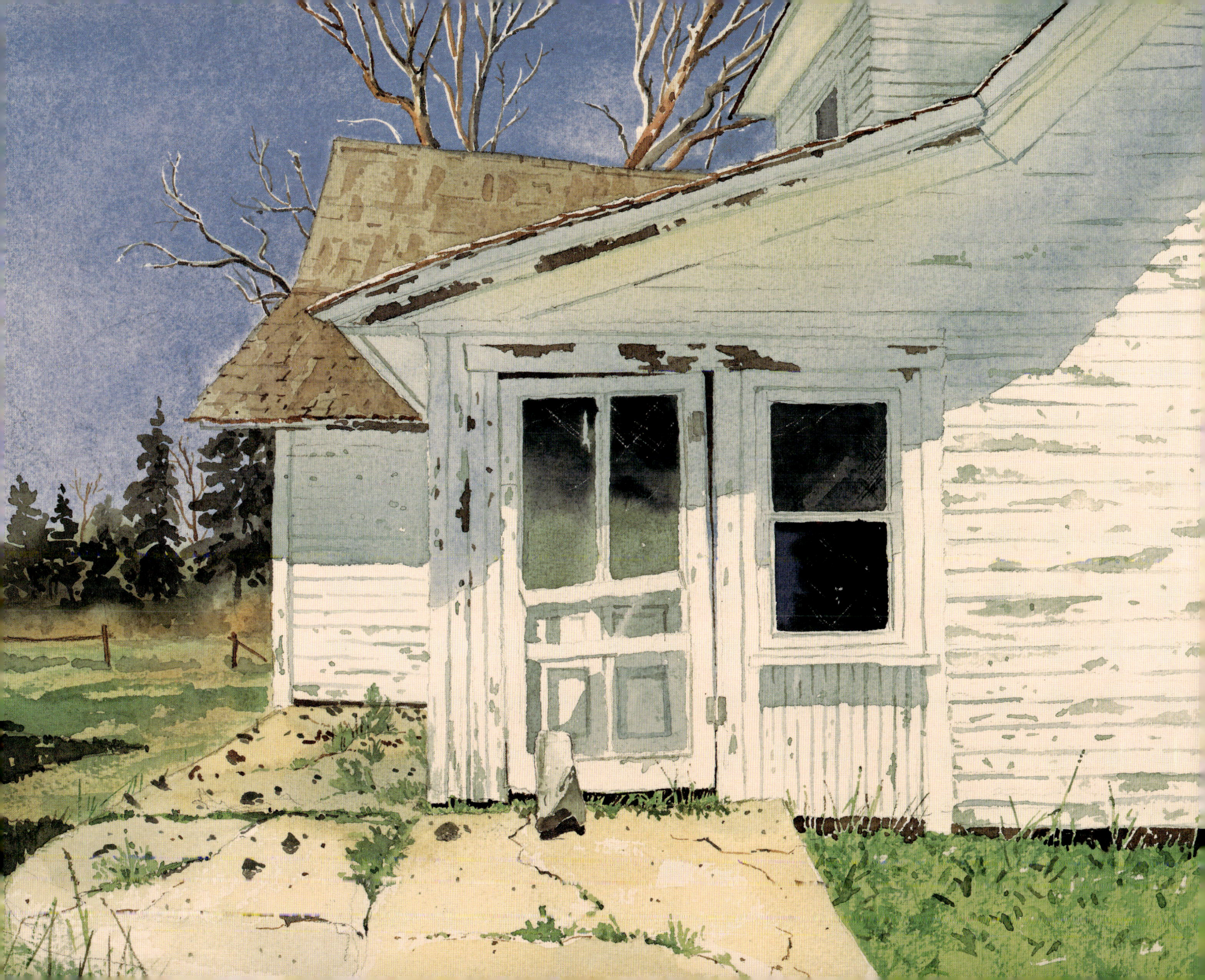

GHOSTS OF COWLES

Cowles is a sleepy community northeast of Red Cloud in Webster County on a north-south spur of the Burlington Railroad. There are only about nineteen families, mostly German, living there today. The settlement was named after W. D. Cowles, a railroad freight agent. This sketch is of an early building in this little settlement, which at one time must have been the pride of the village. Handsome brick archways were constructed by a skillful mason and opened into a portico before the entrance to the building. A crumbling, old kiosk stands in front of the ghostlike building.

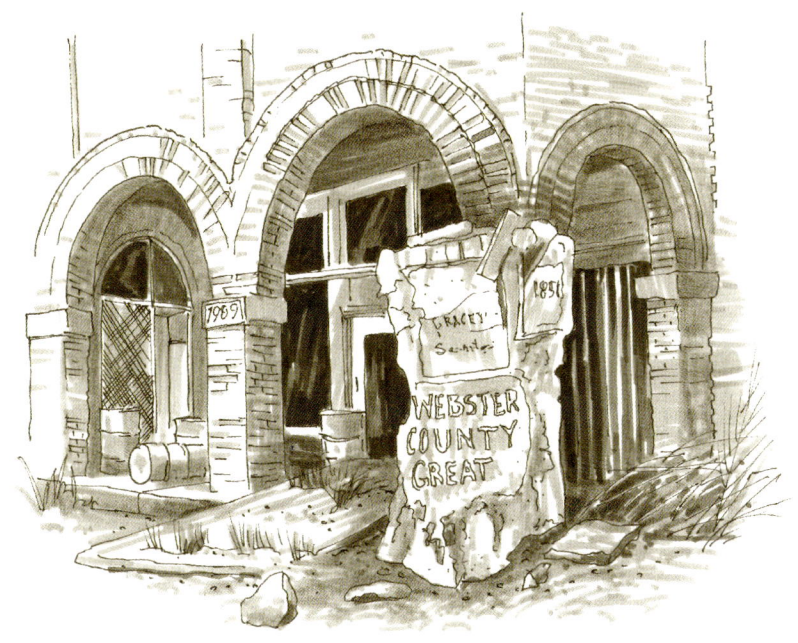

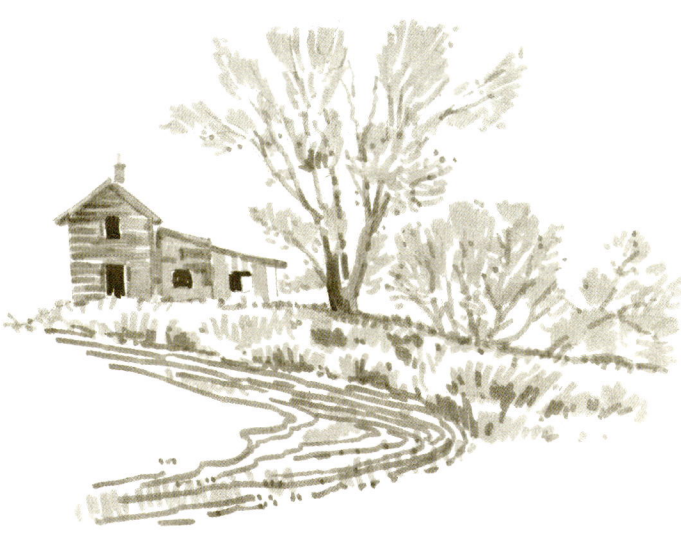

It was probably at this curve of the line just west of Red Cloud that the engineer blew his steam whistle as he approached the railroad station. If it was a Sunday morning, it was the "call to worship," and the train carried the circuit-riding priest from Orleans, Nebraska, to administer the sacraments. When people heard the whistle, they hurried to prepare St. Juliana Falconieri Catholic Church for service. On cold mornings, the parishioners pulled hay from a bale and twisted it into fuel for the church stove.

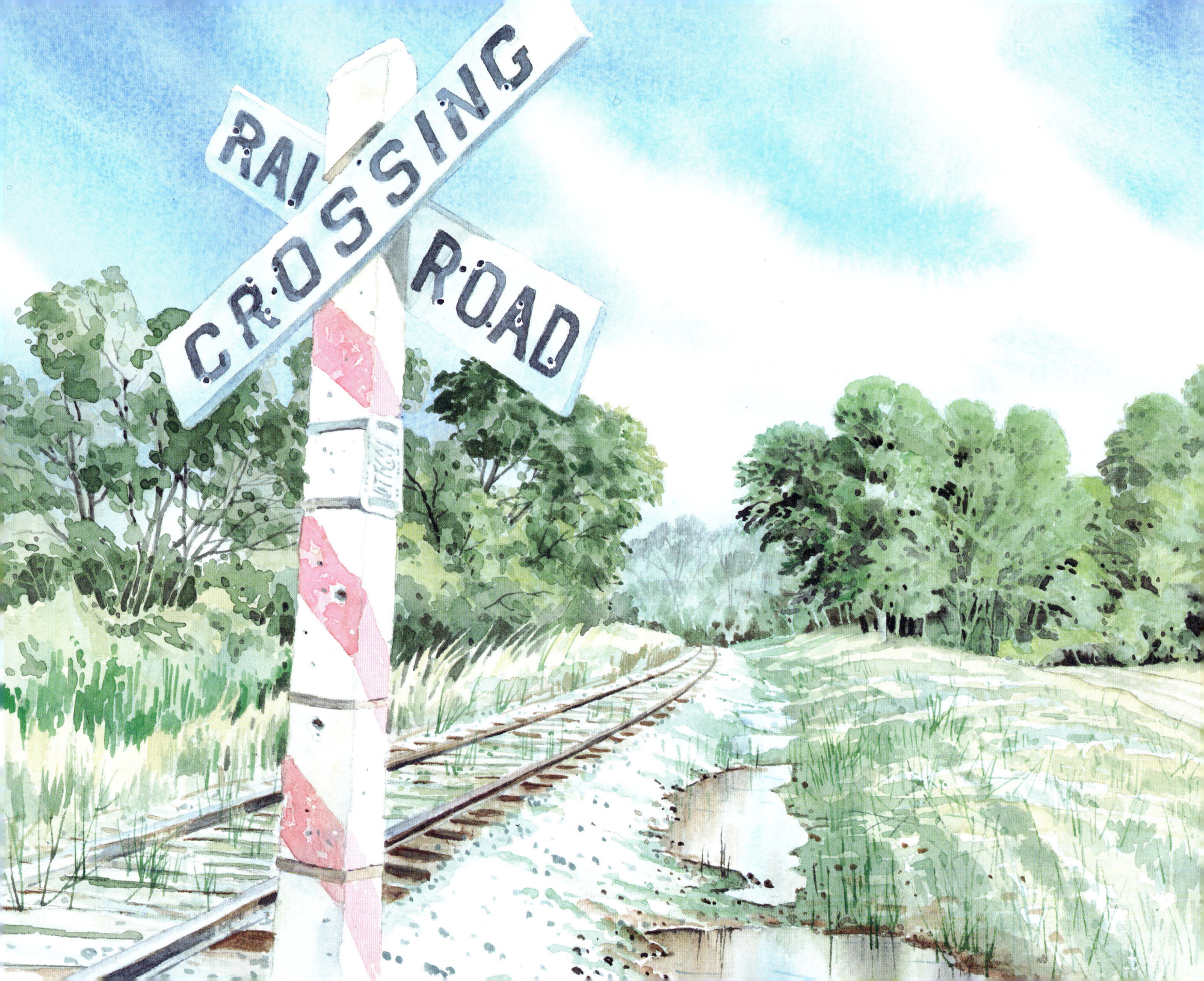

If they turned in early, they had a good while to enjoy the outside weather; they never went to sleep until after ten o'clock, for then came the sweetest morsel of the night. At that hour Number Seventeen, the westbound passenger, whistled in. The station and the engine house were perhaps an eighth of a mile down the hill, and from far away across the meadows the children could hear that whistle. Then came the heavy pants of the locomotive in the frosty air. Then a hissing—then silence: she was taking water.

On Saturdays the children were allowed to go down to the depot to see Seventeen come in. It was a fine sight on winter nights. Sometimes the great locomotive used to sweep in armoured in ice and snow, breathing fire like a dragon, its great red eye shooting a blinding beam along the white roadbed and shining wet rails. When it stopped, it panted like a great beast. After it was watered by the big hose from the overhead tank, it seemed to draw long deep breaths, ready to charge afresh over the great Western land.

"THE BEST YEARS"

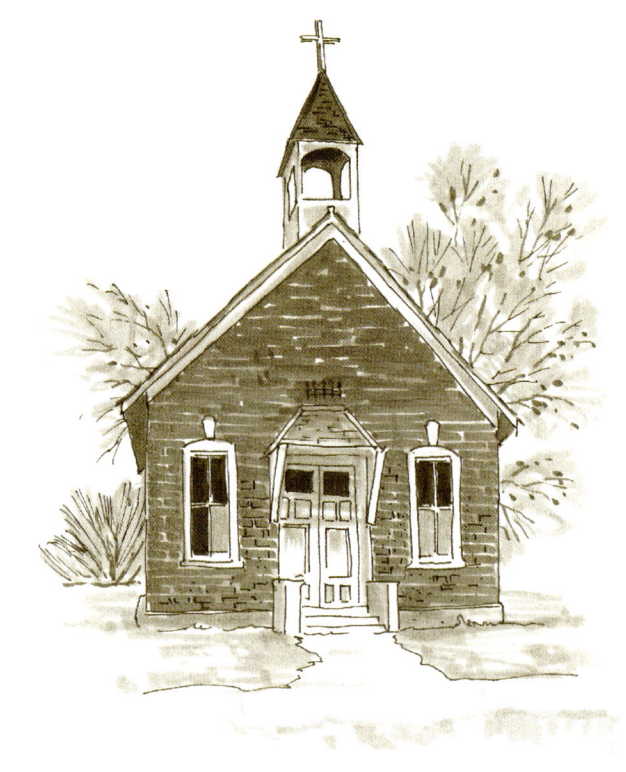

Red Cloud's population is now half of what it was during Cather's lifetime. At one time a bustling city served by several banks and five newspapers, it is now a sleepy town with few shopping options available. The townspeople are friendly and optimistic. Cutter's Cafe not only serves up great food, but its customers are an important source of humor, farming news, rumors, and the gossip that spreads faster than any modern news medium. If you want to get opinions on the latest political issues or the price of wheat, you will find a long table of locals having their second cups of coffee in Cutter's at about nine o'clock.

HIGH NOON AT CUTTER'S CAFE

I open the door and step into the café. Before I can close the door, a woman's voice from behind the bar calls out, "Hi there! How are you?"

Shelly is her name, and I watch her bounce her infant granddaughter on the counter between pouring coffee for her extended family of regular customers. Five or six people are gathered at the bar having lunch. Booths line the sides of the café, but I soon realize they are for the out-of-town folk who stop here. Townspeople eat at the bar, where they exchange news and rumors. It is understood by most that the longer table in the center of the room is for farmers who come to town for their daily cups of coffee and to exchange scuttlebutt when their seasonal chores of planting or haying are not calling.

Shelly reaches to reclaim the pacifier the infant has thrown. "Let's see. Which end goes in?" she jokes.

I take a seat on a green bench in a side booth. The springs are broken. I try to find a comfortable position for my body, but it keeps slipping sideways into a vinyl-covered pothole.

Farmers' ball caps with names like Napa Auto and Figger's Farm Supply of Red Cloud decorate the walls and ends of each booth, and little baskets of colorful, plastic flowers hang above each table. There is a collection of antiques on the shelf above—things like wooden egg crates, antique telephones, and old typewriters. Shelly arrives at my table with a cheery "Hi, darling, whatcha have?" I'm afraid she is going to ask me for my Bug Eaters cap that my father gave me twenty-five years ago. I am fond of that cap. People are friendly here—actually darn right overbearing. "Well," I say to myself, "get over it, you're family now."

I'll have the beef brisket and broccoli soup special. "Whatcha drinking?" she said.

If it's homemade, bring me a piece of your chocolate meringue pie with my coffee.

The food is warm and I think I like this place. I pay my bill and leave a generous tip. Not many customers today.

"Hurry back," she shouts from the back of the café at the jingle of the bell above the door.

As I cross the street to my parked car, I pass a man in bib overalls in the center, on his way over to the café. "How are you?" he yells at me.

You know something? I think he meant that!

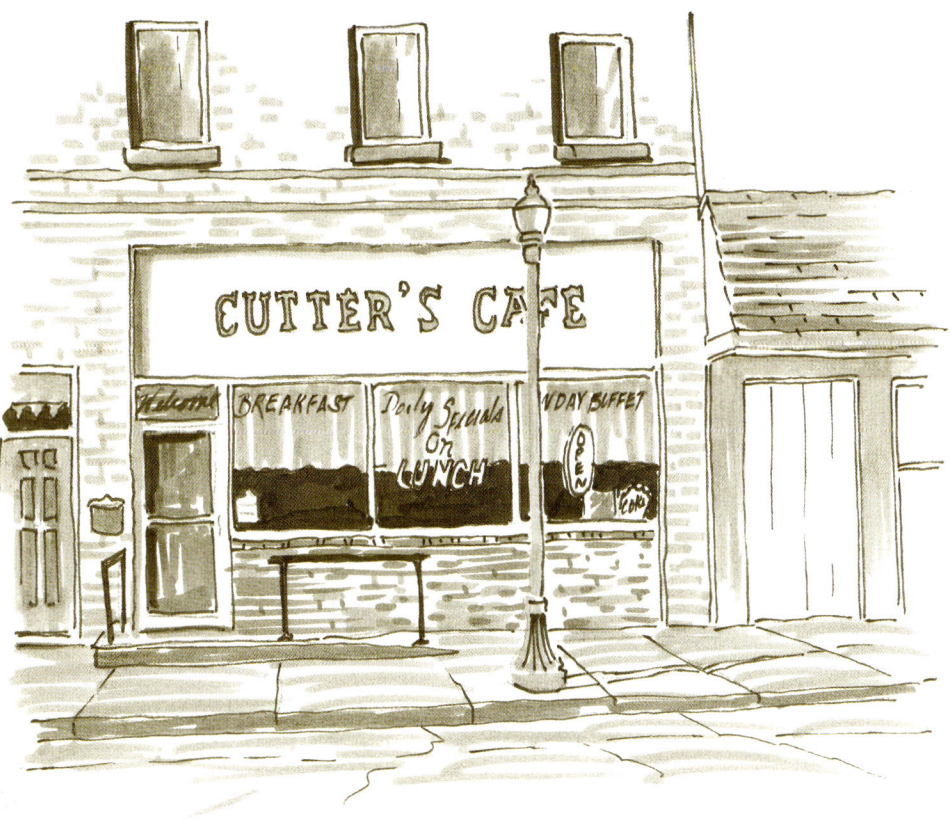

Silas Garber, the prototype for Captain Forrester in *A Lost Lady*, founded the Farmer's and Merchant's Bank. Though it closed in 1932, the bank weathered many trials, including the Panic of 1893, which caused many bank failures and inspired Cather's human interest piece for the *Nebraska State Journal*:

A man stood on the street corner staring at a notice pasted on the door of a bank that had failed. He was tall and powerfully built and his head was set squarely on his broad shoulders. He had on an old soiled summer suit and a mud bespattered overcoat. His pantaloons were tucked into his boots, and an old stiff hat was jammed on the back of his head. He kept his hands in his pockets and whistled softly as he read the notice. He had not lost any money in the bank, he had never had a cent in a bank in his life and he seldom had money in his pocket. He owed money for the clothes he had on, and for those he had worn out years ago. He owed money to every man he had ever done business with, except the police. That was one comfort, a fellow might owe every one else, but the "cops" and the patrol were free luxuries. He would never pay any one a cent while he could help it, not he. He would take his living off the world till he was through with it, then he would take a town lot two by six over in Wyuka, on trust too. He thrust his hands deeper into his pockets and walked off whistling.

"ONE WAY OF PUTTING IT," *NEBRASKA STATE JOURNAL*, NOVEMBER 12, 1893

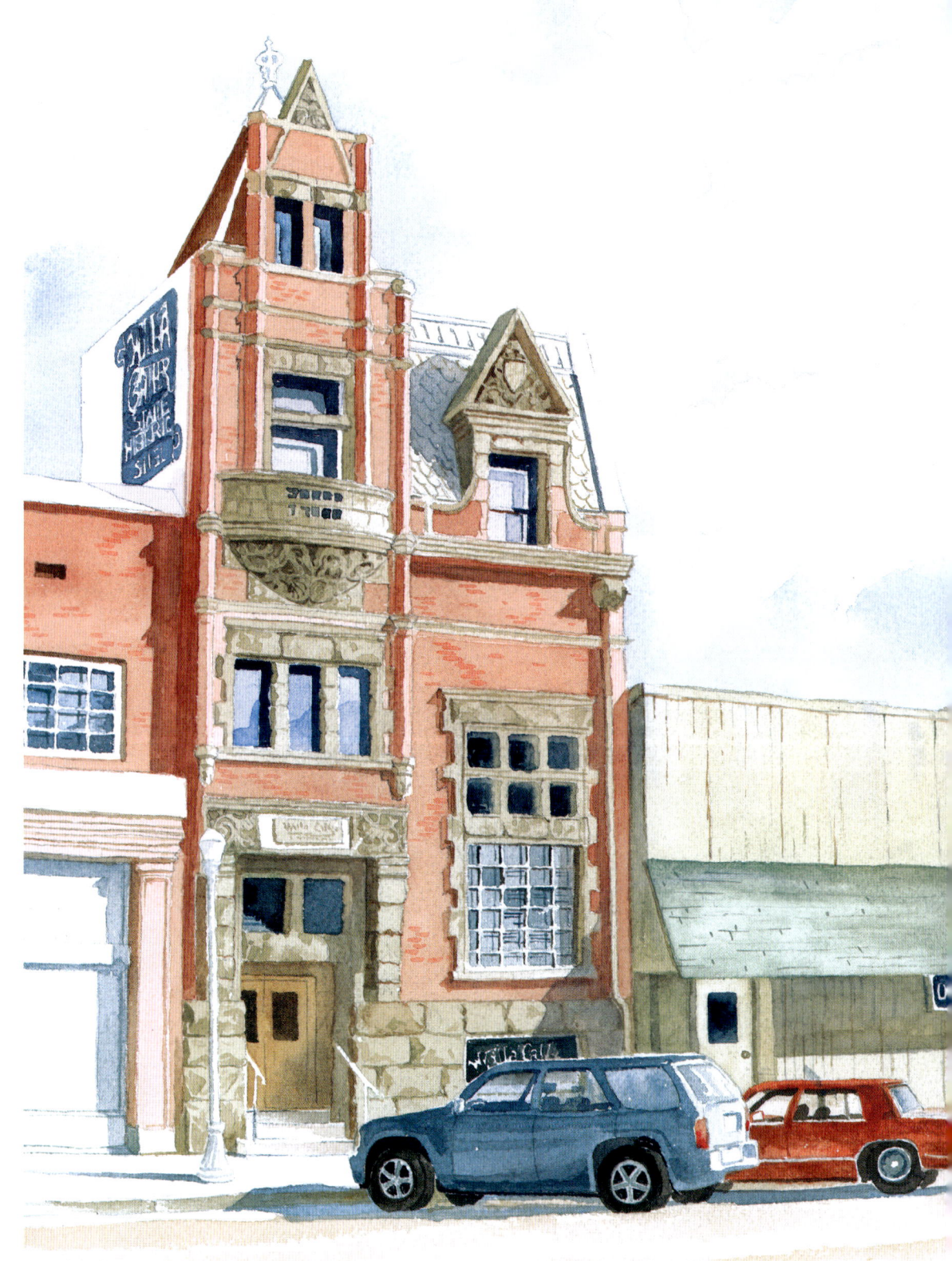

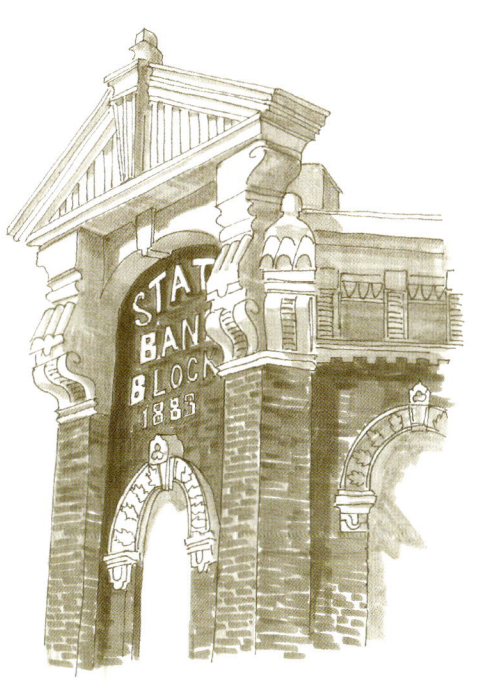

THE WEBSTER COUNTY COURTHOUSE

This courthouse, designed in the French Renaissance style, followed earlier, more temporary structures. Construction began in 1914, and Anna Sadilek and John Pavelka were married here.

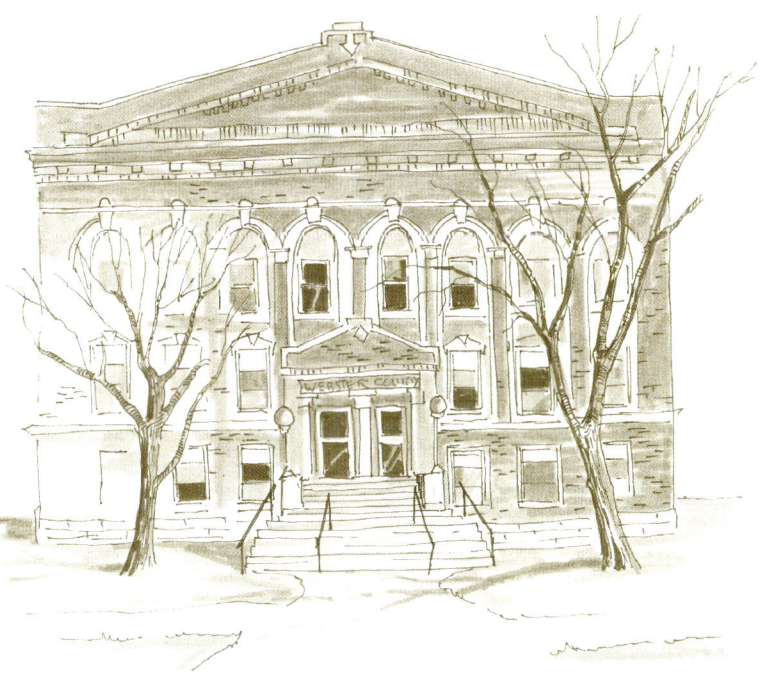

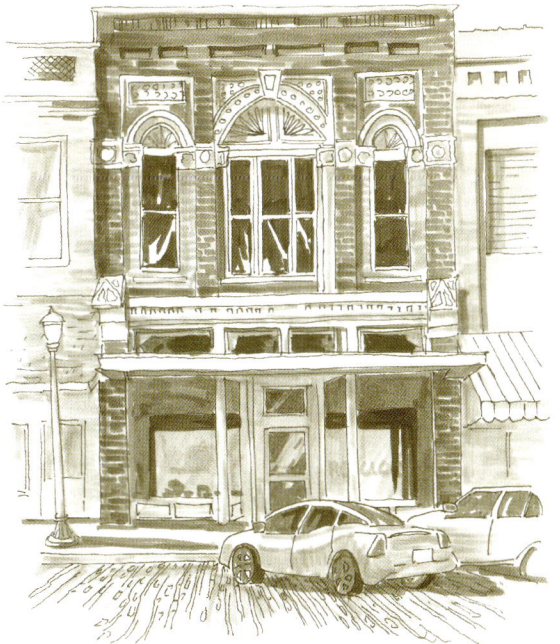

JIM BURDEN'S GRANDPARENTS' HOME

Jim Burden, age thirteen, speaks of his move with his grandparents from the country to Black Hawk:

Our own house looked down over the town, and from our upstairs windows we could see the winding line of the river bluffs, two miles south of us. That river was to be my compensation for the lost freedom of the farming country.

MY ÁNTONIA

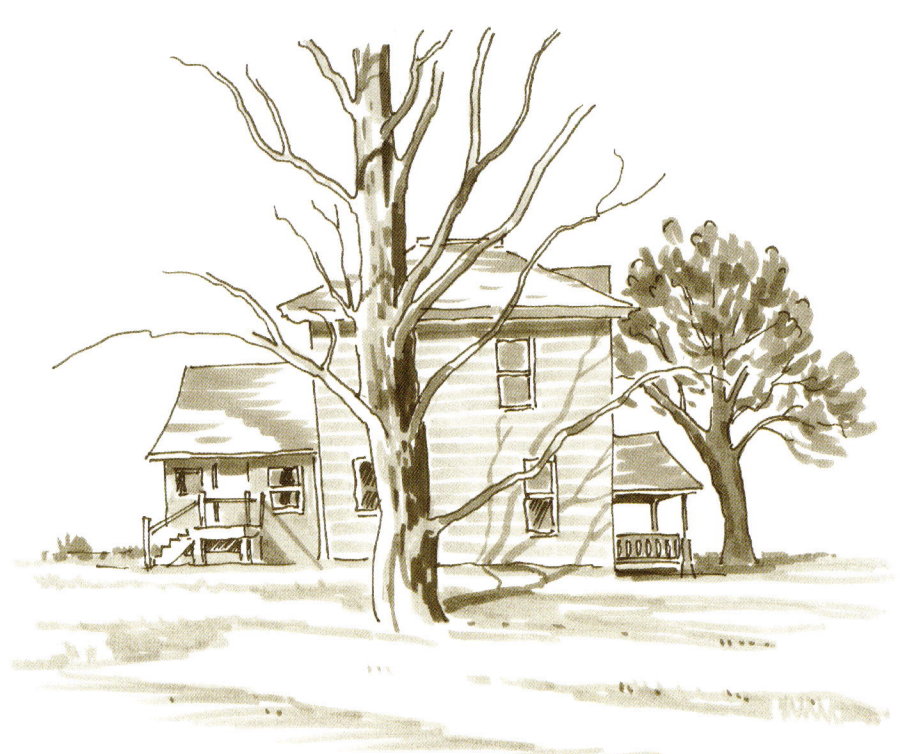

JIM BURDEN'S WHEELCHAIR

Cather often mixed fact and fiction, moving events and locations to fit her fancy, creating characters and settings from more than one individual or place. So it is not surprising if there is some confusion when we try to identify exact characters and story sites.

Willa Cather asked Jim Burden, a man living in Red Cloud, for permission to use his name in her novel, *My Ántonia*. Here, fact and fiction seem to part ways. In the introduction to her novel, Cather indicates that Jim Burden was legal counsel for a great western railway and was living in New York. She said they had grown up together.

The real James Burden was born in 1858 and was fifteen years older than Cather. He was a postmaster early in his career, and in 1904 he entered the mercantile business in Red Cloud. Jim Burden was confined to a wheelchair for most of his life and was greatly admired for his courage and bravery. When he died in 1920, his obituary stated, "When he first came to Red Cloud years ago he was a cripple, all but helpless. He never failed to do what was possible to a man on crutches. He took chances that even men with the full use of their limbs might have shunned."

Whatever the inspiration Cather took from Jim Burden, she artfully employed the fictionalized version as an effective male narrator for her own childhood stories.

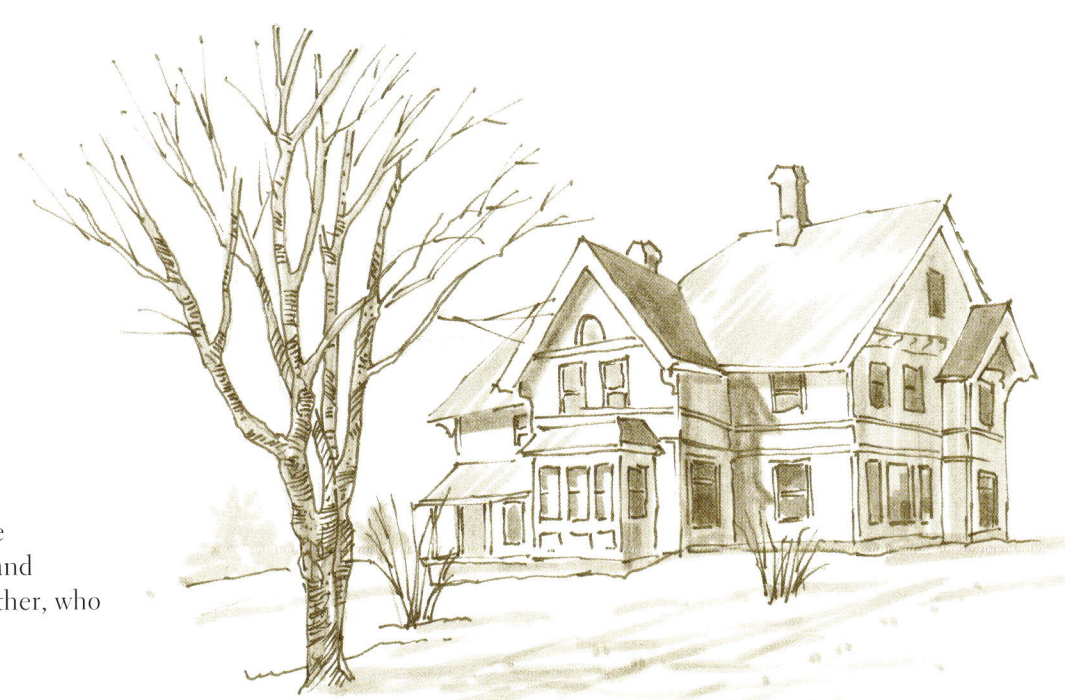

The Miner family members were models for the Harlings. The Miner daughters—May, Carrie, and Irene—were all musical and good friends of Cather, who lived around the corner on Cedar Street.

A HOUSE ON QUALITY HILL

A hill in the northwest corner of Red Cloud was known as "Quality Hill," "Quality Knob, or "Sacred Knob" by townsfolk for this was where the wealthy lived.

After supper she walked toward the town and turned into the street that people jokingly called Quality Street, because Mrs. Ramsay lived at one end of it and the Gordons at the other. Mrs. Ramsay was sitting in her high-backed chair beside the big front window, the shades up and the silk curtains drawn back. This had always been her way, though her house was so near the sidewalk that every passer-by could gaze in; her neighbours sometimes said it looked as if she were giving a reception to the street.

LUCY GAYHEART

GOSSIP GETTER: AN EARLY FORM OF HOME ENTERTAINMENT

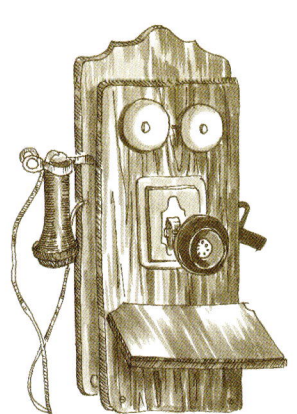

In those days, information traveled faster than one might think in a little town. Telephone lines were strung from poles over the prairie, and with a magneto to generate a small current in a telephone, people were able to keep in touch. Most subscribers were on party lines along with several other users. Eavesdroppers on the party line could listen in on a conversation and pass any juicy gossip on to others with the speed of today's Internet.

Grandmother often said that if she had to live in town, she thanked God she lived next the Harlings. They had been farming people, like ourselves, and their place was like a little farm, with a big barn and a garden, and an orchard and grazing lots—even a windmill. . . .

We found Mrs. Harling with Charley and Sally on the front porch, resting after her hard drive. Julia was in the hammock—she was fond of repose— and Frances was at the piano, playing without a light and talking to her mother through the open window   *MY ÁNTONIA*

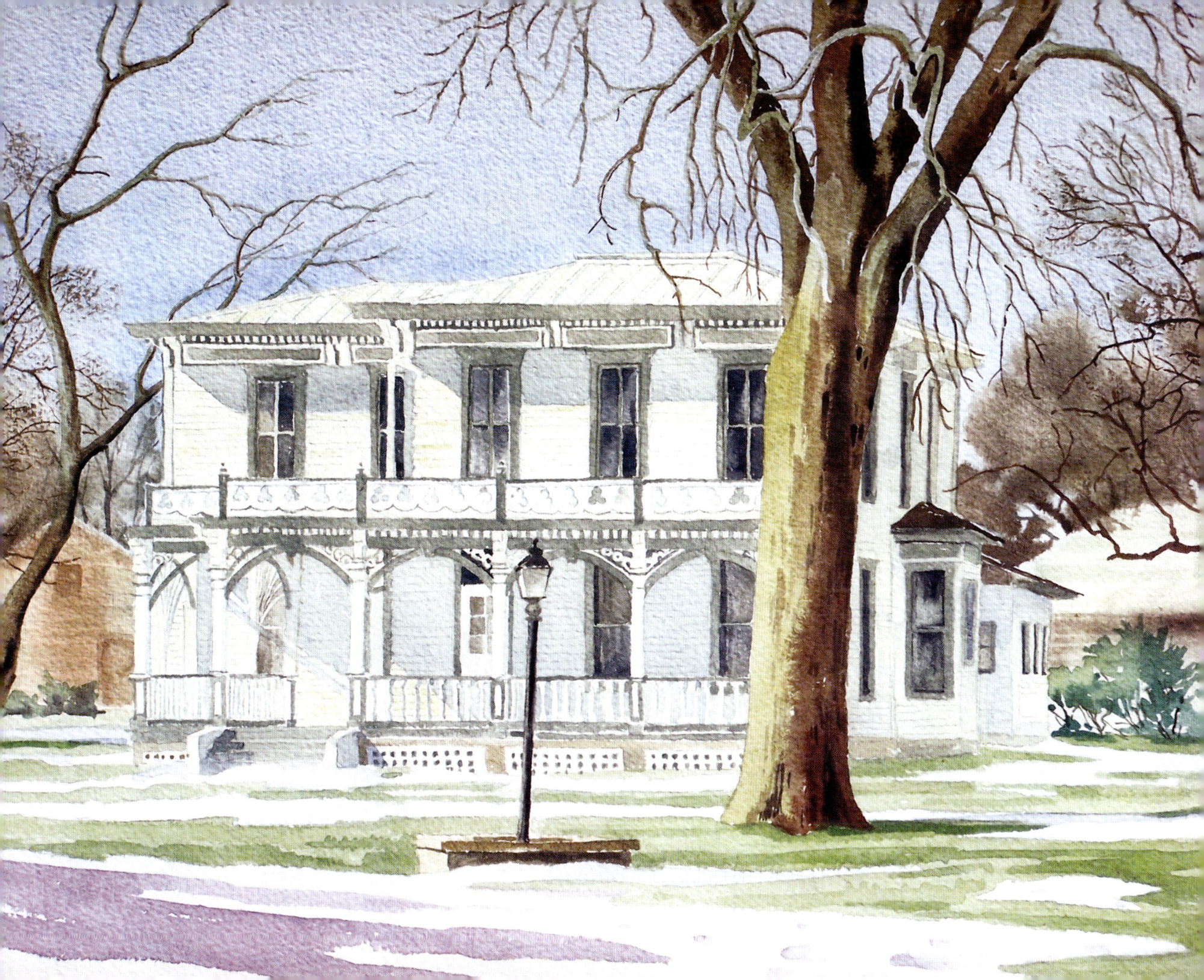

FIRE CHIEF RED CLOUD

I found this old relic under the cover of ash and elm trees in the tall grass south of the Red Cloud cemetery. Whimsically, I call it "Fire Chief Red Cloud."

Willa Cather did not include descriptions of fires in her stories of the prairie. Still, this was an ever-present danger to the pioneers. Without modern fire protection, fires traveled swiftly if not extinguished within moments. Buckets of water sat conspicuously in public buildings and families placed them close to Christmas trees decorated with burning candles.

In 1887 a volunteer fire department was organized in Red Cloud, and a Firemen's Hall was built on the corner of Sixth and Webster. In *A Reader's Companion to the Fiction of Willa Cather,* John March describes the building as a "two-story brick building measuring twenty-five by sixty feet. The fire truck was downstairs and the IOOF (Independent Order of Odd Fellows) hall was upstairs." The community raised money for the volunteer fire department by hosting dances and dinners. Susie Gray in *One of Ours* sold tickets for one such event and in *My Ántonia*, Jim Burden was persuaded by his friends to go to the dances, even though his grandparents disapproved of such indecorous behavior. March writes, "Dances and dinners at the Firemen's Hall, such as those mentioned in *My Ántonia, The Song of the Lark, One of Ours*, and "On the Divide," were indeed held in the Red Cloud, Nebraska, Firemen's Hall.

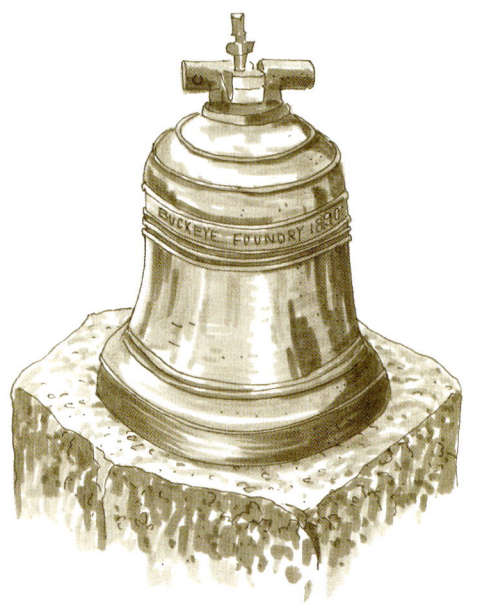

THE FIREHOUSE BELL IN CITY PARK

A 1,200-pound fire bell was cast and installed in the tower of the two-story building. A rope hung from the bell that was available to anyone who might need to sound an alarm, but it was also a source of temptation and amusement to pranksters.

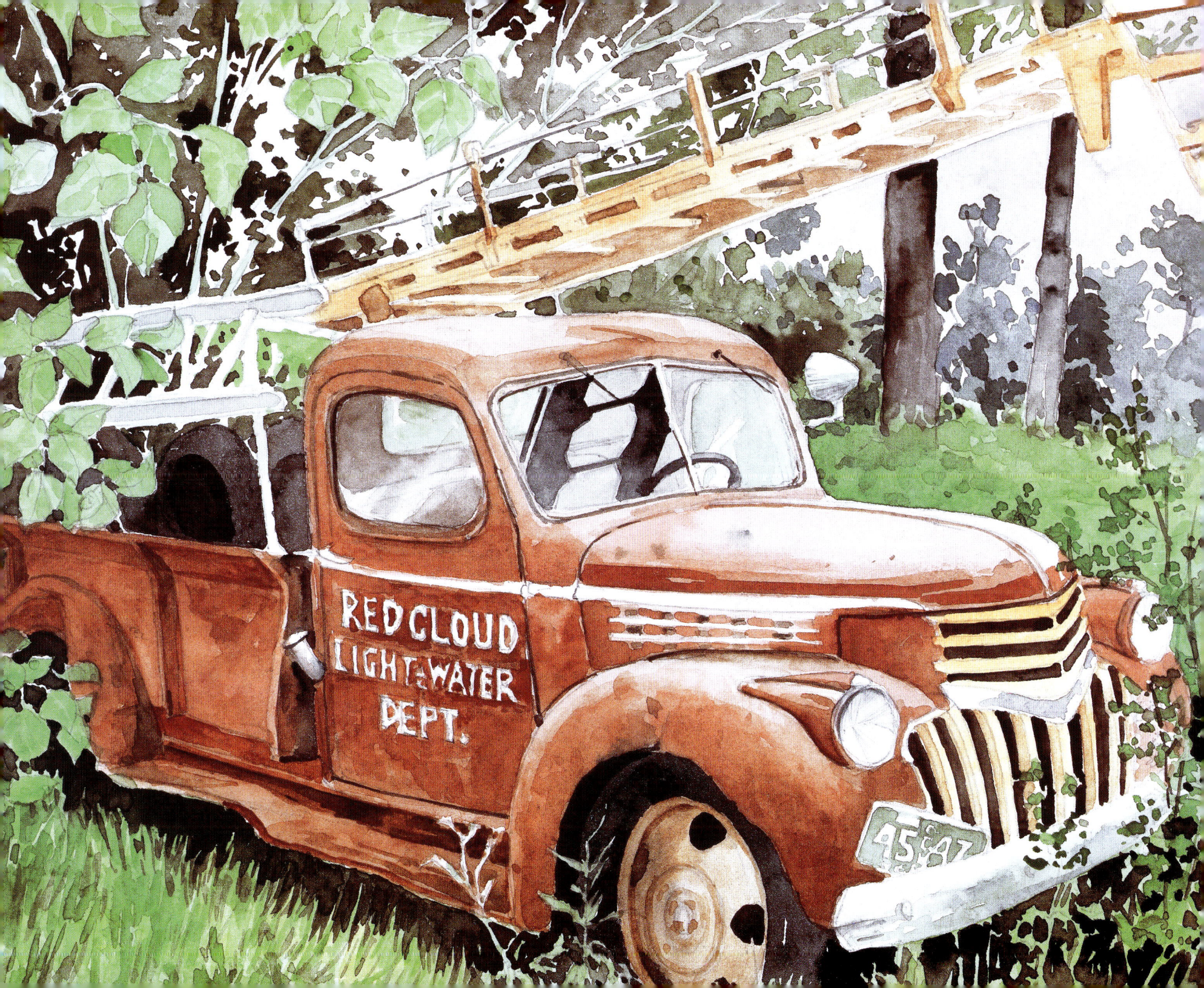

Far out at the north end, nearly a mile from the court-house and its cottonwood grove, was Dr. Archie's house, its big yard and garden surrounded by a white paling fence. . . .

Dr. Archie was very proud of his yard and garden, which he worked himself. He was the only man in Moonstone who was successful at growing rambler roses, and his strawberries were famous.

THE SONG OF THE LARK

This home actually belonged to Dr. McKeeby, a friend of Cather's and her model for Dr. Archie. Dr. McKeeby first practiced law in Red Cloud then later switched to medicine.

The McKeeby home was a mail-order house. We would call it a manufactured home today—all of the parts were precut then shipped and assembled on the building site.

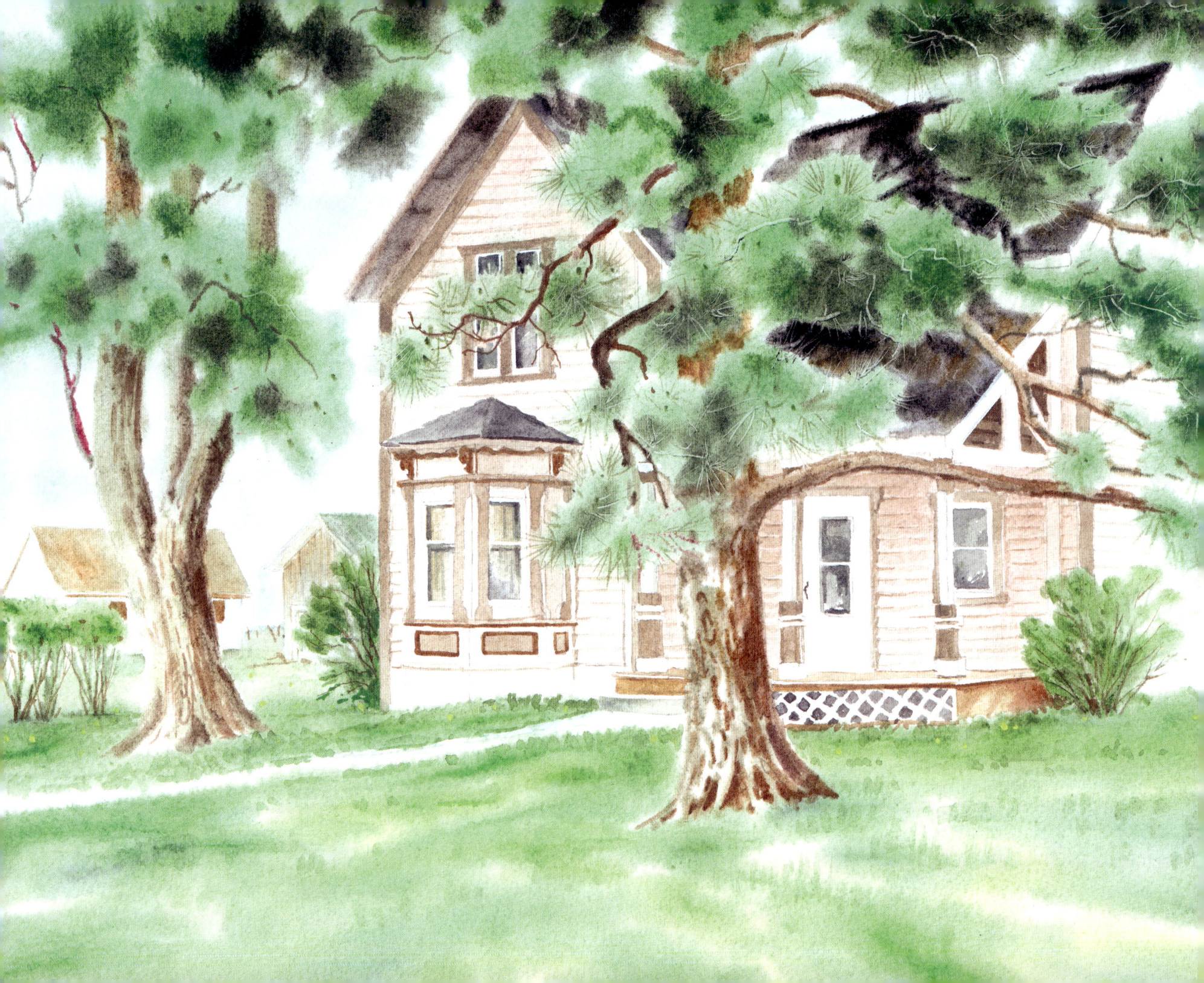

Dr. Howard Archie had just come up from a game of pool with the Jewish clothier and two traveling men who happened to be staying overnight in Moonstone. His offices were in the Duke Block, over the drug store. Larry, the doctor's man, had lit the overhead light in the waiting-room and the double student's lamp on the desk in the study. The isinglass sides of the hard-coal burner were aglow, and the air in the study was so hot that as he came in the doctor opened the door into his little operating-room, where there was no stove. The waiting-room was carpeted and stiffly furnished, something like a country parlor. The study had worn, unpainted floors, but there was a look of winter comfort about it. The doctor's flat-top desk was large and well made; the papers were in orderly piles, under glass weights. Behind the stove a wide bookcase, with double glass doors, reached from the floor to the ceiling. It was filled with medical books of every thickness and color. On the top shelf stood a long row of thirty or forty volumes, bound all alike in dark mottled board covers, with imitation leather backs.

SONG OF THE LARK

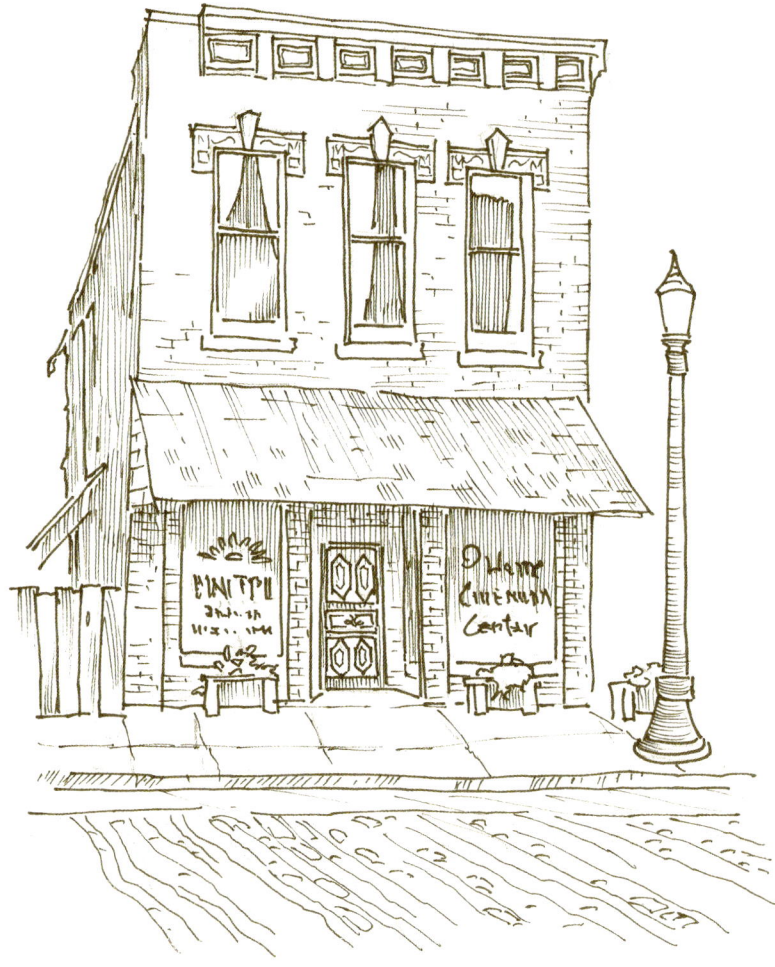

Thirty or forty years ago, in one of those grey towns along the Burlington railroad, which are so much greyer to-day than they were then, there was a house well known from Omaha to Denver for its hospitality and for a certain charm of atmosphere. Well known, that is to say, to the railroad aristocracy of that time; men who had to do with the railroad itself, or with one of the "land companies" which were its by-products. In those days it was enough to say of a man that he was "connected with the Burlington."

A LOST LADY

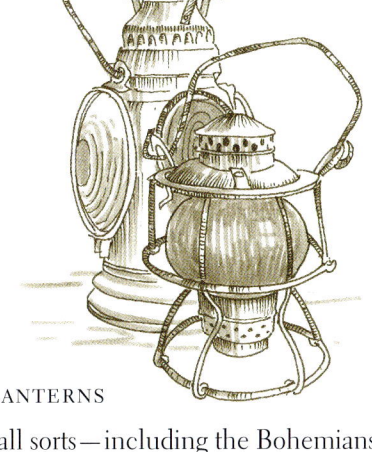

THE BURLINGTON AND MISSOURI RAILROAD

The railroad was the artery that provided a town its lifeblood. Red Cloud was a sleepy settlement until the arrival of the railroad gangs in 1878, and once the rails were laid, the town grew rapidly into a bustling city of nearly three thousand people. Eight passenger trains passed through each day. Since the trains did not have food service, passengers would disembark to take their meals in the local cafés. The Burlington and Missouri Railroad became an important economic asset to the community.

To settle the land with permanent residents, promoters promised immigrants good jobs and plenty of land in the West, but dreams were often shattered when visions of nice homes and bountiful farmlands were not realized. Oftentimes, the unfamiliar language and customs of a new country were as difficult as the long winters or the backbreaking work. For mutual support, families were drawn to their own ethnic "islands" on the prairie.

TRAINMAN'S LANTERNS

Immigrants of all sorts—including the Bohemians, Germans, and French—were people that Cather knew well, and she used them as prototypes for fictional characters in her stories. Most of the immigrants arrived in Red Cloud on trains from the East. Cather begins *My Ántonia* with Jim Burden's nighttime arrival in Black Hawk; the drama of the bewildered travelers arriving in a strange land in the dead of night were accentuated by the engine's clanging bell, belching steam, and swinging lanterns carried by railroaders on the platform. Additionally, the lives of the railroaders provided important structure for *The Song of the Lark*, as well as other tales.

While the railroad was the cause for the early success of Red Cloud, it also became the death knell of the community. The railroad management controlled the destiny of the hamlet, and when the townspeople sided with the strikers in a labor dispute, management decided to remove Red Cloud as a division point. Today, the mainline of the Burlington runs through Hastings, forty miles away.

Mr. Gayheart set off through the snow flurry, a daughter on either arm. He liked to reach the Opera House early and watch the people come in. (The theatre in every little Western town was then called an opera house.) On the way he told Lucy the manager of the house had put in folding chairs in place of the old straight-back wooden ones; otherwise she would find the hall just the same as when she played on the stage for her own commencement exercises, nearly four years ago.   *LUCY GAYHEART*

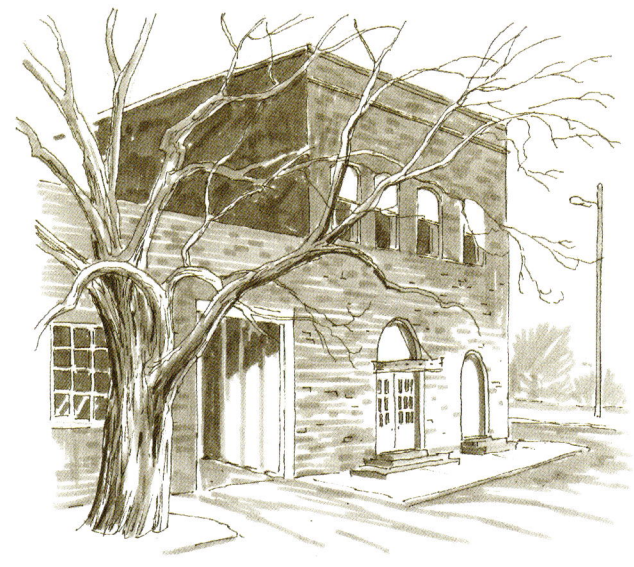

THE BLADEN OPERA HOUSE

Willa Cather called it the Moonstone Opera House in *My Ántonia, Lucy Gayheart,* and *The Song of the Lark.* The Red Cloud Opera House opened on October 26, 1885, and occupied the second floor of the Moon building, above the Morhart and Fulton hardware store and Mizer's grocery store on Webster Street. It seated about 450 people in straight-back chairs bolted five to a board. In the beginning, the auditorium was lighted with oil lamps equipped with tin reflectors. Later, gaslights were installed; they were fed through concealed pipes connected to a large gas tank located in the alley.

The Red Cloud Opera House boasted famous performers, orators, and musicians. William Jennings Bryan, the Democratic Party nominee for president, made three appearances here. Cather also appeared in a number of local productions. The cost of admission to the Opera House was between ten and fifty cents or one might rent the entire facility for ten dollars.

The Opera House was restored and reopened in 2003. The first floor, formerly the hardware and grocery stores, became the home of the Willa Cather Pioneer Memorial and Educational Foundation.

When I go about among little Nebraska towns . . . the thing I miss the most is the opera house.

FROM A LETTER WRITTEN TO HARVEY E. NEWBRANCH, WHO PUBLISHED IT IN THE DIAMOND JUBILEE EDITION OF THE *OMAHA WORLD HERALD,* OCTOBER 27, 1929.

The opera house in Bladen, sixteen miles north of Red Cloud on the Divide, is a two-story brick building that was both lodge hall and auditorium. It opened on March 25, 1913, featuring the Fisher Shipp Concert, and was considered by some to be the finest opera house between Omaha and Denver. Cather and her friends often visited Bladen, and it is believed that Cather's initials were carved in the back of an auditorium chair.

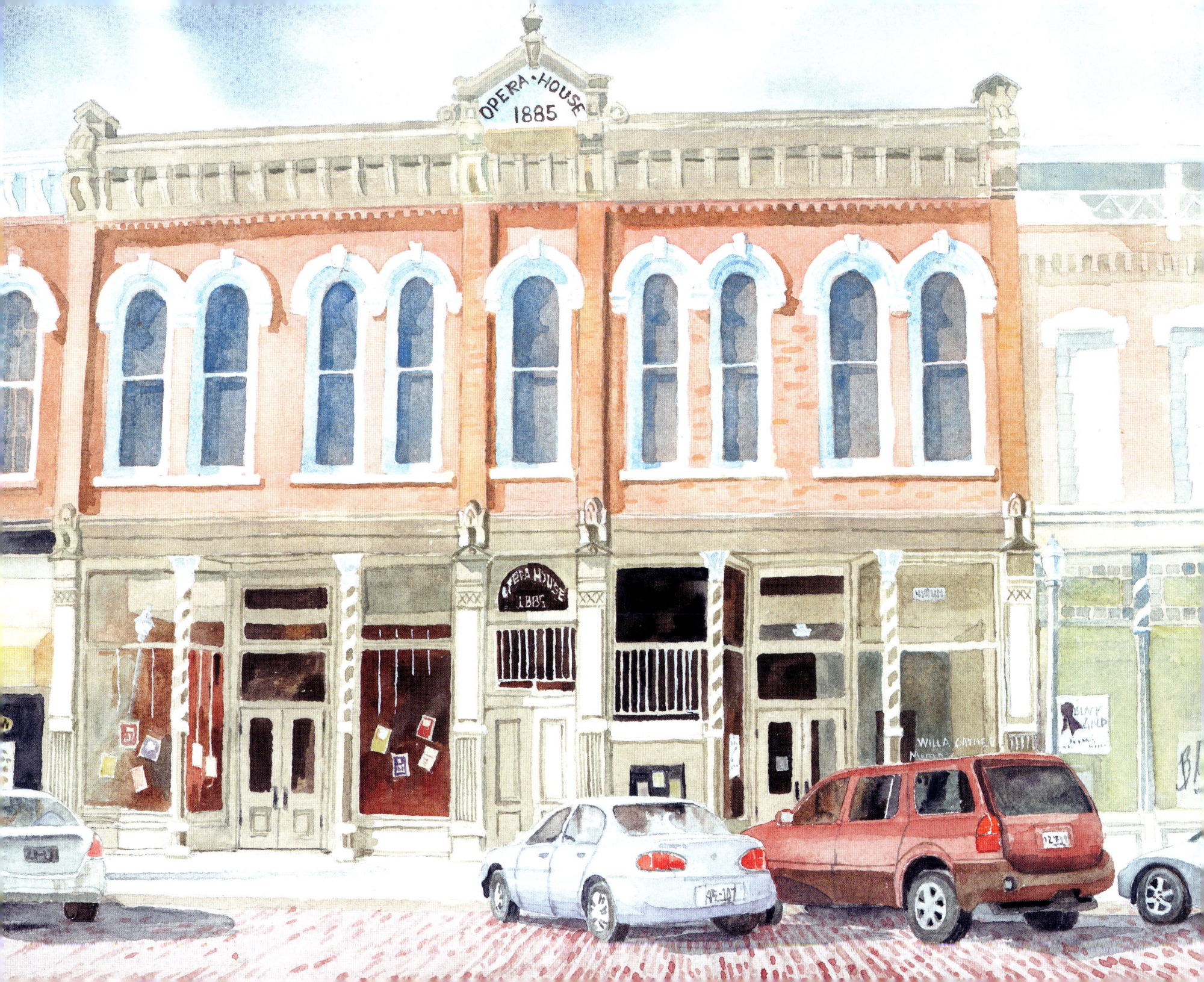

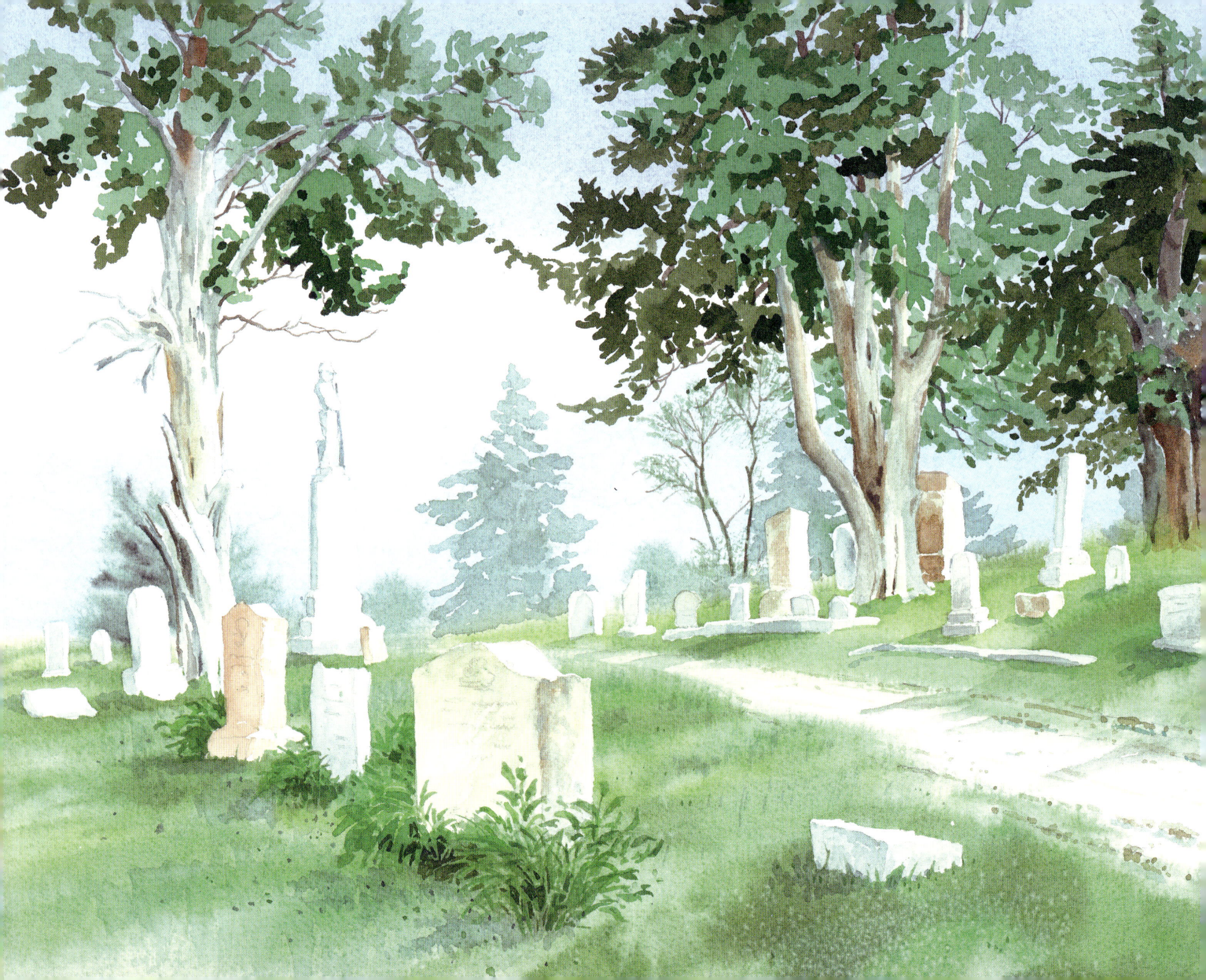

Churches and Cemeteries

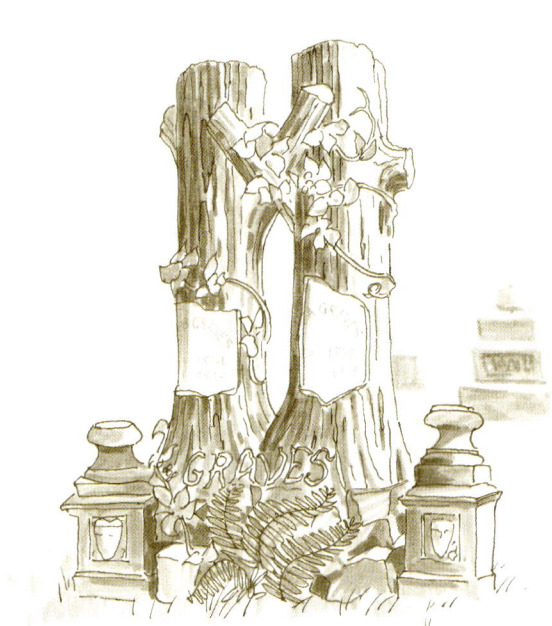

RED CLOUD CEMETERY

A funeral train was going toward Wyuka. The hearse was very plain and the driver was not in livery. In the carriage behind the hearse sat a man wearing a tall silk hat. He sat twirling his moustache and looking steadily out of the window. He was her son, that was why he was there. His wife had a nervous headache and could not accompany him. After they had entered the cemetery he hastily drew out a note book and jotted down a few figures, the result of his solemn cogitation. When the hack stopped he got out and stood by the open grave. He thought that it was very cold and that funerals were horrible things and wondered if civilization would never find a way of doing away with them. He thought of the time she had been all in all to him of what she had endured and suffered for him, and then how the greater love had come and gradually the need for her had passed out of his life, and he hated himself that he did not feel more deeply. After it was all over he got back into the carriage telling the driver to drive him to his office.

"ONE WAY OF PUTTING IT" NEBRASKA STATE JOURNAL, DECEMBER 17, 1893

The modest frame church sits alone on the prairie. This type of scene was a recurring visual in Cather's writing, and she reveals her own faith as she writes admiringly about the Christmas story in the *Nebraska State Journal*:

It is a beautiful story, this of the holiest and purest childhood on earth, beautiful even to those who cannot understand it, as dreams are sweet to men without hope. After all, if we cannot hear the carol and see the heavenly messenger, it is because our ears are deaf and our eyes are blind, not that we turn wilfully away from love or beauty. No one is antagonistic by preference. Almost any of us who doubt would give the little we know or hope to know to go down upon our knees among the lowly and experience a great faith or a great conviction.

"ONE WAY OF PUTTING IT" *NEBRASKA STATE JOURNAL*, DECEMBER 17, 1893

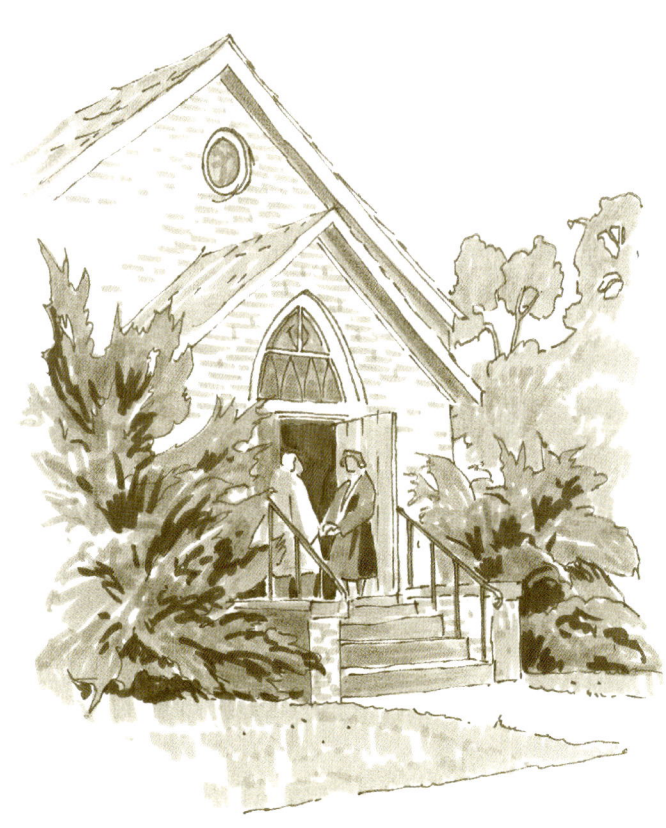

THE GRACE EPISCOPAL CHURCH

Cather joined this church in 1922 and was a member until she died in 1947. She commissioned the stained-glass window of "The Good Shepherd" in memory of her father for the north wall of the little chapel.

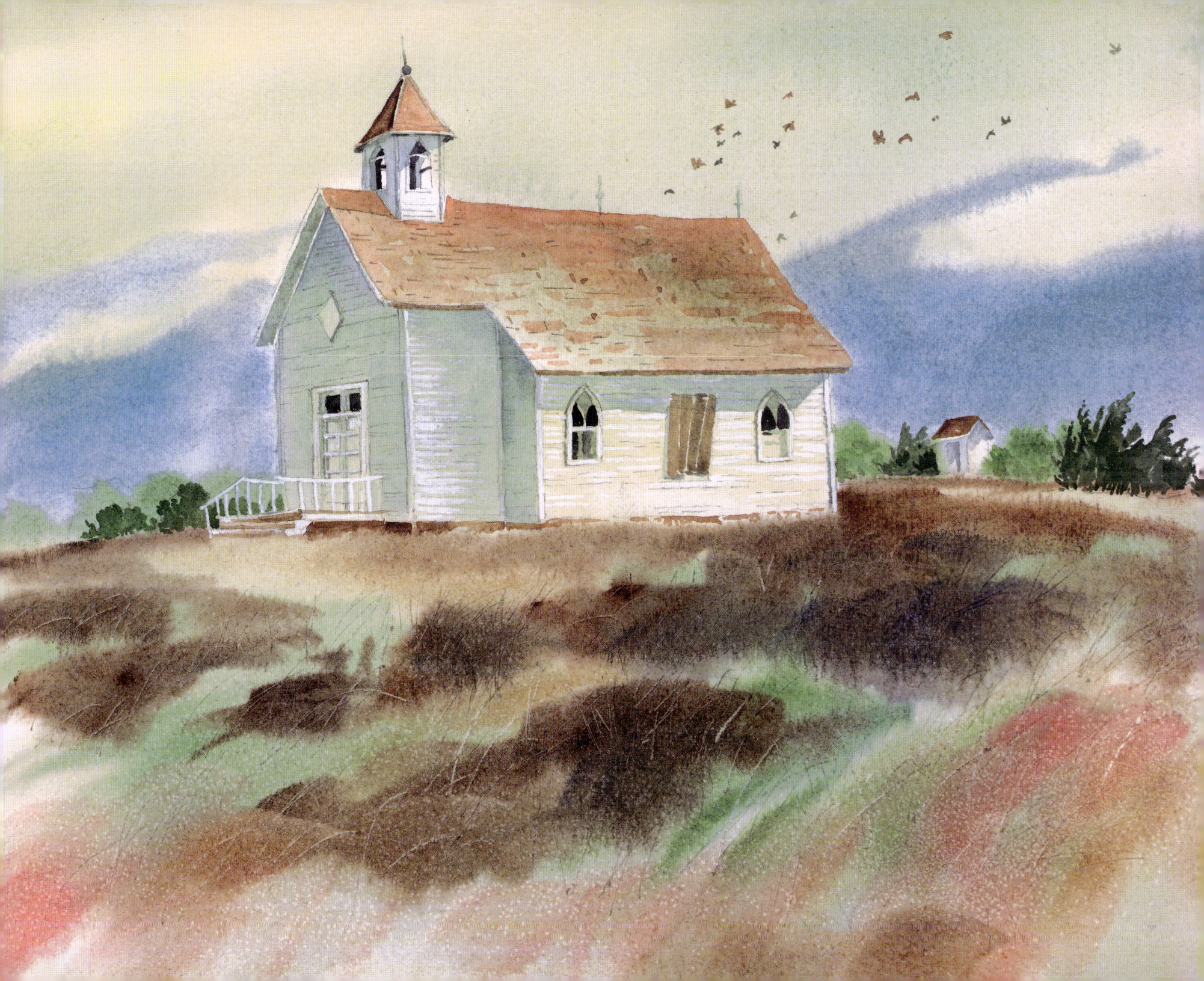

On Sunday we could drive to a Norwegian Swedish church and listen to a sermon in that language, or to a Danish or a Swedish church. We could go to the French Catholic settlement in the next county and hear a sermon in French, or into the Bohemian township and hear one in Czech, or we could go to church with the German Lutherans.

INTERVIEW WITH CATHER, 1926, NEW YORK. *WILLA CATHER IN PERSON: INTERVIEWS, SPEECHES, AND LETTERS,* EDITED BY L. BRENT BOHLKE

When the little Danish church was built, a local artist named Ondrak was hired to paint a mural above the altar. Ondrak, a Czech immigrant, made his living as a house painter and had only done a few crude murals in homes. "Christ in the Garden" was chosen for the commissioned picture, and when it was finished, Willa's father commented, "Look at that halo. Just like a ring of cheese." Ondrak was proud of his work, however, and when a tornado destroyed most of the little church, Ondrak saw the destruction, and sadly cried out, "My Yesus! My Yesus! Blown all to hell!"

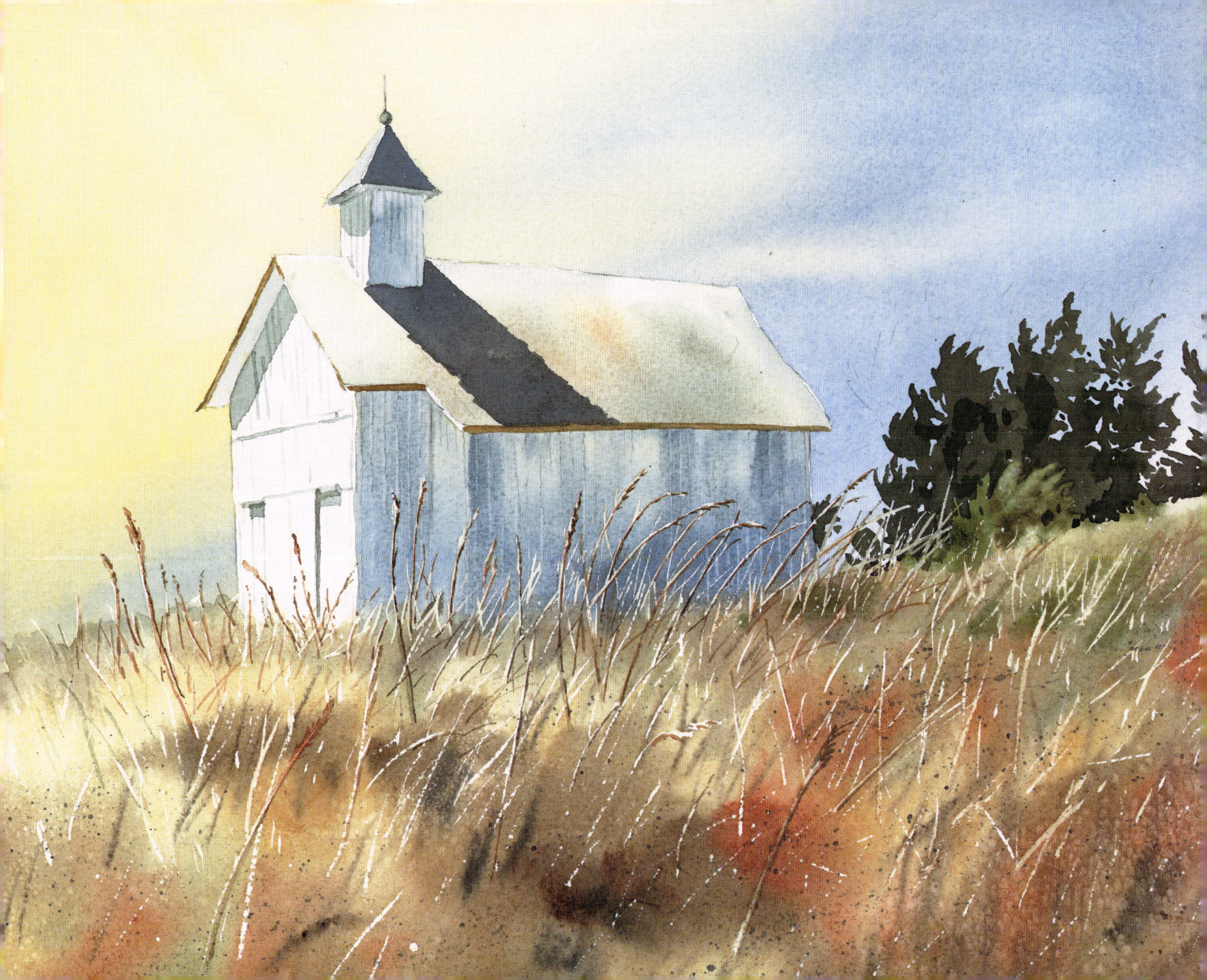

When I got as far as the Methodist Church, I was about halfway home. I can remember how glad I was when there happened to be a light in the church, and the painted glass window shone out at us as we came along the frozen street. In the winter bleakness a hunger for colour came over people, like the Laplander's craving for fats and sugar. *MY ÁNTONIA*

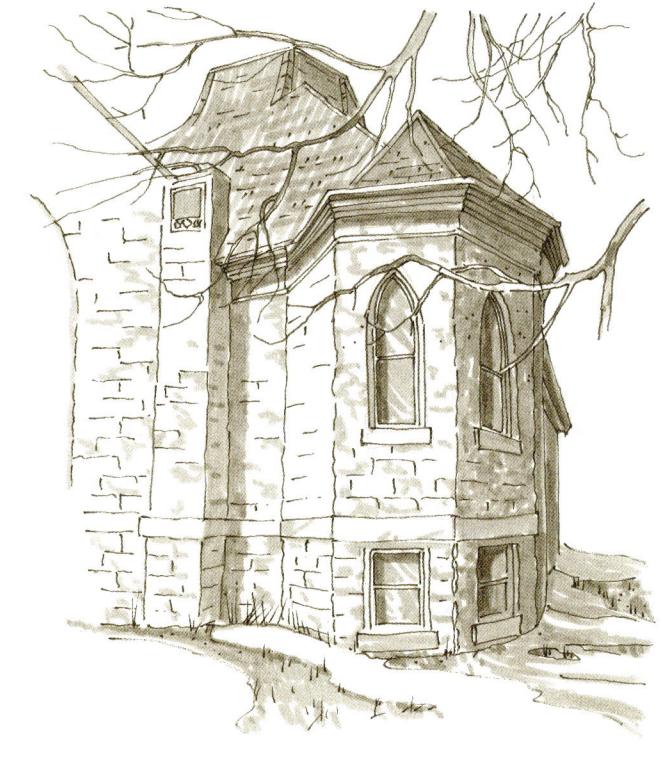

One Sunday I rode over with Jake to get a horse-collar which Ambrosch had borrowed from him and had not returned. It was a beautiful blue morning. The buffalo-peas were blooming in pink and purple masses along the roadside, and the larks, perched on last year's dried sunflower stalks, were singing straight at the sun, their heads thrown back and their yellow breasts a-quiver. The wind blew about us in warm, sweet gusts. We rode slowly, with a pleasant sense of Sunday indolence. *MY ÁNTONIA*

As I contemplated the scene for this painting, I thought of Cather visiting her friends in several ethnic churches on Sunday mornings. These little wooden churches were the important centers of immigrant cultural and spiritual life. Today, they stand next to their prairie cemeteries as their own white, clapboard monuments to past generations.

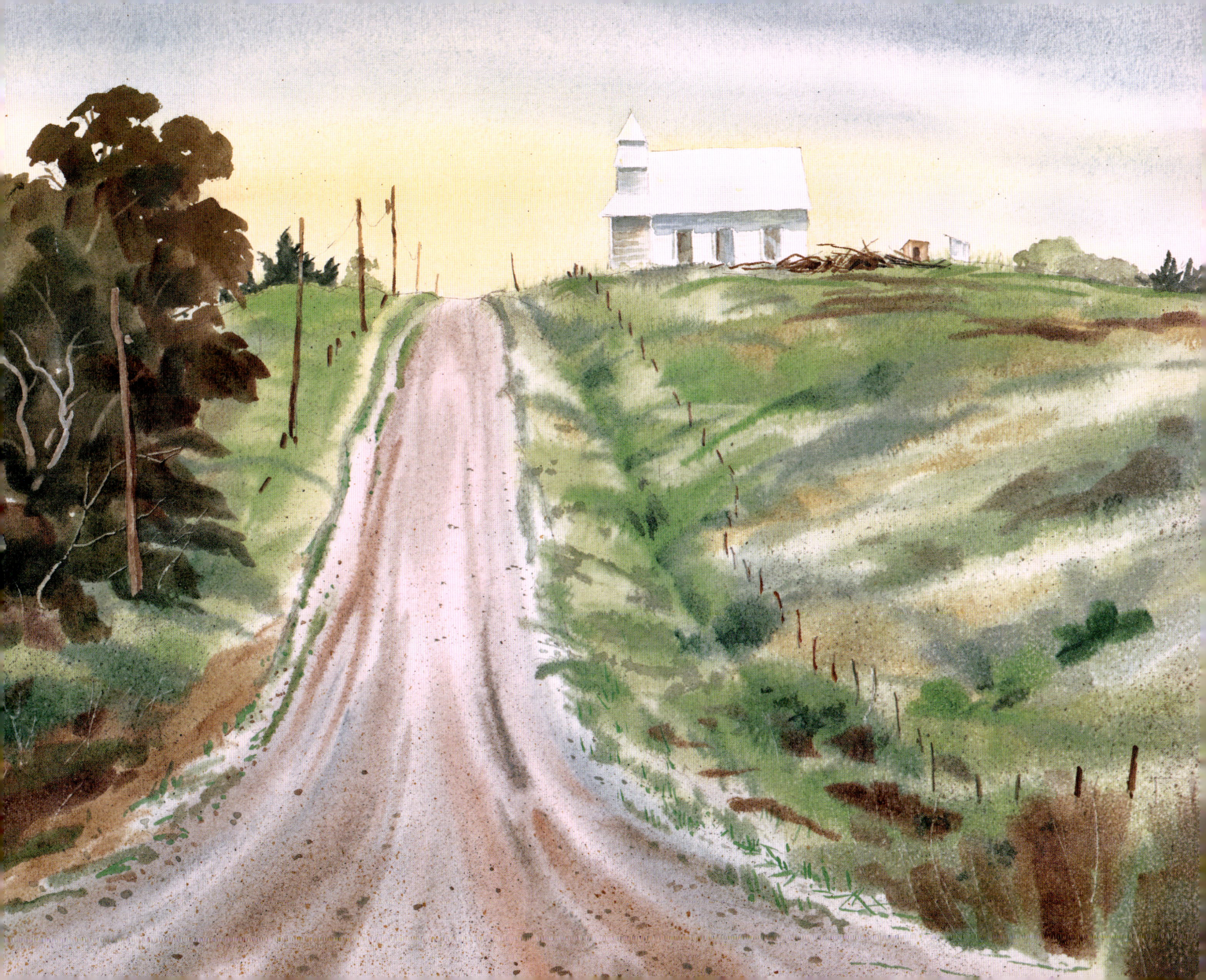

Each prairie church had their boys' and girls' "necessary rooms" out back—often hidden in a row of cedar trees. I was amused to find this one with a window.

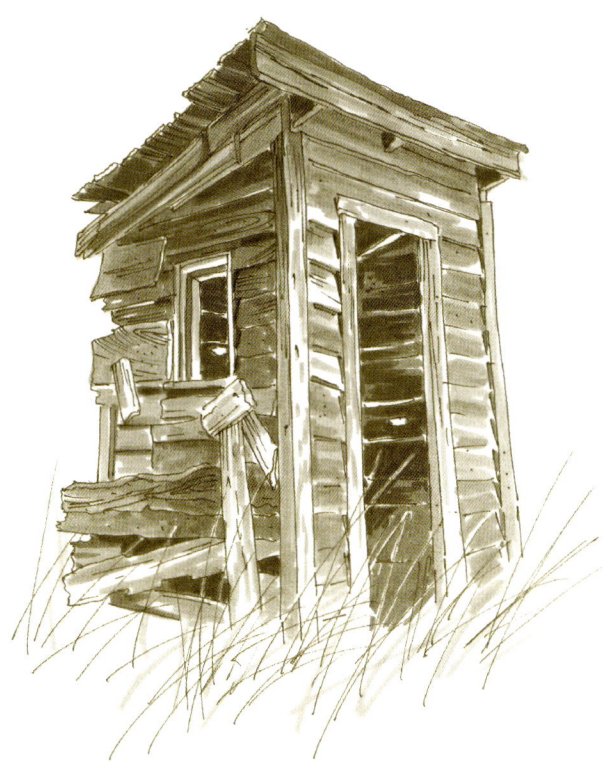

The area around the Divide was known as the "New Virginian" settlement since it was an "island" in the prairie settled by farm families that moved out from Winchester, Virginia. Like the ethnic communities, the church provided a cultural and spiritual center.

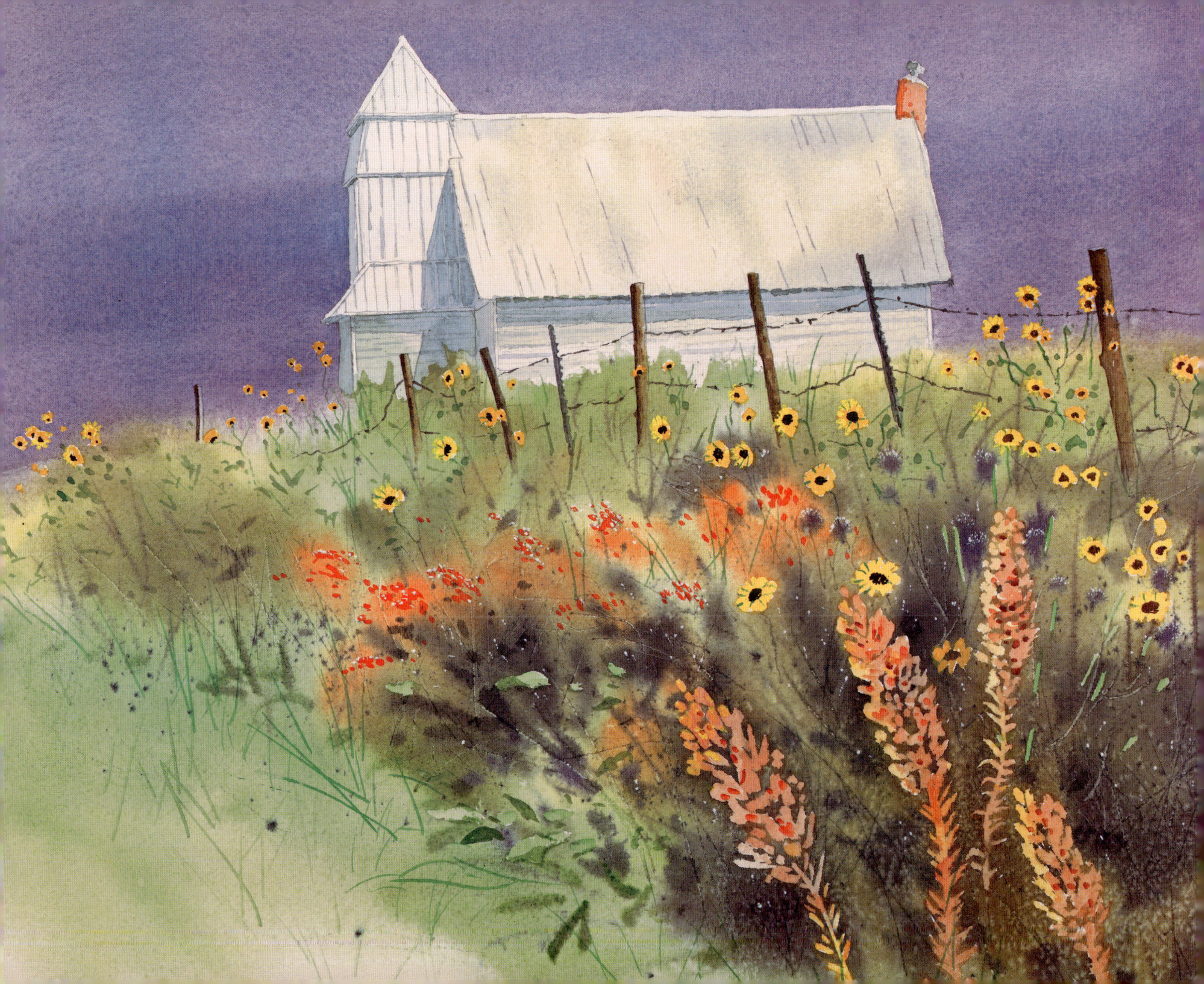

For the first time it struck Doctor Ed that this was really a beautiful graveyard. He thought of city cemeteries; acres of shrubbery and heavy stone, so arranged and lonely and unlike anything in the living world. Cities of the dead, indeed; cities of the forgotten, of the "put away." But this was open and free, this little square of long grass which the wind for ever stirred. Nothing but the sky overhead, and the many-coloured fields running on until they met that sky. The horses worked here in summer; the neighbours passed on their way to town; and over yonder, in the cornfield, Rosicky's own cattle would be eating fodder as winter came on. Nothing could be more undeathlike than this place; nothing could be more right for a man who had helped to do the work of great cities and had always longed for the open country and had got to it at last. Rosicky's life seemed to him complete and beautiful.   "NEIGHBOUR ROSICKY"

This is one of my favorite Cather stories. Anton Rosicky was not an anxious man but filled with kindness, compassion, and hope. This cemetery could have been his resting place. It is beautiful in every season, and today, as on most days, it is quiet and serene. The wind and tall prairie grass wave an eternal "good-bye" to those sleeping beneath.

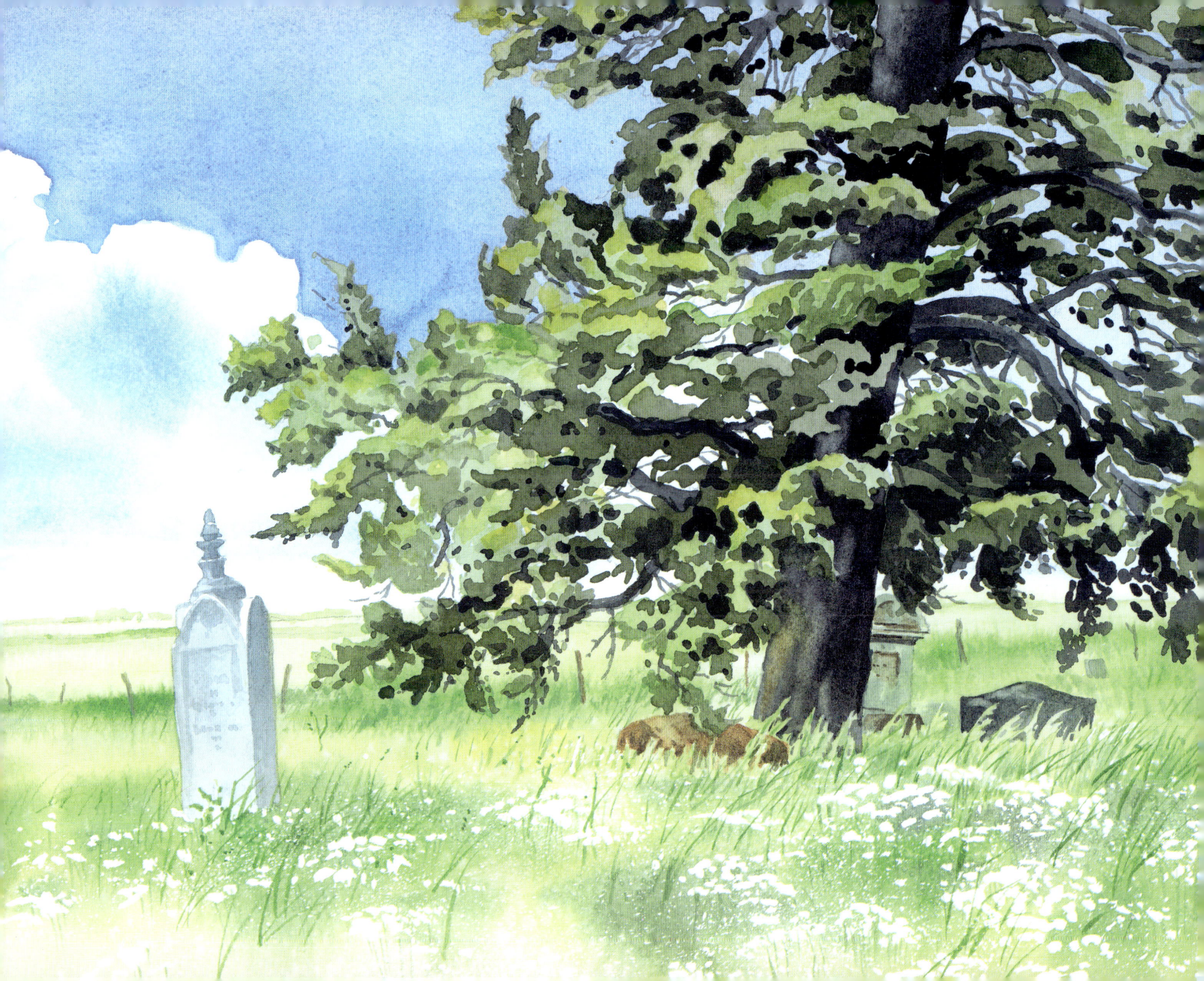

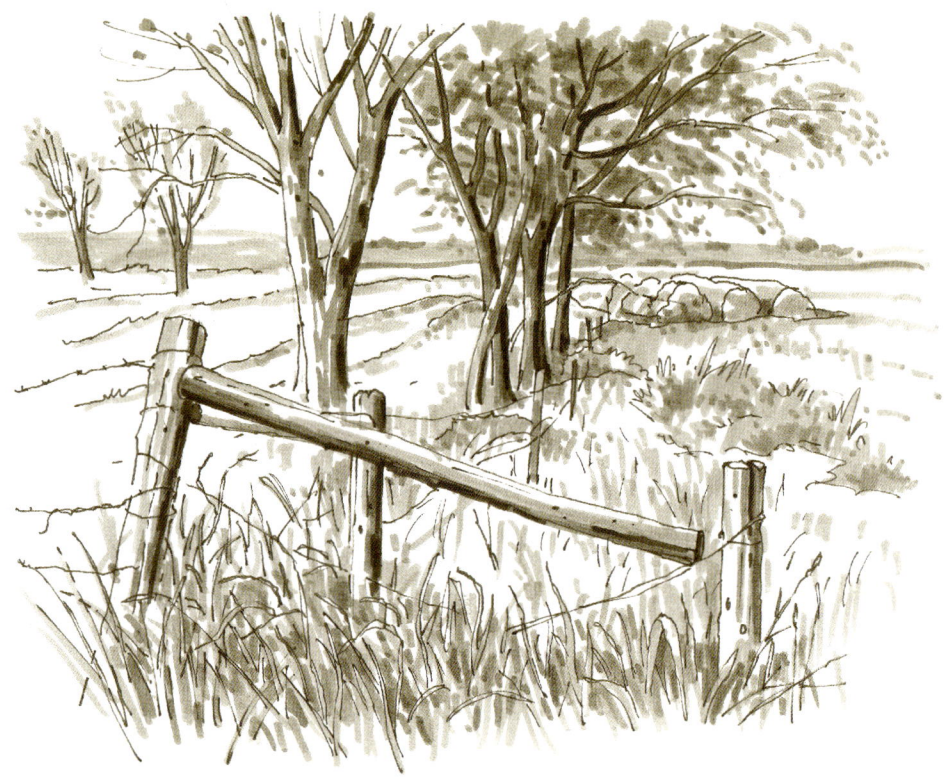

The prototype for Mr. Shimerda in *My Ántonia* was Francis Sadilek, who was generally believed to have committed suicide on April 6, 1914, although the *Red Cloud Chief* indicated that it had been an accidental shooting.

Francis Sadilek was a good man—a tailor and a violin player from the old country—but beset by sorrow and a longing for Bohemia. His body was interned near a rural crossroad, which by folklore tradition would prevent a spirit from rising and haunting the area. Later his remains were removed to the Red Cloud Cemetery, where he rests next to his wife and son.

The death of Mr. Sadilek had a profound effect on Cather, and she adopts his tragic story for *My Ántonia*. She paints the following sad picture of Mr. Shimerda's grave at the crossroads:

Mr. Shimerda's grave was still there, with a sagging wire fence around it, and an unpainted wooden cross. As grandfather had predicted, Mrs. Shimerda never saw the roads going over his head. The road from the north curved a little to the east just there, and the road from the west swung out a little to the south; so that the grave, with its tall red grass that was never mowed, was like a little island; and at twilight, under a new moon or the clear evening star, the dusty roads used to look like soft grey rivers flowing past it.

After he had gone eight miles, he came to the graveyard, which lay just at the edge of his own hay-land. There he stopped his horses and sat still on his wagon seat, looking about at the snowfall. Over yonder on the hill he could see his own house, crouching low, with the clump of orchard behind and the windmill before, and all down the gentle hill-slope the rows of pale gold cornstalks stood out against the white field. The snow was falling over the cornfield and the pasture and the hay-land, steadily, with very little wind—a nice dry snow. The graveyard had only a light wire fence about it and was all overgrown with long red grass. The fine snow, settling into this red grass and upon the few little evergreens and the headstones, looked very pretty.

"NEIGHBOUR ROSICKY"

The local mortician and funeral director sometimes faced difficulties burying the dead in rural cemeteries when the weather was bad, and, therefore, the responsibility of a pall bearer was a serious commitment. My father told me of a time when due to heavy rains, the motor hearse was unable to climb the last hill to the country cemetery. The pall bearers were forced out in the rain to carry the casket the last half mile, plodding through slick, gummy mud that formed channels of trickling water in the old wheel tracks.

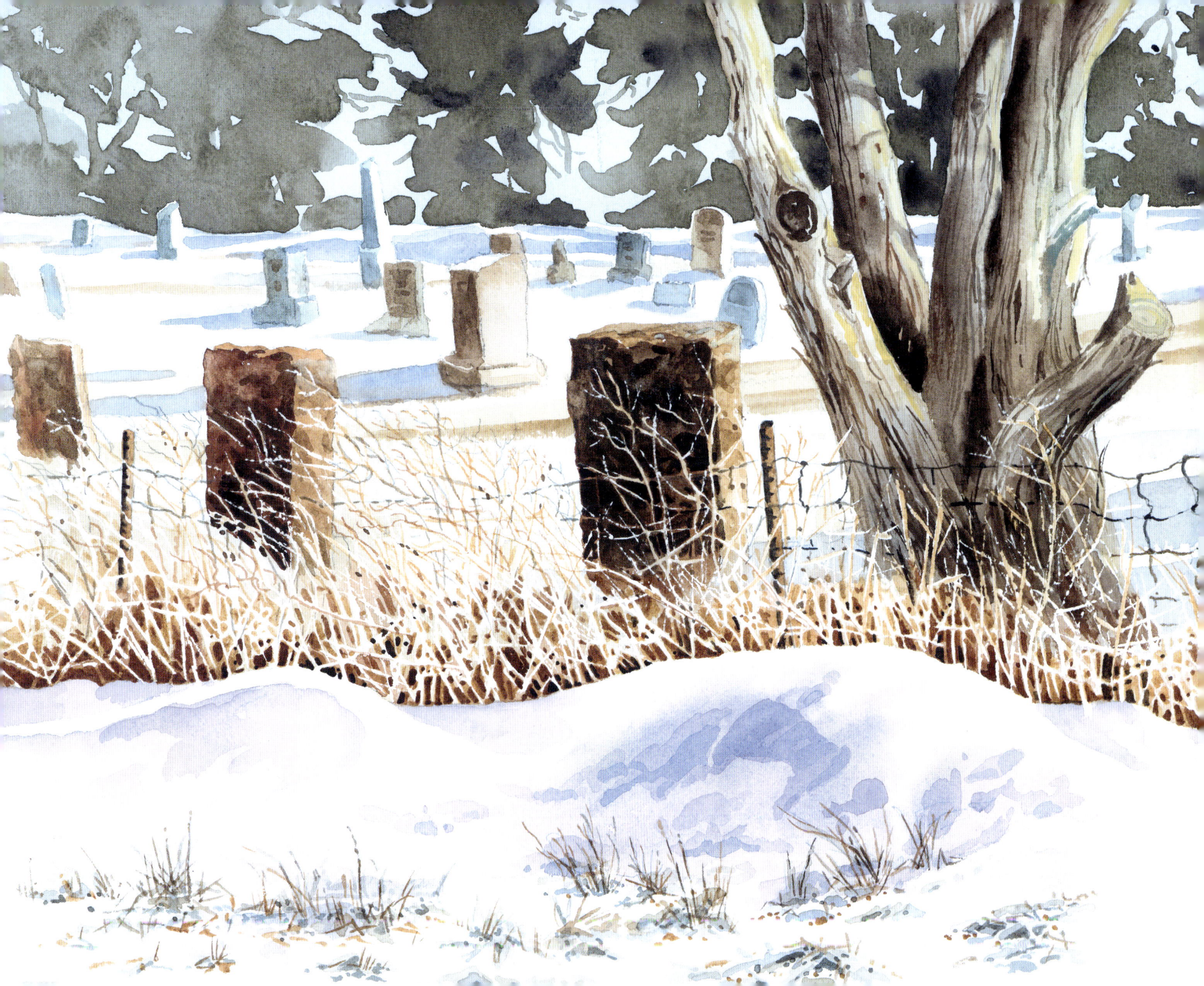

When people ask me if it has been a hard or easy road, I always answer with the quotation, "the end is nothing, the road is all."

INTERVIEW WITH CATHER IN *WILLA CATHER IN PERSON: INTERVIEWS, SPEECHES, AND LETTERS*, L. BRENT BOHLKE

Bibliography

Bennett, Mildred R. *World of Willa Cather*. Lincoln: University of Nebraska Press, 1961.

Bohlke, L. Brent, ed. *Willa Cather in Person: Interviews, Speeches, and Letters*. Lincoln: University of Nebraska Press, 1986.

Cather, Willa. *April Twilights*. Boston: The Gorham Press, 1903.

——. "The Best Years." In *Five Stories*. New York: Alfred A. Knopf, 1956.

——. "The Bohemian Girl." *McClure's Magazine*, April 1912.

——. *Death Comes for the Archbishop*. New York: Alfred A. Knopf, 1927.

——. "El Dorado: A Kansas Recessional." *New England Magazine*, June 1901.

——. "The Enchanted Bluff." *Harper's Monthly Magazine*, April 1909.

——. "Eric Hermannson's Soul." *The Cosmopolitan*, April 1900.

——. *Five Stories*. New York: Vintage Books, 1956.

——. interview by the *Philadelphia Record*, August 10, 1913.

——. "Light on Adobe Walls." An unfinished essay.

——. *A Lost Lady*. New York: Alfred A. Knopf, 1923.

——. *Lucy Gayheart*. New York: Alfred A. Knopf, 1935.

——. *My Ántonia*. Boston: Houghton Mifflin, 1918.

——. "Neighbour Rosicky." In *Obscure Destinies*. New York: Alfred A. Knopf, 1932.

——. *Obscure Destinies*. New York: Alfred A. Knopf, 1932.

——. *One of Ours*. New York: Alfred A. Knopf, 1923.

——. "One Way of Putting It." *Nebraska State Journal*, November 12, 1893.

——. "One Way of Putting It." *Nebraska State Journal*, December 17, 1893.

——. *O Pioneers!* Boston: Houghton Mifflin, 1913.

——. "A Resurrection." In *Willa Cather's Short Fiction 1892–1912*, edited by Virginia Faulkner. Lincoln: University of Nebraska Press, 1970.

——. *Shadows on the Rock*. New York: Alfred A. Knopf, 1931.

——. *The Song of the Lark*. Boston: Houghton Mifflin, 1915.

——. *Sapphira and the Slave Girl*. New York: Alfred A. Knopf, 1940.

——. *Uncle Valentine and Other Stories*. Lincoln: University of Nebraska Press, 1973.

——. "A Wagner Matinée." *Everybody's Magazine*, March 1904.

——. "The Way of the World." *The Home Monthly* 6, April 1898.

March, John. *A Reader's Companion to the Fiction of Willa Cather*. Westport CT: Greenwood Press, 1993.

Robinson, Phyllis C. *Willa: The Life of Willa Cather*. Garden City NY: Doubleday & Company, 1983.

She was a tall, lank brown woman, dressed in deep mourning, and she stood in a marble-cutter's shop looking for a tombstone for her lord who was not.

"I want something plain, plain and neat," she said in a harsh metallic voice as she ran her rusty black glove over a stone beside her. The marble dealer tried in vain to influence her selection, for he had known and liked the dead man. But she suspected that he wanted to impose on her, and let him know in decided language that she had read up thoroughly in the matter of tombstones and knew what she wanted. She finally selected the ugliest one in the shop and began beating the dealer down in the price. She had evidently gone shopping for tombstones often and had learned all the technical terms, such as "plinth" and "base." She used them very freely and was evidently not a little proud of her knowledge. When she saw that the dealer had lowered his price for the last time, she opened a stiff black pocketbook, which was of real leather, as its disagreeable odor left no doubt, and gave him the number of the lot in the cemetery. Then she repeated in a loud, high voice the text she wished cut upon it.

"'I would rather be a doorkeeper in the house of the Lord than dwell in the tents of the wicked.' It was his favorite scripture text." And clearing her throat violently she went across the street to buy muffin rings. The marble dealer turned with a sigh to the ugly mass of stone that was to cover the grave of a man he had always honored, and wondered if doorkeeping paid.

WILLA CATHER, "ONE WAY OF PUTTING IT,"
NEBRASKA STATE JOURNAL, NOVEMBER 12, 1893

A *Prairie Cemetery*

They don't come here often anymore
Whispering their last goodbyes,
And
Leaving as quickly as they came.
Only the murmur of wind in the pines
And,
Snapping grasshoppers in the dry grass
Interrupt the stillness

RICHARD SCHILLING

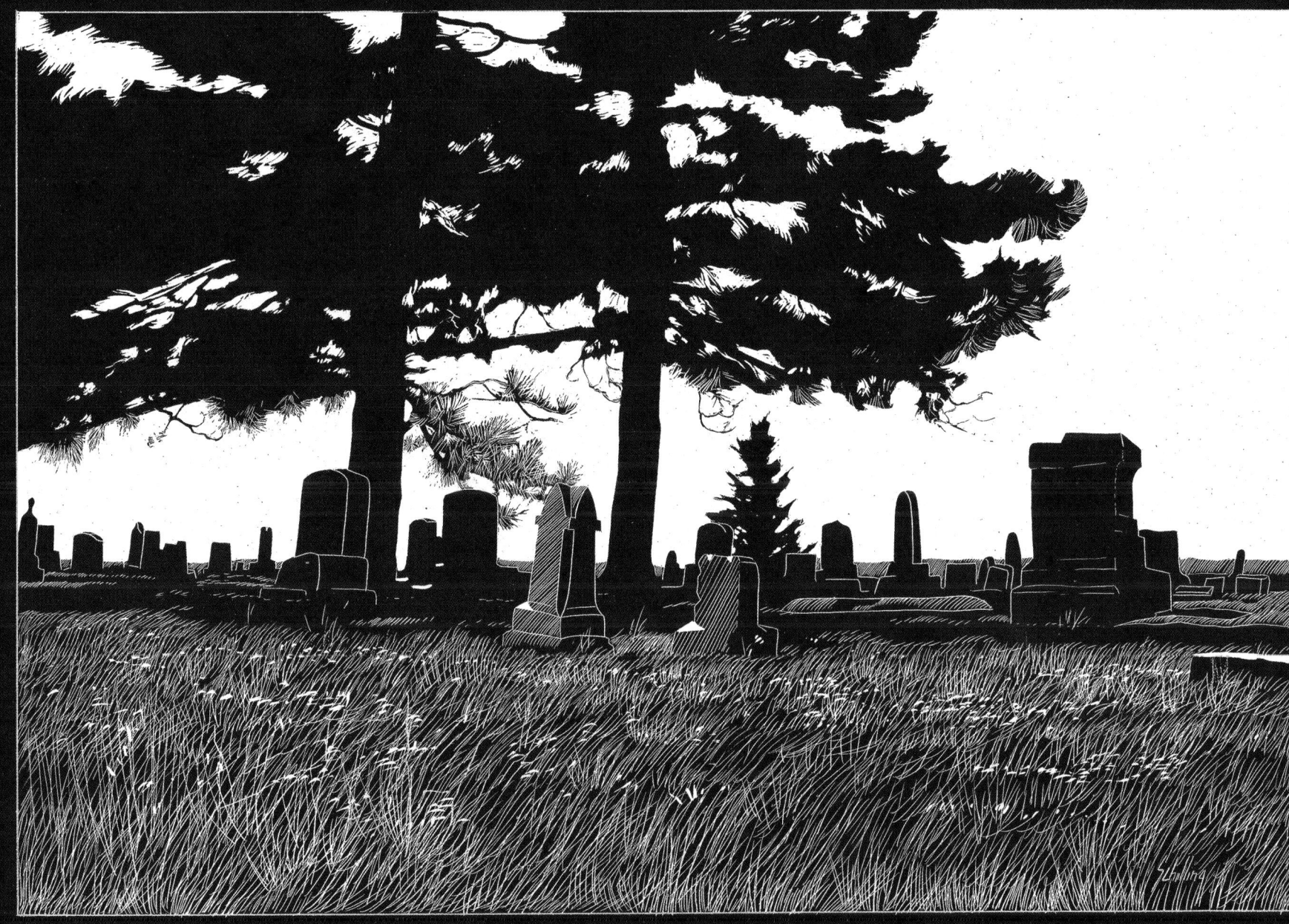